Data Base
Management Systems

Data Base
Management Systems
A Guide to Microcomputer Software

David Kruglinski

Osborne/McGraw-Hill
Berkeley, California

Published by
Osborne/McGraw-Hill
630 Bancroft Way
Berkeley, California 94710
U.S.A.

For information on translations and book distributors outside of the U.S.A., please write to Osborne/McGraw-Hill at the above address.

DATA BASE MANAGEMENT SYSTEMS
A GUIDE TO MICROCOMPUTER SOFTWARE

1234567890 DODO 898765432
ISBN 0-931988-84-5
Cover art by Terry Hoff
Text design by Karen van Genderen

To Michel

Contents

Acknowledgments

Special thanks go to those software publishers and distributors who made copies of their packages available for evaluation. These include Rick Merlich of DJR Associates (distributors of FMS-80), Bob Cohen of Condor Computer Corporation, and Clyde Holsapple, a consultant to Micro Data Base Systems. Dr. Holsapple was very helpful in correcting the flaws in Chapter 7, despite disagreement over the scope of the term "data base." A Solomon II package, PL/I source code, and schematic diagrams were provided by Gary Harpst of TLB.

Denise Penrose of Osborne/McGraw-Hill contributed her editing skill and a massive infusion of patience. The loan of a computer by Rex Erickson of Compu-lab was much appreciated as were some suggestions by Elaine Snyder of Creative Resources in Technology (CRT). Angel Rodriquez volunteered his R + E Cycles as a "beta test site" for several of the examples.

1

What a Data Base Is

You may already use word processing programs, electronic spread sheets, accounting systems, chess, biorhythm analyzers, and many other programs that run on your new microcomputer, but a few important business tasks remain outside the scope of these packaged programs. For example, you might want to select certain customers from your accounts payable system for special collection purposes. Or you may want to classify customers according to sales volume and select low volume customers for a special promotional mailing. You might want a printed report that lists high-priced inventory items, the customers who buy them, and the dates of purchases in the last six and twelve months.

A simpler example will convey the basic functions common to each of these tasks. If you want to keep a Christmas list, you could buy a mailing list program. But such a program won't help you keep track of shirt sizes, children's names, liquor brand preferences, and so on. To include such information, you may decide that it's finally time to learn programming, and then spend four days writing a BASIC program that works—but just barely.

Storing this kind of information in a computerized Christmas list is a good example of data management. An electronic file on disk contains information about your friends, particularly their names, addresses, phone numbers, and personal preferences. A program allows you to manipulate the information: to add new names, change and delete existing names, and print labels for cards.

Now suppose you write another BASIC program to keep track of your phonograph record collection, printing lists of albums by artist and music type. You quickly learn one of the oldest techniques in programming: taking an old program and changing it slightly to do something new. You may need only two days to write the record library program because you copied the structure of the Christmas list program.

Fortunately, computer experts long ago recognized a need to solve these problems without days of programming. They created the *data base*. Initially designed to aid professional programmers, the data base was later implemented for computer *users*. Now, with a microcomputer in nearly every home and office, even a nonprogrammer can benefit from data base technology. But this does not exclude the programmer. In fact, the data base increases the productivity of professional programmers, enabling them to develop systems

1

for microcomputers as sophisticated as those running on large computers.

A data base identifies a set of data that the computer can access and operate on. It is a tool for handling problems like the two described above, that is, problems that involve information stored on disk. It cannot help you with loan amortizations or with differential equations; it won't play computer games or invert matrixes, and it won't let you eliminate all of your office filing cabinets. However, a data base *will* make problems like the Christmas list and the record catalog seem trivial (you can set up each of them in less than an hour) and complex business applications, like sales order processing, less intimidating.

A SHORT HISTORY OF DATA BASE DEVELOPMENT

The development of software for microcomputers is about fifteen years behind that of large computer systems and about seven years behind that of minicomputers. Just as data processing (DP) departments, which use standard COBOL programs, simple disks, and tape files, begin to realize the expense of inflexible software, so, too, are today's microcomputer owners using BASIC encountering the same problem. While computer manufacturers rescued large computer system users by offering sophisticated data base systems for $40,000 or more, software publishers now offer data base packages to microcomputer owners for $700. Just as some DP shops still struggle with software from the 1960s, in fifteen years some microcomputer owners will be using yesterday's software.

Mainframe computers are often supported by large staffs of professional programmers. Company management often depends on their expertise, and many DP shops wish to preserve that dependent relationship. Recognizing this political reality, software houses have traditionally not offered packages that permitted computer end-users to bypass the programmers. Consequently, the first data base systems used existing languages (for example, COBOL) and were complex and difficult to learn. Only recently have query languages been introduced, languages which allow the nonprogrammer to access data, but which still require a DP staff to set up the system.

In the early days, a data base was known as a *management information system.* The idea was to put all the company's data into a vast pool where executives could "go fishing" for any information they wanted. The information would, of course, instantly reflect any changes resulting from payrolls, sales invoicing, and so on. But this system was not adequate because the software was not sophisticated enough and because executives didn't know what questions to ask. After failing to implement a general management information system, computer professionals reconsidered and applied the data base concept to specific sets of operations.

One such data base operation is information retrieval. For example, the United States Census Bureau sells tapes describing in minute detail all U.S. foreign trade. After feeding this data into a data base, an oil executive can ask the computer to list all petroleum shipments into the port of Los Angeles in descending order of volume and by country of origin. Using old programming techniques, the programmer would have had to anticipate each question. Each time the executive wanted new information from the foreign trade data, the programmer would have had to write a new program. By the time the program was finished, the executive would have forgotten why he or she wanted it.

Data base is also used in applications programming such as inventory, invoicing, airline reservations, and accounting. The main benefits of using data base instead of conventional programming are the cost and time saved in setting up the systems and later making changes to them. Because DP departments spend the majority of their time "maintaining" old systems, anything reducing that burden is welcome.

DATA BASE DEFINED

The question may arise of how a microcomputer Christmas card list can have anything in common with a management information system on a big computer. The answer is simple. In both cases a person requests and receives information from the computer. What happens inside a computer to make this possible?

Imagine, for example, that the computer is a tiny room where an efficient hobbit has his office. In one corner of the office he has a big filing cabinet containing every bit of data that anyone has given him. The filing cabinet has a sign on it saying "Data Base," and the hobbit has been given the title "Data Base Manager." His job is simply to look up things when people ask him to. If you ask him which of your friends like "Old Grandma" bourbon, he obligingly rummages through the "Christmas" file in the bottom drawer and types out the list of names.

Now imagine that you go to work on Monday morning and ask your accountant for a list of who owes you what. The accountant asks the company data base manager to review an accounts receivable ledger and produce the required information. The company data base manager sets to work, digging into each customer's folder to determine the amount owed and the date it was due. Occasionally, an invoice or

credit memo doesn't make sense, but the accountant is only a phone call away for specific questions. At last, the data base manager finishes the report and delivers it to the accountant, who delivers it to you. A few minutes later, the sales manager calls the data base manager requesting a list of customers in Maine in ascending order by year-to-date sales. The data base manager goes back to the same files and assembles the information.

Obviously, the hobbit and the company data base manager are colleagues. The company data base manager is really a computer program called a Data Base Management System (DBMS). The filing cabinet is really a disk containing the data base. A DBMS separates data from the programs and people who use them and permits many totally different views of the same data. This approach is shown in Figure 1-1; it contrasts dramatically with the older method shown in Figure 1-2, in which each program is connected to the physical data. In the first case, the programs have a *logical view* of the data that is independent of how the data is *physically* laid out on the disk. The data on disk can be changed or supplemented without requiring program changes.

Remember that the DBMS is the computer program you buy and that the data base is your data after the DBMS has stored it on disk. You may have to write your own programs as well, or you may not, depending on which DBMS package you select.

DBMS OBJECTIVES

Benefits other than elegance must justify the expense of purchasing and setting up a DBMS. Consider the following benefits as objectives for examining and evaluating each prospective DBMS package.

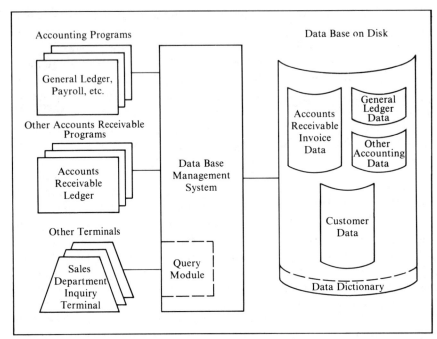

FIGURE 1-1.
The data base
environment

Presents an Accurate Model Of the Data

Presumably a DBMS would not exist if it did not present an accurate model of somebody's data. If you have a single application in mind for your DBMS, you can match the system to the requirements, but if you are getting a DBMS for general purposes, you have some homework to do. Chapter 2 will help you understand the strengths and weaknesses of some very different data structures.

Organizes Data with Simplicity

The structure of the data in a DBMS should be as simple as possible. The simpler the struc-ture of the data base, the easier it is to manipu-late the data.

Provides Timely Response To Queries

A DBMS must run fast enough. If you dis-play data on the screen, a two-second delay is acceptable. If you need a report involving a search of all the data in a file, you must be the judge of how long it should take. Are five min-utes, ten minutes, or several hours too long? The data base may be set up so that often asked questions are "cheap" and seldom asked ques-tions are "expensive." By doing a little research and experimentation with dummy data, you can answer these questions before purchasing a particular DBMS package.

Reduces Cost

Disk storage is getting cheaper, and programmers are getting more expensive. Most DBMS packages reduce the need for both. While a DBMS does reduce data redundancy, you may not notice the extra disk space because in pre-data base systems the redundant data was usually stored in temporary files. For example, to list employees in numeric and alphabetic order, the program would not have maintained two employee files. Instead it would have sorted the primary numeric file into a temporary alphabetic file for printing. Conversely, in the DBMS environment, one employee file appears to be in two different sort orders.

The real saving is in programming time. With a DBMS, solutions to simple problems take hours rather than days. Complex applications require one programmer instead of a team. Reducing the cost of a set of business programs

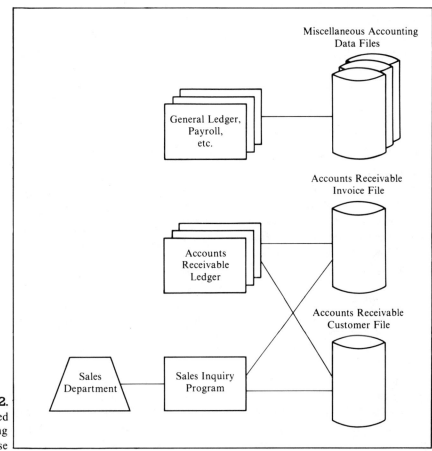

FIGURE 1-2.
File-oriented
programming
before data base

from $6000 to $3000 (including the cost of the DBMS) might make it possible for a small company to invest in custom programming.

Uses Only Nonredundant Data

Redundant data requires little disk space but has great potential for errors. If you record a shipment for ten units of product X and you immediately decrement the product's "units on hand" by ten, you are in fine shape unless the shipment is canceled. In that case you must add the ten units back to inventory. In a good DBMS, no units on hand figure exists. Instead, you look at the opening balance for the month, then total up all shipments currently on file, and subtract. If an order is canceled, the amount of the order simply is not subtracted.

Safeguards Data Integrity

A data base is often composed of a number of files, records, data items, and interconnections. If something goes wrong—a power failure, for instance—a part of the data base may be unreadable. The DBMS should check itself and immediately let you know if it finds something wrong. The most common approach involves controlling the "opening" and "closing" of the data base. For example, just before business ends on Friday, the computer operator terminates (closes) data base processing, and the DBMS and the operator both record the time and date. When the data base is reactivated (opened) Monday morning, it displays data from the previous close. The operator can check whether the date and time match the entries in the logbook. If the data base is opened twice in a row with no intervening close, then the DBMS itself knows there is a problem.

On a lower level, if a data base has a place for price, it would make no sense for the price to be less than zero, nor would it be reasonable for the price to be XYZ or any other nonnumeric value. The DBMS should always be on the watch for inconsistent data, not allowing its entry and, if it should slip in, alerting the user to its presence.

Permits Access by Users

As a DBMS user, you should be able to ask a wide variety of questions about the data. Questions like "What parts have a value greater than $50?" or "What is the total value of inventory?" are commonly asked by nonprofessional computer users. Most data base management systems have a *query language* for asking these questions. This language should be simple to use and easy to learn.

If you query the data base, you usually get one screenful of data. Sometimes you need a report—a nicely formatted printout. A shop owner, for instance, might need a current price list to leave on the counter. An accounts payable clerk might need a list of overdue accounts for collection procedures. A DBMS should permit an inexperienced computer user to create these reports via a report generator.

Provides Privacy and Security

A diskette-based, single-terminal computer system is easy to protect by simply locking up the diskettes in a safe. With larger systems, security becomes complex. Good data base management systems include features that restrict unauthorized individuals from changing or viewing data. This is usually done with passwords, each with its own level of security.

Provides Fail-Safe Operation

Suppose you use a DBMS to run a telephone answering service. Incoming messages are entered directly into the computer and are later retrieved for clients. Now suppose that one busy day the power goes off. What happens to the messages in the computer? If the DBMS includes a transaction logging function, the messages are stored on magnetic tape on a dedicated drive. After the power failure, you simply reload the morning's backup disk and then "play" the logged transactions into the data base, reconstructing them to the point of failure. If you don't have a tape drive, you can use a special disk file, but if the disk crashes you are out of luck—you've lost the day's data.

Remember that no computer system is 100 percent fail-safe. If something went wrong with the tape drive just described, the game would be over. According to Murphy's law, the tape drive will fail just at the most critical moment.

Interfaces with the Past

If you have never had a computer before, you don't have to worry about this. If, however, you have a set of programs and data to transfer to the data base, you may not want to rekey all the data. A DBMS should be able to accept data from conventional files, and it should be able to output data in file format for use by existing non-data base programs.

If you have a set of conventional accounting programs running on your microcomputer, you probably have a vendor file, a customer file, a payroll master, and a general ledger account file. You can bring all these files into the data base and then rearrange them as necessary for queries and reports that your old system never gave you. Until you convert to a complete data base accounting system, you will have to keep getting fresh copies of the files as the old system updates them.

Interfaces with the Future

Without a DBMS, even the most trivial change can require rewriting dozens of programs. Once the rewrite is done, new bugs appear, sometimes causing downtime and lost data.

Data base management systems can make change less painful. Often you can rearrange or add data elements without touching any programs except those which use the new elements. Most demands on a working system are requests for new reports. If the data base has a powerful report generator, these requests can be fulfilled in a matter of hours.

Permits Shared Usage of Data

The DBMS should allow data to be shared. In an organization with a single-terminal computer, a DBMS should permit different people to use the same data. Perhaps the purchasing staff and the accounts payable clerk can share the same vendor file. With multiuser systems, a salesperson can print a list of the most active customers from one terminal while a clerk checks customer credit from another.

Offers Language Flexibility

In addition to the high-level query language described above, a lower-level programming language should prevent programmers from saying "We just can't do that." The lower-level language may be an established language, like COBOL or BASIC, with "hooks" into the DBMS, or it may be a proprietary language included in the DBMS package.

Produces Self-Documentation

All too often programmers write systems that no one else understands. They may be motivated by job security or by ignorance, but the result is always unacceptable. If the software automatically produces documentation, you are ahead of the game.

In all DBMS systems, the data dictionary provides a good start toward computer-produced documentation. By keeping a book with printed copies of these dictionaries you will know the structure of your data base at all times. Require anyone who makes a change to make a new listing and to put it in the book.

MICROCOMPUTER LIMITATIONS

As you may have gathered, some microcomputer data base management systems meet most of the objectives set for large computer systems. Why then, you might ask, do people pay millions for a large computer when they could buy a $5000 microcomputer with a $700 data base package? Part of the answer is *networks.* Large computer systems can connect to thousands of terminals all over the country. But a microcomputer running under CP/M is restricted to one computer and one terminal.

Although microcomputer manufacturers have released network and multiuser microcomputer systems, many of these systems simply share an expensive hard disk among several terminals. Only one of the data base management systems in this book has true multiuser capability as found on large systems and minicomputers. (Chapter 2 describes what a multiuser DBMS has to do.) Data base management systems are limited primarily because the networks are not standard; a TeleVideo network does not have the same software as an Ohio Scientific network, and neither resembles an Altos multiuser MP/M system. Suppliers of data base management systems are unwilling to support custom versions and instead aim for the largest markets. Sometimes a hardware firm offers a DBMS tailored to its own computers, but this action excludes the package from the general software market and makes computer owners prisoners of their computer company.

With the advent of hard disks for microcomputers, response time is often less than with large computers, and storage capacity is up to eight megabytes per file with 8-bit CP/M. If your application does not require sharing of information or 100 megabytes of disk storage, you could save a great deal of money by using a microcomputer. If you need a modest network, buy a 16-bit microcomputer and wait for the next generation of data base software. Chapter 9 gives some hints of what is to come.

TERMINOLOGY

The terms used in the software industry often originate in software user manuals. As you would expect, there is little agreement on the term data base. This section establishes how terms will be used in this book. These terms will be used consistently, even though particular vendors describe their systems with other terms. If these definitions seem confusing at first, don't worry; they will become clearer as you read the book.

Data Base Management System (DBMS)

A DBMS is a package of computer programs and documentation that lets you set up and use a data base.

Data Base

A data base is a collection of interrelated data. Specifically, the data base is the complete collection of data, pointers, tables, indexes, dictionaries, and so on. If you keep track of both your customers and your products, these are part of the same data base, unless you never intend to relate the two in any way.

Database

Don't confuse the one-word term with the two-word term data base. A database is a part of a data base. Consider it as a two-dimensional table like that shown in Table 1-1. The rows are records, and each column is a field. The table is usually stored on disk as a file. A dictionary describes all the fields, and one or more indexes enable quick access to any record. The table, the dictionary, and the indexes are all considered part of the database. A customer list and a list of products would be two databases. Not every vendor's data base can be broken down into databases.

File

As in CP/M, a file is a collection of data on disk accessed by a unique name. It generally contains a sequence of records of identical format, each containing a series of fields. It might instead contain a data dictionary, an index, a screen layout, or any combination of the above.

Record

A record is a group of related fields of information treated as a unit. Each row in Table 1-1 is a record.

Field

A field identifies a location in a record where a data item is stored. This field has certain characteristics, such as length and type (numeric or character string), and is represented by a column in Table 1-1.

Data Item

A data item is another name for a field used in conjunction with large DBMS systems and network DBMS microcomputers.

Byte

A byte is the smallest piece of information in the data base of interest to the user. Normally it is equivalent to one character, but sometimes it consists of two numeric digits. A megabyte is 1 million bytes and is used up faster than you might think.

	Field	Field	Field	Field	Field
Record 1	Name	Street	City	State	ZIP
Record 2	Name	Street	City	State	ZIP
Record 3	Name	Street	City	State	ZIP
Record 4	Name	Street	City	State	ZIP
Record 5	Name	Street	City	State	ZIP

TABLE 1-1. Records and Fields

Schema

A schema is a logical picture of the data base showing the relationships between various records. The detailed contents of the records come from the data dictionary. Schemas are used in Chapter 2 to illustrate essential data base concepts.

Data Dictionary

The data dictionary is a full description of the fields in a database or data base. The data dictionary describes the relationships between various fields in a data base. It also describes each field by name, report heading tag, length, data type, high and low limits, and so on.

Index

An index is a table of record numbers. These record numbers, called *pointers,* are arranged to help you find a particular record quickly by key. The index permits retrieval of records in sequential order and allows insertion of new records. But be careful. Some indexes do not have this "add" capability.

Key

A key is a unique identifier for a record. It can be a single field or a group of fields.

2

Data Base on the Microcomputer

In this book, a DBMS is any software package which meets most of the objectives identified in Chapter 1 and runs under the CP/M operating system. These criteria are broad enough to include any package that is actually called a DBMS and a few that are not. Some computer professionals exclude packages that lack some feature they think necessary, and some software vendors exclude all packages except their own. We will present some standards for judging and comparing a wide variety of individual DBMS packages.

The DBMS may be classified in three categories—File Management System (FMS), Relational Data Base Management System (RDBMS), and Network/Hierarchical Data Base Management System (NDBMS). We will now discuss each of these three categories of DBMS in turn.

FILE MANAGEMENT SYSTEM (FMS)

File management systems (also called data management systems or information management systems) were available before the term data base became popular. Unfortunately, some of these have recently been "upgraded" to DBMS status by manufacturers who recognize the appeal of a more complex program. Essentially, an FMS automates the construction of business computer programs, concentrating on file definition, data entry programming, sorting, and creating reports. The idea is to allow nonprogrammers to put together straightforward business systems.

The traditional FMS supports the creation of single-file systems and often provides an index for direct access. For example, if you receive mail and phone inquiries in response to an advertisement you placed in a computer magazine, you can use an FMS to make a customer contact list with one record per customer. Each record should include the following:

ID number
Name
Address line 1
Address line 2
City
State
ZIP
Phone
Date contacted
Product of interest (number)

You define the file by telling the computer the name and length of each field and whether the field is numeric or alphabetic. This is done via the menu; you choose one of the displayed options, as shown in Figure 2-1. (This file definition process has been renamed the *data dictionary* in the data base world.)

After you have defined the fields, you may enter data for as many customers as you like. To search for a particular customer, you enter the ID number, and the program either scans the whole file of customers from the beginning of the file, or uses the index to find the target customer directly. Once the record is found, you may delete it or change it using another menu as is shown in Figure 2-2.

The FMS lets you define and print reports— a customer list for the sales staff, for example— simply by using menus. You specify the fields to be printed, including the column headings and the report title. The FMS stores these specifications to disk for future use. Thus, you could ask for a list of customers interested in product 5230 and print mailing labels or form letters.

This may sound like a trivial application, but programming it in BASIC could take you days. Many record-keeping chores lend themselves to the FMS approach, and nonprogrammers can easily set them up. If your FMS isn't powerful enough, however, you could reach a dead end on a tough assignment. This point has not been lost on the FMS designers, who have been increasing the power of their packages. At least one FMS contains its own programming language.

Most recently published FMS programs can handle multiple files. You could process an invoice file and then look up the customer name in another file based on the customer number. Some systems let you build systems with transaction files, multiple master files, historical transaction files, and even your own menus, but it is sometimes difficult to analyze your needs against FMS capabilities. You can learn what compromises to make with an FMS by evaluating the capabilities of the spectrum of data base systems.

Much attention has been focused lately on *program generators* that purport to have made programmers obsolete. Actually, the program generator is just a special type of FMS. Except for a time-consuming intermediate step where a number of BASIC programs are "generated" to disk, the end result of the program generator and the FMS is the same. In the conventional FMS, the data dictionary, report formats, and

```
ENTER VARIABLE DESCRIPTION ID NUMBER 3

ENTER STORAGE FORMAT
  0 = FLOATING POINT
  1 = INTEGER
  2 = STRING
  3 = DATE
  4 = MONEY
  5 = COMPUTATIONAL
? 1                    Typing "1" indicates INTEGER storage

ENTER LENGTH OF FIELD 6
```

FIGURE 2-1.
Using a menu to define a field

```
RECORD FOUND!

 1.   ID Number:         643212
 2.   Name:              Leonard J. Fulton
 3.   Address line 1:    5546 55th Place S.
 4.   Address line 2:
 5.   City:              Seattle
 6.   State:             WA
 7.   Zip:               98108
 8.   Phone:             (206) 762-1212
 9.   Date contracted:   08/10/82
10.   Product:           2347

ENTER OPTION CODE
 0 = RETURN TO MAIN MENU
 1 = GET ANOTHER RECORD
 2 = CHANGE THIS RECORD
 3 = DELETE THIS RECORD
? 2

ENTER FIELD NUMBER TO CHANGE 3

3. Address line 1:     [5546 55th Place S.] 5456 55th Place S.

ENTER OPTION CODE
 0 = RETURN TO MAIN MENU
 1 = GET ANOTHER RECORD
 2 = CHANGE THIS RECORD
 3 = DELETE THIS RECORD
? 0
```

FIGURE 2-2.
Using a menu to
change a field

menu control are all stored in special disk files. The FMS program looks at this control information, reads your response to its menu, and then figures out how to do the data entry and print the reports. In the program generator system, all the control information is coded right into the generated BASIC program. You can always customize the program after it has been generated, but if you decide to change the record layout, for instance, you will not be able to regenerate the code without losing your customizations.

For more information about program generators, refer to Chapter 8, which describes one program generator, pointing out its strengths

and weaknesses compared to an FMS. Chapter 6 describes a file management system package, FMS-80, published by DJR Associates, Inc.

RELATIONAL DATA BASE MANAGEMENT SYSTEM (RDBMS)

You can consider the Relational Data Base Management System as one step up from the FMS, but be careful: some features of the FMS are absent in the RDBMS. Like the FMS, the RDBMS works with individual files, known as *databases.* Unlike the FMS, the RDBMS lets you operate on an entire database with a single command. If you have a field called PRICE in the data dictionary, for example, you can say REPLACE PRICE WITH PRICE*1.1, causing all prices to be increased by ten percent. In addition, you can use several databases at the same time. This is the real power of the RDBMS.

When RDBMS programs became available, only a few experimental systems ran on large computers, although the concept was being highly praised in the literature. However, the larger data processing community had just become familiar with the network/hierarchical style DBMS and was not ready to convert to RDBMS. The microcomputer industry has recently adapted the relational concept to its machines with considerable success.

The main reason for the success of the RDBMS is its simplicity. Easier to learn than other data bases, RDBMS allows you to build complex systems one step at a time. The name comes from a mathematical concept called a *relation*, which is simply a table. This table is stored in the computer as a file, or database,

where the records are the horizontal rows, and the fields are the vertical columns, as shown in Figures 2-3 through 2-9.

Suppose you are the Internal Revenue Service and you want to use your RDBMS to identify taxpayers who did not report all their interest income. You compile a list of taxpayers from their 1040 forms (Figure 2-3) and then a list of interest payments from the 1099 forms prepared by the banks (Figure 2-4). First you sort the 1099s and 1040s by Social Security number, then you update the 1099 relation (Figure 2-5) against the 1040 relation, giving the result shown in Figure 2-6. The last step (Figure 2-7) shows only those taxpayers with a discrepancy. You are now ready to call in those hapless souls for their audit.

Two hundred million taxpayers might be a burden for your microcomputer, but this sample of ten runs quite smoothly. Once the 1040 and 1099 relations are in the machine, it takes just a few minutes to manipulate them with simple commands to get the information you need. Save the commands to repeat the procedure with new data.

Social Security Number	Name	Address	Interest Reported
336-42-8487	JEFFREY S. GORDON	BELLEVUE WA 98006	1302.57
339-50-9482	DIANA B. GARRETT	KIRKLAND WA 98033	335.80
301-58-7409	PATTI THOMPSON	REDMOND WA 98052	2.89
338-42-9034	DAVID STARK	REDMOND WA 98052	24177.77
302-40-2980	LARRY DALBY	NORTH BEND WA 98045	0.00
331-40-6201	SUSAN L. MILLBOURN	BELLEVUE, WA 98004	0.00
339-52-7850	JOHN CURTIS WOLFE	SEATTLE, WA 98177	0.00
337-35-0156	GERALD T. BREYMEYER	REDMOND, WA 98052	0.00
338-42-1446	JOSEPH GOELLER	DUVALL, WA 98019	0.00
331-50-8713	MICHAEL J. MILLER	BELLEVUE, WA 98008	0.00

FIGURE 2-3.
Unsorted 1040 information

Bank Number	Account Number	Social Security Number	Interest Paid
192	654978	336-42-8487	1258.36
192	654513	338-42-9034	2588.39
213	987465	336-42-8487	44.21
213	132654	339-50-9482	10.57
213	126427	338-42-9034	21589.38
358	556778	339-50-9482	558.99
358	789872	301-58-7409	2.89
358	651159	338-42-9034	7885.33

FIGURE 2-4.
1099 information sorted by bank

Social Security Number	Bank Number	Account Number	Interest Paid
301-58-7409	358	789872	2.89
336-42-8487	192	654978	1258.36
336-42-8487	213	987465	44.21
338-42-9034	192	654513	2588.39
338-42-9034	213	126427	21589.38
338-42-9034	358	651159	7885.33
339-50-9482	213	132654	10.57
339-50-9482	358	556778	558.99

FIGURE 2-5.
1099 information sorted by Social Security number

Social Security Number	Name	Interest Reported	Interest Paid
301-58-7409	PATTI THOMPSON	2.89	2.89
302-40-2980	LARRY DALBY	0.00	0.00
331-40-6201	SUSAN L. MILLBOURN	0.00	0.00
331-50-8713	MICHAEL J. MILLER	0.00	0.00
336-42-8487	JEFFREY S. GORDON	1302.57	1302.57
337-35-0156	GERALD T. BREYMEYER	0.00	0.00
338-42-1446	JOSEPH GOELLER	0.00	0.00
338-42-9034	DAVID STARK	24177.77	32063.10
339-50-9482	DIANA B. GARRETT	558.99	569.56
339-52-7850	JOHN CURTIS WOLFE	0.00	0.00

FIGURE 2-6.
Interest reported vs. interest paid

Social Security Number	Name	Interest Reported	Interest Paid	Discrepancy Amount
338-42-9034	DAVID STARK	24177.77	32063.10	7885.33
339-50-9482	DIANA B. GARRETT	558.99	569.56	10.57

FIGURE 2-7.
Taxpayers with interest
discrepancies

Bank Number	Bank Name
192	MT. ST. HELENS
213	FIRST NATIONAL
358	FARMERS' TRUST

FIGURE 2-8.
Bank numbers
and names

Bank Number	Bank Name	Account Number	Interest Paid
192	MT. ST. HELENS	654978	1258.36
192	MT. ST. HELENS	654513	2588.39
213	FIRST NATIONAL	987465	44.21
213	FIRST NATIONAL	132654	10.57
213	FIRST NATIONAL	126427	21589.38
358	FARMERS' TRUST	556778	558.99
358	FARMERS' TRUST	789872	2.89
358	FARMERS' TRUST	651159	7885.33

FIGURE 2-9.
1099 information joined
with bank names

The beauty of the RDBMS is that you do not have to anticipate all your needs when you set up your files. In the tax example, all you had was a list of 1040 information and a list of 1099 information. Rather than ask for cheaters, you could have asked for an alphabetical list of taxpayers reporting interest income, a list of all banks with depositors in Bellevue, Washington, total interest payments by bank, and so on. You could get all this from two simple databases.

Two important RDBMS operations are the "projection" and the "join"; together they give you an electronic "cut and paste" capability. Projection creates a new relation by selecting certain columns from an existing relation, while join combines two separate relations. Figure 2-6 shows a projection from Figure 2-3 (with Interest Paid added on). If we combine Figure 2-4 and Figure 2-8 (a list of bank names and numbers) we get the join shown in Figure 2-9. If a particular bank number was associated with several different bank names, join would give you invalid results because you would not know which name to use.

The projection in Figure 2-6 is really a new relation, completely separate from the original. If Susan Millbourn got married and changed her name and you updated the first relation, the second relation would still show the old name. At least one RDBMS has solved this problem by letting you create a view of a database, a "virtual" table, one that does not exist in its own right, but that allows changes to the real data to be made visible. You can't do this with a microcomputer RDBMS yet, but you can approximate it by building a secondary index for a database, allowing the same rows to appear in a different sort order. Figure 2-10 shows the 1099 relation with an Account Number index, giving you a second view of the same data. Usually, you may have as many secondary indexes as you like.

To work properly as a relation, a database has to be in *normal form*, which means you must organize it according to some mathematical rules. This organization is done as part of the data base design process. Look at Figure 2-11, which shows two sales orders, each with multiple line items for products sold. This is not at all a relation because it is not a table with rows and columns. Figure 2-12 shows the *first*

Account Number	Social Security Number	Bank Number	Account Number	Interest Paid
126427	301-58-7409	358	789872	2.89
132654	336-42-8487	192	654978	1258.36
556778	336-42-8487	213	987465	44.21
651159	338-42-9034	192	654513	2588.39
654513	338-42-9034	213	126427	21589.38
654978	338-42-9034	358	651159	7885.33
789872	339-50-9482	213	132654	10.57
987465	339-50-9482	358	556778	558.99

FIGURE 2-10.
1099 information indexed by
account number

```
   Order  Customer                              Order    Product
   Number  Number      Customer  Name            Date     Number    Quantity

   158204   28000   ADDISON PACIFIC SUPPLY     01/18/82   21-405      24
                                                          21-510      18
                                                          44-020       4
                                                          56-785      18
                                                          80-702      12

   158205   88000   BIRD ELECTRIC CORP         01/19/82   21-405      12
                                                          32-840       2
                                                          44-020       8
                                                          62-320      24
```

FIGURE 2-11.
Unnormalized relation

normal form of the relation, the simplest way of making a table.

In any relation, there is a unique way of identifying the rows: You specify one or more fields as the *key*. In Figure 2-12 the key is Order Number and Product Number. If you know those two values, you can look up Customer Number, Customer Name, Order Date, and Quantity. These fields are said to be functionally dependent on the key. The customer information and date, however, are dependent only on the Order Number—a part of the key, not the whole key. Splitting the relation in two as shown in Figure 2-13 eliminates this dependence and gives the *second normal form*. If you know the Order Number, you can look up the Customer Number, Customer Name, and Order Date in the header database, and you can look up the Product Number and Quantity in the detail database.

Now there is only one problem. Customer Name is dependent on Customer Number, so Customer Name is transitively dependent on Order Number. Splitting the relation again (Figure 2-14) solves the problem and yields the *third normal form*, which is the best model of

the data. Here you have to go into the customer database to look up the name every time you print an order header. It is a little more work, but there is less redundancy.

Computer scientists have pursued this logic further with more complex data structures, identifying the fourth and fifth normal forms plus a few others. They attack this with the zeal of a physicist searching for new subatomic particles, but there is little in this work that concerns the microcomputer owner. The relational idea is so basic that you can begin to see how it works just from studying examples.

So far, the microcomputer RDBMS has made the database and the file one and the same. This approach works well, but it is not the only way to build an RDBMS. Data base theory says that the physical data structure need not be related to the logical structure, but if the two structures are similar, the system is very efficient. Chapters 4 and 5 describe in detail two relational data base management systems: Condor II, published by Condor Computer, and dBASE II, published by Ashton-Tate.

Order Number	Customer Number	Customer Name	Order Date	Product Number	Quantity
158204	28000	ADDISON PACIFIC SUPPLY	01/18/82	21-405	24
158204	28000	ADDISON PACIFIC SUPPLY	01/18/82	21-510	18
158204	28000	ADDISON PACIFIC SUPPLY	01/18/82	44-020	4
158204	28000	ADDISON PACIFIC SUPPLY	01/18/82	56-785	18
158204	28000	ADDISON PACIFIC SUPPLY	01/18/82	80-702	12
158205	88000	BIRD ELECTRIC CORP	01/19/82	21-405	12
158205	88000	BIRD ELECTRIC CORP	01/19/82	32-840	2
158205	88000	BIRD ELECTRIC CORP	01/19/82	44-020	8
158205	88000	BIRD ELECTRIC CORP	01/19/82	62-320	24

FIGURE 2-12.
First normal form

Order Number	Customer Number	Customer Name	Order Date		Order Number	Product Number	Quantity
158204	28000	ADDISON PACIFIC SUPPLY	01/18/82		158204	21-405	24
158205	88000	BIRD ELECTRIC CORP	01/19/82		158204	21-510	18
					158204	44-020	4
					158204	56-785	18
					158204	80-702	12
					158205	21-405	12
					158205	32-840	2
					158205	44-020	8
					158205	62-320	24

FIGURE 2-13.
Second normal form

Order Number	Customer Number	Order Date		Order Number	Product Number	Quantity
158204	28000	01/18/82		158204	21-405	24
158205	88000	01/19/82		158204	21-510	18
				158204	44-020	4
				158204	56-785	18
Order Number	Customer Name			158204	80-702	12
				158205	21-405	12
28000	ADDISON PACIFIC SUPPLY			158205	32-840	2
88000	BIRD ELECTRIC CORP			158205	44-020	8
				158205	62-320	24

FIGURE 2-14.
Third normal form

NETWORK/HIERARCHICAL DATA BASE MANAGEMENT SYSTEM (NDBMS)

Of all microcomputer data base management systems, the NDBMS is, for better or for worse, the closest copy of commercial data base systems in general use on large computers. (This is no accident because the leading package started with standards set by a computer industry group called CODASYL, Conference on Data System Languages.) If you use an FMS, you are used to looking at your data as physical files, just as you would if you were a BASIC or COBOL programmer. You have a collection of records, each divided into fields. The RDBMS continues with this approach but uses different names. The NDBMS, however, takes a radical departure and makes you look at the data as a whole in a new, logical way. The physical layout of the data is of no concern to you, so you can forget about files. Records, fields, and data items still remain.

You have already seen that the relation is the basic unit in the RDBMS. The NDBMS has the *set* as its basic unit. The best way to understand sets is to study an example borrowed from James Martin's book, *Computer Data-Base Organization.**

Martin is obviously a connoisseur of fine wine, as well he might afford to be. You, however, have spent your last nickel on a new 20-megabyte hard disk, and you have to settle for less in the way of personal luxury. Your wine comes not from France but from California and New York; it isn't distinguished by region, but by brand name. In order to illustrate we will use four fictitious wineries named Tuttle,

Jarrett, Vigeant, and Smith. Tuttle and Jarrett are California wineries and Vigeant and Smith are New York wineries. To simplify things further, let's suppose that all vintages are 1982. The schema in Figure 2-15 represents the structure of your wine cellar and shows three levels of hierarchy. The arrows indicate a "one-to-many" (1:N) relationship, that is, many brands from one state or many bottles of one brand. Figure 2-16 is a view of some sample data, which looks something like an upside-down tree.

Applying an NDBMS structure to the example in Figure 2-15, you define the two sets as shown in Figure 2-17. The top one, SET1, has as its *owner* one state—in this case either California or New York—and has for its *members* the different brands of wine made in the owner state. Each brand, in turn, is the owner in the bottom set, SET2, with individual bottles as members. You can establish sort orders within the sets, for example sorting bottles alphabetically by name, price, first-in first-out, and so on. There is actually another set, SET0, with the system as its owner and the states as members.

In the RDBMS you specified the organization of the data with a data dictionary, one entry per field, with all the records in the database assumed to be the same. In the NDBMS things are more complex because you have to learn a Data Description Language (DDL), which describes the structure of the data. Figure 2-18 shows an idealized description of the wine cellar data base. First you see the record definitions, then the set information describing how the data records are related. Contrast this with the RDBMS approach where you specify the relationships when you actually use the data.

Once the data base is defined, the next step is to use it. Because the NDBMS does not

---

*James Martin, *Computer Data-Base Organization*, second edition (Englewood Cliffs, New Jersey: Prentice-Hall, 1977).

emphasize direct interactive data retrieval, you have to write some programs. The large computer systems have a Data Manipulation Language (DML) specifically geared to working with data structures. As a microcomputer owner, you will have to use an available host language, such as BASIC, COBOL, or PL/I, instead. Since these compilers don't know

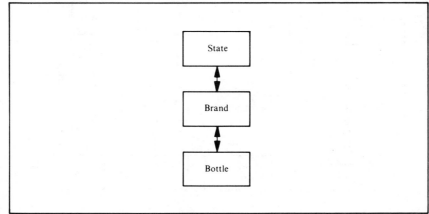

FIGURE 2-15.
Wine cellar
schema

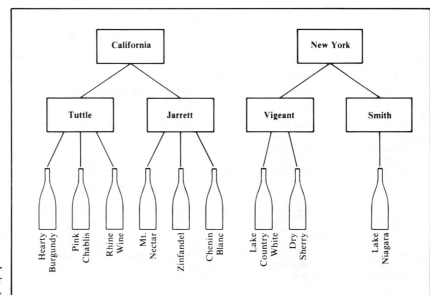

FIGURE 2-16.
Wine cellar
hierarchy

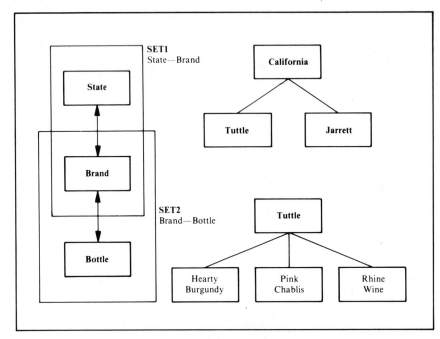

FIGURE 2-17.
SETs

```
RECORD          STATE
ITEM            SNAME           CHAR      12 bytes

RECORD          BRAND
ITEM            BNAME           CHAR      12 bytes

RECORD          BOTTLE
ITEM            NAME            CHAR      30 bytes
ITEM            PRICE           REAL       8 bytes
ITEM            COMMENTS        CHAR      30 bytes

SET             SET1            One-to-many, not sorted
OWNER           STATE
MEMBER          BRAND

SET             SET2            One-to-many, not sorted
OWNER           BRAND
MEMBER          BOTTLE
```

FIGURE 2-18.
Data dictionary for
the wine cellar

about data base, you have to shoehorn in your data access commands with CALLs to the data base software. A CALL statement is just a way to exchange information with another program, in this case the DBMS, which is already in the computer's memory.

In order to make the wine example as simple as possible, assume that your host language has DML words built-in. A program written in this imaginary language lists all wines by state and brand, as follows:

```
OPEN THE DATA BASE
PRINT "Wine List by State, by Brand"
FIND FIRST MEMBER OF SET0
DO WHILE NOT END OF SET0
   PRINT "State ="; STATE
   SET OWNER OF SET1 BASED ON MEMBER OF
   SET0
   FIND FIRST MEMBER OF SET1
   DO WHILE NOT END OF SET1
     PRINT "Brand ="; BRAND
     SET OWNER OF SET2 BASED ON MEMBER OF
     SET1
     FIND FIRST MEMBER OF SET2
     DO WHILE NOT END OF SET2
       PRINT  "Name = "; NAME;
       PRINT  "Price = "; PRICE
COMMENTS        FIND NEXT MEMBER OF SET2
           END DO
         END DO
       END DO
       PRINT "End of list"
       CLOSE THE DATA BASE
```

Most of these statements will be familiar to you if you have programmed in BASIC or Pascal, but the statement SET OWNER OF SET2 BASED ON MEMBER OF SET1 may be new. Remember that the wine brands are both members of SET1 and owners of SET2. If the program is stepping through the brands in SET1 and gets to Jarrett, it is now ready to make a switch and consider Jarrett the owner of SET2 so it can step through those bottles. You

can read the statement backward as "Make the member of SET1 the owner of SET2," if this seems helpful.

Looking at the program again, notice that there are three concentric "loops," one for each set, and that the program follows the structure of the tree, exploring each branch in sequence.

The wine example so far has been strictly hierarchical, assuming that no one brand is made in more than one state. If you learn that Vigeant wineries are located in both New York and California, things become more complicated. You could retain the structure used in Figure 2-16 and consider the two Vigeants as separate brands, as shown in Figure 2-19 (dropping Tuttle out of the picture for the moment). However, if you wanted to ask the question "What wines does Vigeant make?" the model of your data breaks down. You must then move on to the network model, of which the hierarchical model is just a special case.

Figure 2-20 shows the first example of a network model in which Vigeant wineries are now members in both the New York and California sets. Unfortunately, you no longer know whether Lake Country White comes from New York or California—this structure is clearly not an accurate model of your wine cellar. In fact, you have now established a "many-to-many" (N:M) relationship between states and brands. (The N:M relationship taxes a large NDBMS, but a microcomputer NDBMS handles it easily.) Books about large data base systems caution against the N:M relationship because of the kind of problem shown here. Chapter 7 details a successful use of a many-to-many relationship.

Consider a different model as shown in Figure 2-21. It lets you list all wines by state and by brand. The model is accurate, since it does not lead to false conclusions about the origins of your wine. On the other hand, this model does

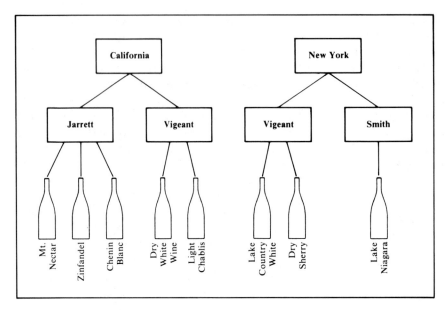

FIGURE 2-19.
Two Vigeants

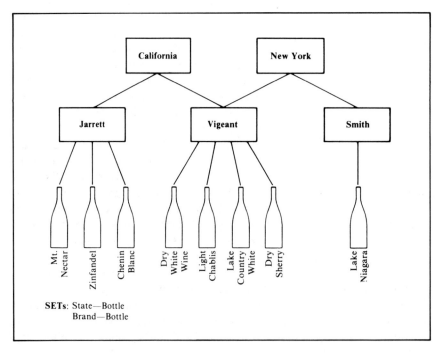

FIGURE 2-20.
First try at a
network

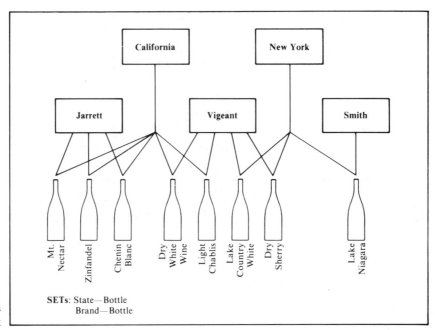

FIGURE 2-21.
Second try at a
network

not allow you to easily find all Vigeant wines from California.

The last attempt to establish a network model is shown in Figure 2-22, the most accurate and complete model. However, although the problem is simple, the complexity of its solution is overwhelming. If you choose any of the new models shown in Figures 2-20, 2-21, and 2-22 you must rewrite the list program completely. As an exercise, try laying out the wine cellar problem using a relational model.

As you can see, the planning and setting-up of an NDBMS require much analysis and design. You must be certain that the fundamental structure of your data will not change, and you must be able to write programs in an established computer language. In return you get the full use of all the features of both the language and the DBMS, and there is little to restrict you in developing your system. Also, this set data structure lends itself to efficient storage and quick access. Chapter 7 describes in detail a Network/Hierarchical Data Base Management System, MDBS III, published by Micro Data Base Systems.

FEATURES OF DATA BASE MANAGEMENT SYSTEMS

The remainder of this chapter discusses specific features of data base management systems. Some of these features are considered necessary elements, while others are considered useful options for particular applications. Careful reading of this section will provide essential

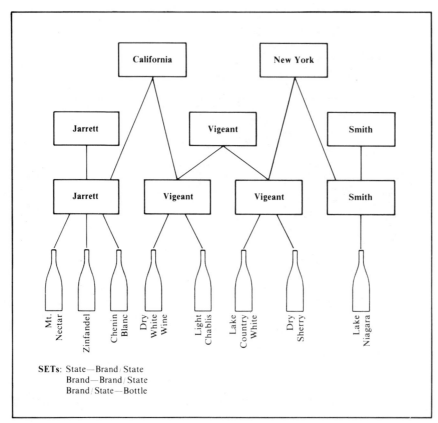

SETs: State—Brand/State
Brand—Brand/State
Brand/State—Bottle

FIGURE 2-22.
Last try at a
network

information for evaluating systems. The features defined in this section have been used to create a checklist for evaluating the software in Chapters 4 through 7.

DBMS Trade-offs

In order to understand a DBMS, you may consider each of the following trade-offs as "independent." This means that an RDBMS can be either command-driven or program-driven, and if it is program-driven, the language could be established or built-in. However, you may not be able to find both the type of language and type of DBMS in the same package; for example, a menu-driven RDBMS, a NDBMS with a built-in language, and so forth. There may also be some overlap, that is, a particular package may operate in both menu-driven and program-driven modes.

FMS, RDBMS, and NDBMS Compared

In general, the FMS (File Management System) is the easiest to learn and simplest to use. It is a menu-driven system that works especially well for home and office problems, such as address lists, coin collections, and inventory. The RDBMS (Relational Data Base Management System) gives you most FMS capabilities plus some additional data manipulation ability, but it requires that you learn a new "language." You must also understand some abstract data modeling concepts in order to take advantage of its power. An RDBMS is handy if you need to experiment with your data or if you can't plan your whole system in advance. Setting up routine, but foolproof, business systems with an RDBMS is hard work, but those systems will be more flexible in the end.

Both the FMS and RDBMS are suitable for use by people who are not computer professionals. The NDBMS trades ease of use for power, enabling a programmer to create complete applications, such as complete business accounting systems that are efficient and flexible.

Menu-, Command-, and Program-driven Systems Compared

The menu-driven DBMS is certainly the easiest system for an inexperienced user. But just having a menu is no guarantee of understanding it. Look at the menu in Figure 2-23 and see if you can understand it. Menus work best when there are a limited number of options and the options follow a "tree"; that is, a choice from the main menu brings up a secondary menu with new choices, and so on. Commands, on the other hand, are more concise and flexible but require that you learn them. Take the command RENAME FILE1 TO FILE2. This could be done easily with a menu where the computer asks you for the old filename and then the new filename. The command to calculate gross margin percent, STORE 100*(MARGIN/GROSS) TO PERCENT, would be more difficult to structure as a menu.

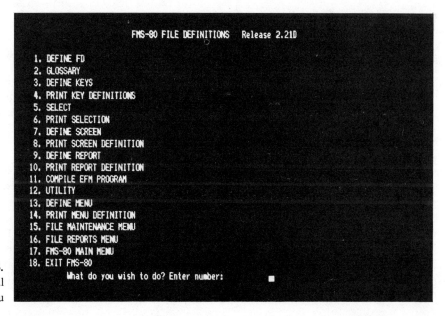

FIGURE 2-23.
A typical
DBMS menu

With either a command-driven or a menu-driven system, you are controlling every data processing step from your keyboard. Suppose you have worked out a complicated procedure that you want to repeat often. Almost every DBMS offers you a way of saving a sequence of commands or menu choices as a disk file, which can be edited and invoked by its name when you wish to run it. This disk file could be considered a program, but not in the same sense as a BASIC or COBOL program. A real program is a sequence of instructions which allows you to operate on data record-by-record. With the addition of control instructions, a program can test for conditions and then alter its logic flow, as in the following example in BASIC, which prints the numbers 0 through 9:

```
100 I = 0
110 PRINT "THE VALUE OF I IS ";I
120 I = I+1
130 IF I < 10 GOTO 110
140 STOP
```

Any DBMS which uses this type of program is said to be *procedural*. Any DBMS which offers menu choices, fill-in-the-blanks, or global commands like LIST ALL PRICE is described as *nonprocedural*. Packages allowing both procedural and nonprocedural control are the most flexible.

Built-in and Established Languages Compared

This comparison only applies to the program-driven DBMS. Established languages such as BASIC, COBOL, Pascal, and PL/I are well known by programmers. Because these languages were invented before the DBMS, there are no data manipulation commands that tie into the data base. One manufacturer of large computers releases a special version of the

programming language that integrates all the commands for its DBMS, but microcomputer companies that write compilers may not write the DBMS. Consequently, the DBMS program could contain a statement like

```
E0=CALL(A2,"DEFINE,OPENLIST,"F$,N$,P$,R$,4)
```

where E0, A2, F$, and so on, are variables in the host BASIC program. This statement opens the data base and relates the internal BASIC variables to the data dictionary fields. You must remember, however, that F$ is the freight bill number and P$ is the purchase order number.

In contrast to the established languages, the built-in DBMS languages are not restricted by old standards but instead introduce their own commands and structures tailored to the data base. One useful feature, the connection of the data dictionary with the language, enables you to enter data base fields either by name or by sequence number without having to "declare" those fields in your program.

DBMS Performance Criteria

This section provides important criteria for comparing one DBMS with another and for matching program capabilities with particular applications.

Access Times

Access time is the elapsed time between your request for data and the appearance of the data on the screen. If you asked for the account balance for customer 0231, for instance, there would be a slight delay before the dollar figure came up. Access times depend on your computer hardware, particularly on the disk. When comparing benchmark results from several

DBMS packages, make sure that the hardware configuration is the same for each. A hard disk can access data many times faster than a floppy disk, and a 4-MHz microprocessor chip makes a program run twice as fast as a 2-MHz chip, provided the disk can keep up. New memory advances such as "semiconductor disk" and "cache buffers" sometimes have more impact than a hard disk.

Another criterion of access time is the access method—direct, indexed, or sequential. (Chapter 3 presents a detailed description of each method. Making meaningful comparisons depends on knowing what access method you are using.) Direct access is the quickest and depends only on the disk and not on the DBMS. The speed of indexed access depends on the algorithm used. Indexed access with DBMS packages written in BASIC can be almost as fast as assembly language packages, indicating that the disk access is critical. Among packages there are many sequential and indexed access times. A slow package ought to have some offsetting advantages to merit your consideration.

Processing Speed

Disk speed considerations apply both to processing speed and to access times, with sorting and indexing being the most important speed tests. You should practice with large files that are very much out of order to seriously measure sort times, but you can buy an external sort program if the built-in sort is too slow. Do not forget that the network/hierarchical class of DBMS does not intrinsically require any sorting.

You have some control over processing speed when you set up the data base. Knowing the most frequently asked questions will help you to arrange the data for quick access. Beware of operations like the RDBMS "join"

which could run endlessly if carelessly invoked.

Modern DBMS packages are no longer written in interpretive BASIC, but rather, packages are written in assembly language or a compiled language such as CB-80. Both are fast, but the compiled programs need more memory space and must swap code from disk more often than assembly programs do. You will notice more delays when going from function to function with the compiled program.

Unless otherwise noted, all access and performance benchmarks in this book assume the use of a 4-MHz Z-80 system with double-density, 8-inch diskettes. Systems that use 5 1/4-inch diskettes will be slower; hard disk systems will be faster.

Data Storage Capacity

The size of a microcomputer data base is generally limited by the CP/M operating system. Version 2.2, the most widely used, has a built-in limitation of almost eight megabytes per file. However, unless you have a large capacity hard disk, you won't notice this limit. Instead you will worry about squeezing your data into the disk space you have. The FMS and RDBMS are very predictable for disk usage because they work with files, records, and fields. If you define a customer address as 25 characters in the data dictionary, that is how much space every record requires, even if a particular address is shorter. Usually the DBMS stores numbers as strings of digits, one digit per byte, but a few packages manage to compress two digits into each byte. To determine the space required for each file, simply add up the lengths for all the fields in a record and multiply by the number of records per file. Double this number to allow yourself room for indexes and some work space for sorting, extracting, and reorganization.

With an NDBMS the procedure is more

complex. You have to allow space for internal pointers, but this space is partially offset by less redundancy in the data. It usually takes some experimentation to come up with good space estimates.

Built-in Limitations

The limitations of the DBMS vary widely from one package to another, and each must be examined in light of your specific applications. Maximum fields per record could be important if you are doing a payroll system. If you need current quarter-to-date and year-to-date totals for each employee, as well as personnel information, a DBMS with a 32-field limit won't be sufficient. A maximum of 256 bytes per record, as imposed by some BASICs, could severely limit many systems. A numeric accuracy limit of ten digits could give you trouble if you were doing an accounting system for a large corporation with balances over 99,999,999.99. For example, you must consider whether exponents are allowed. Also, consider how many files may be used at the same time. An FMS that allows only one eliminates them from the data base class altogether. If your DBMS permits only two, you will probably quickly outgrow it.

Consider what data types are available. Most packages offer character, numeric, and logical types, but a few systems have short integer, Julian date, dollar, and so on.

Necessary DBMS Features

You will find the following features in all the DBMS commercial packages described in Chapters 4 through 7 of this book.

Data Dictionary

The data dictionary is the heart of the data base. It tells you almost everything about the

data. The FMS and the RDBMS use a dictionary to describe an individual file or database, but the NDBMS uses it to describe the entire data base—all the data in the system. In the latter case, the data relationships are encoded into the dictionary.

Each field has a dictionary entry with the following minimum information:

- The field name or number
- The data type (alphabetic, numeric, and so on)
- The length in bytes or digits.

This is the minimum amount of information an entry can contain. In addition, the dictionary may list the

- Edit mask (the number of decimals, leading zeros, and so on)
- Upper and lower limits
- Validation fields in other files
- Password security levels
- Screen row and column.

Query Facility

There must be a way for nonprogrammers to view and update the data. The more powerful this facility, the better, but power should not compromise ease of use. The FMS uses menus; the RDBMS and NDBMS use commands—actually a special query language—to access the data base.

Report Generator

The most common request in a data processing department is for special reports that list data in a certain order with subtotals and totals plus column headings on each page. A contract programmer may charge $500 to write a COBOL program to print an average report, but you can use a DBMS to do the job in less than an hour. There is considerable power variation in the report generator of each DBMS but there is a trade-off between power and ease of use. If your DBMS has a language, either established or built-in, you can use it to program any reports that the report generator will not create, at a cost substantially less than the contract programmer's figure.

A good report generator should let you select certain data for printing, both from the fields and from the records. If you have a name and address file, you could select name and city from the fields, then all out-of-state vendors from the records. You can see by now that the report generator is just an extension of the query language, oriented to paper instead of to a video screen.

File Compatibility with Other Programs

The DBMS must be able to read data from BASIC and COBOL programs as they are found in existing accounting systems, and it must be able to write data for use by these programs. BASIC uses records of the delimited type with commas between the fields and quotes around the strings like the following example:

```
127788,"Jones,"  "Robert G.,"  "8811
    Prairie Ave."
```

The COBOL equivalent, also associated with some BASICs and PL/I, looks something like the following first-field record:

```
127788 JonesRobert G8811 Prairie Ave.
```

The program expects that the last name will always be 12 characters long. A DBMS should be able to read and write both record types.

Restructure Ability

In order to understand this feature, imagine it is 1973 and that your job is to put together a gas station data base for an auto club, listing price per gallon in different cities and states. Since gasoline is only $0.39 a gallon and disk storage is very expensive, you allow two positions for the price, and the price field is sandwiched between the state and brand fields. The system runs well until 1979, when the price goes beyond $1.00 per gallon. You must now restructure the data base to reflect the new price.

Fortunately, the DBMS designers foresaw that changes would be necessary (the gas price increase, for example) and provided a way to restructure the data base. The programmer changes the price field to four digits after changing the data file to provide the space for the new digits. This fix should hold for at least five years.

Effective Error Handling

When you do something wrong, your DBMS should not crash or destroy all your data. Of course, you will have made frequent backup copies, but it is irritating to have to use them all the time. A good DBMS gives clear, helpful error messages and lets you correct the problem. It is difficult to recover from hardware problems, but full disks and directories, off-line printers, and so on, should be allowed for. If the disk fills up, the DBMS should warn you and let you delete unwanted files.

Authors of data base management systems for large computers work hard to ensure recovery after a system failure. As the data base is being updated, special *transaction records* are logged to disk or tape. After a disaster, the disk files are reloaded from the prior night's backup, and the transaction is "played" into a special recovery program that reconstructs the data base to the point of failure. The only problem with this system is that about half of the programming effort for the project goes into planning for this recovery, but the program often does not work when the time comes. This error recovery feature has been implemented in one microcomputer DBMS, and it operates more smoothly than most large-system recovery schemes.

Good Documentation and Support

Buyers of an expensive DBMS for a large computer are expected to send their staff to a long training course. As a microcomputer owner, you probably don't have a staff, nor do you have time for a two week trip to Chicago. With your DBMS you rely on your manual and your dealer. An ideal manual should offer a tutorial that leads you through the system one step at a time. The manual should also have a reference section, organized by command or function.

As you may have noticed, mail order prices on DBMS software are often lower than local prices. Mail order is an excellent choice for experienced software users who may not need the support a dealer offers. As with all mail order purchases, you should be sure to obtain sufficient information from the software publisher before you buy. Novices, however, will appreciate the expertise of a dealer. If you pay a dealer full list price to guarantee this support, make sure your dealer thoroughly understands the package.

Many books have been published about particular software packages. You can buy at least three different books on CP/M at the moment, plus books on CBASIC, WordStar, and others. Some books on data base packages have started to appear, and some dealers offer courses for local users.

Desirable DBMS Features

The next section outlines desirable DBMS features. Not all of these features are contained in the packages evaluated in Chapters 4 through 7 of this book. These features are presented as benchmarks for evaluating these packages and other DBMS software you might consider.

Multiple Files

Imagine yourself using an FMS which handles only one file at a time, like the customer contact list described in Chapter 1. Suppose you set up the contact list and a product list, each as independent files. Figure 2-24 shows simplified samples of both lists. Now suppose you want a report showing customer name and product name together (Figure 2-25). With your single-file system, there is no way of matching by product number. The only alternative is a multifile system—one that will let you process two or more files together.

An FMS may be a multifile system, but many are single-file systems and don't really qualify as DBMS systems unless they have other redeeming features. The RDBMS is, by definition, a multifile system, but the file concept does not even apply to the NDBMS. The NDBMS is unique but has a lot of the properties of multifile systems. Complex turnkey software packages can only be developed on a multifile DBMS with a programming language interface.

Full-Screen Editing

Microcomputers were invented before the video terminal became popular. As a result, early software was oriented to the teletype, the standard input/ouput device at the time. In addition, software transported from larger

```
Customer                                            Product
 Number              Customer Name                of interest

 101273        Academy Press, Inc.                  PER-1020
 103918        AFCO                                 GRA-1200
 131415        Bargreen Rest. Equip. Co.            MIP-0040
 156720        Blackstock Lumber Co.                NOR-6671
 180009        Broadcast Music, Inc.                PER-1020

Product
 Code                Product Description              Price

 GRA-1200      Job Cost Package                     1000.00
 GRA-2010      C-BASIC/2                             150.00
 HAX-0020      General Mathematics-1                 14.95
 MIP-0040      WordStar for Apple                   315.00
 NOR-6671      Inventory Ctrl & Analysis            999.00
 PER-1020      VisiCalc for Atari                   199.95
 ZEN-6450      Peachtree Accts. Recvbl              395.00
```

FIGURE 2-24.
Separate customer contact
and product files

```
Customer
 Number      Customer Name         Product of interest       Price

 101273   Academy Press, Inc.      VisiCalc for Atari         199.95
 103918   AFCO                     Job Cost Package          1000.00
 131415   Bargreen Rest. Equip. Co. WordStar for Apple        315.00
 156720   Blackstock Lumber Co.    Inventory Ctrl & Analysis  999.00
 180009   Broadcast Music, Inc.    VisiCalc for Atari         199.95
```

FIGURE 2-25.
Combined customer and
product information

computers was written for 80-column punched cards. This situation continued for a long time, and only recently has it become standard for software to use cursor addressing to display characters anywhere on the screen. Word processor programs and electronic spread sheets are prime examples of a technology permitting the programmer to use his or her CRT as the artist uses a canvas.

Consider, for the moment, the prospect of entering data without full-screen editing. If you are using an old-fashioned program to enter name and address data, the computer asks you first for the last name, then scrolls to the next line, asks you for the first name, and keeps scrolling and asking until the record is finished. Next the entire record is displayed on the screen, each field with an identifying number next to it. You may now change any field by keying in its number. Each time you make a change, the entire screen is displayed with the new information.

Full-screen editing, on the other hand, shows you a screen with a series of blanks with descriptive "tags" corresponding to field names. You move freely among the fields by using special keys. After entering a screenful of data, you use another key to "release" the record and start a new one. A display format program controls positioning and validates the entered data. This editing method, patterned after the data entry machines that replaced keypunches, is fast and efficient, and most DBMS authors have adopted it in some form.

One problem with full-screen editing is that video terminals perform cursor addressing in different ways. DBMS authors take special pains to allow for each terminal's "idiosyncrasies," and they must provide a "configuration program" to go with their systems. This program usually has a menu of standard terminals, and you are invited to choose yours. If you develop a DBMS application that uses the full-screen editing capabilities of a Televideo terminal, for instance, you could sell it to an ADM 3-A owner, and the DBMS would perform the correct translation. There is one problem, though: Full-screen editing doesn't work well if you incorporate a slow modem (telephone line connection).

DBMS packages use two types of screen editing. One type, "by the numbers," identifies each field by a number and makes you key in that number to change the field. This is tedious, but

it eliminates most errors since control key sequences (using the CTRL key as an alternate shift key) are not required. The second type, "move the cursor," closely copies data entry machines that replaced the keypunches. It's faster than "by the numbers" but requires more skill from the operator. Sometimes the terminal's arrow keys move the cursor, but sometimes you need ^S, ^D, and so on. (The symbol ^ represents the CONTROL character.)

With the DBMS controlling data entry, data integrity (see Chapter 1) is less of a problem. The operator is simply not able to enter alphabetic characters into a numeric field.

On-Screen Display Format Generation

The display format is what you see when you begin to enter or change data for a given data base record. It consists of the descriptive tags and blank spaces for the fields, all arranged in a pleasing manner. Some systems lay out the display for you, and others let you lay it out with a kind of programming language. The latter method assumes that you have sketched the screen on graph paper and know which rows and columns you will use.

A more convenient method treats the screen like a sketch pad and lets you build the screen yourself by moving the cursor around as if you were using a word processor. You can type in your tags directly, but you must somehow link the blank spaces with the data base fields. A good format generator should let you use graphics, reverse video, highlighting, and other terminal features, and should also permit the range of insert and delete functions common to word processors. It should also allow you to change an old screen.

Password Security

Suppose you have set up an integrated accounting system with your DBMS. The two tasks that consume the most time are accounts payable and payroll, and there are two data entry employees—the accounts payable clerk and the payroll clerk. There is no way to keep the payroll clerk from knowing how much employees are getting paid, and the clerk is probably able to update pay rates. Since pay rates are confidential, you don't want the accounts payable clerk to even see them, let alone update them. The pre-data base solution to the security problem was to keep all the accounts payable programs separate from the payroll programs. The main payroll program had some built-in logic to admit only those typing in a certain password—a crude but effective technique. If you have a DBMS with a programming language interface, you can do

the same thing, but you must program all the password logic yourself.

In a data base environment, all the data is supposed to be shared by everyone, to the extent that someone in personnel could send out a mailer to all employees without having access to private information. You could, of course, program the application with a password for personnel, but then you are not taking full advantage of the data base concept.

Look at the example in Table 2-1 to see how authors of software for large systems have approached the problem.

The numbers under Access and Update are security codes—0 is low security, 3 is high security. If you are the personnel clerk and if you can remember your password, MOTHER, you can use your access code of 1 to look at all fields with your security level or lower, including everything except Pay Rate. Your update code of 1 allows you to change only the Address field if an employee moves. If you are the

TABLE 2-1.
Password
Application for
Employee File

Simplified Employee File		
Field	**Access**	**Update**
Employee number	0	2
Social Security number	1	2
Employee name	0	2
Address	0	1
Date of birth	1	2
Date of employment	1	2
Pay rate	2	3

Password Dictionary			
User	**Access**	**Update**	**Password**
All employees	0	0	FISHING
Personnel clerk	1	1	MOTHER
Payroll clerk	2	2	4300
Personnel manager	3	3	POWER

personnel manager, you can access and update everything, including Pay Rate, and you are the only one who can update Pay Rate.

If you have made a big effort to protect the Pay Rate field, be sure your DBMS does not permit unauthorized people to "list all employees in order by pay rate." Not only data values but also relationships are subject to security.

All this password capability should be built right into the DBMS. Security levels for fields are entered in the data dictionary along with field length, data type, and so on. Passwords are entered in a special section of the dictionary with the understanding that it takes a special high-security code to access and modify the passwords themselves. At present only one DBMS has this password feature built-in, but as data bases move into the multiuser realm, passwords will be all the more necessary.

Multiuser Capability

To have a multiuser DBMS, you must have a multiterminal computer system with a multiuser operating system. But as you may have noticed, the whole multiuser microcomputer world is in a rapid state of development. The early 8-bit multiuser systems did not work very well, and a lot of buyers were disappointed. Now the industry is switching to networks of 8-bit computers and 16-bit multiuser computers. Both these approaches have advantages and disadvantages, and each is best suited to different situations. All this makes life difficult for the DBMS authors, who would really like one standard operating environment such as they have enjoyed with CP/M.

Most existing DBMS systems will operate in either a CP/M multicomputer network or with MP/M, the 8-bit multiuser CP/M. You have to be very careful. If you have two totally separate

software systems, you're home free; you have two copies of the DBMS and two sets of files on different parts of the disk, and neither user knows the other one is there. You could go a step further and assign certain files to be accessed by several users. If you had a data base of community service agencies, for instance, you could assemble a city-wide network with inquiry terminals sharing the information residing on a common disk. With most systems you have to shut down the network to update the data base.

Ideally, a DBMS should allow simultaneous updating and access of the data base. This is easier said than done, as you can see from the following example: Two people are trying to update information for part 3250. Sharon, at her terminal, keys in the part number and watches the description and price appear on the screen. She pauses for a phone call, but before she is finished, Steve, at another terminal, brings up the same part and sees the same description and price. Sharon changes the price about the same time that Steve makes a slight change to the description. Sharon finishes and moves to the next part, and the old description and the new price go back to disk. Just after that, Steve finishes, and the new description and the old price go to disk. Sharon's price change has been erased.

The solution to this problem is the *record lock*, which means that the DBMS "locks out" part 3250 the instant Sharon brings it up on the screen. If Steve wants to update the part, the DBMS makes him wait until Sharon is completely finished.

There are two kinds of record locking, active and passive. Passive locking is usually automatic within the multiuser DBMS. Anytime a record is being accessed by one user, it may be read, but not written to, by other users. Active locking prevents another user from reading or writing a record. It is switched on and off by specific DBMS commands.

In Chapter 3, under the heading "Multiuser B^+- Trees," some technical multiuser update problems that a good DBMS should solve internally are described. Whether a DBMS uses B^+- trees or some other link-pointer scheme, the package's author must produce some of the most complex system programming imagina- ble. That code should be reentrant, meaning that all data base users execute the same copy of the program. In this way, in a multiprogram- ming environment, there are usually several memory partitions. Each user will be able to have his or her program to call DBMS in an individual partition, and the DBMS itself resides in its own partition, accessible by all user programs.

3

Physical Data Access Techniques

A DBMS hides the physical structure of the data and presents only a logical view. Because of this, you might assume that you don't have to know anything about how the data is processed and stored on the disk. But this is not true. Your microcomputer is exerting itself at full capacity to run your DBMS, so if you tell it to do something that is not efficient, it could "go off and think" for eight hours. Rephrasing the question, on the other hand, might get you the answer in eight minutes. Not surprisingly, the same thing happens with a large DBMS, except that a that a mistake might cost $8000 instead of eight hours.

ACCESSING DATA

In order to understand physical data storage, you must first know what a disk file is. Imagine the file to be a long string of beads. Each bead is a character—a number, letter of the alphabet, or special symbol like &, $, or %. The text for this chapter, for example, is a file because it was written using a word processor; the characters you are looking at are strung together, one after the other on the file. The file has a name, CH3,

and you can print it out by typing PRINT CH3. The PRINT program goes to disk, finds out where on the disk the first letter is, prints that letter, goes back for another, then another, and so on, until it is finished. This is the simplest form of the sequential file—great for text, but not so good for organizing information.

Sequential Data Access

In the text file, the data items that you processed in sequence were letters of the alphabet known as characters. But what if you process groups of 70 characters, with each group containing all the information about someone on your Christmas list? You have now divided your text file into records—one record for each individual on the list. Each record is further divided into fields: The first 15 characters comprise the last name, the next ten the first name, and so on, as shown in Figure 3-1. Now the file is still made up of a sequence of individual characters, as shown in Figure 3-2, but anyone looking at the data could quickly figure out what was really going on. If someone told you the record length and the field lengths (the exact number of characters in each), it would

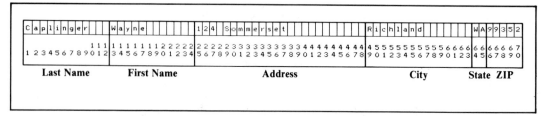

| C | a | p | l | i | n | g | e | r | | | | W | a | y | n | e | | | | | | | 1 | 2 | 4 | | S | o | m | m | e | r | s | e | t | | | | | | | | | | | | R | i | c | h | l | a | n | d | | | | | | | W | A | 9 | 9 | 3 | 5 | 2 |

Last Name   First Name   Address   City   State ZIP

FIGURE 3-1.
Data record
with fields

```
Caplinger   Wayne        124 Sommerset           Richlan
d      WA99352Carlson     Kerry      8331 Washington
St     Eugene      OR97401Shoquist    Stephen       5
170 SE Chestnut Ave      Beaverton     OR97005Clark
   Bob        1600 LK PK Dr #90     Tumwater       WA
98502Clauss     Scott      E 3204 Daisy Ave       Sp
okane      WA99208Ramp       Henry       574 Locustf
ield Rd.    Teaticket     MA02536Coady      Elizabet
h   480 NE Conifer Blvd   Corvallis    OR97330Colem
an    Tim       908 Queen Ave        Yakima
   WA98902Connoly     Janet      3428 SW 28th
   Portland       OR97202Conover    Bruce      4765 S
W 3rd ST     Gresham      OR97030Cook        Bob
   2132 Nashua Circle    Englewood    CO80110
Cozby     Dave      P.O. Box 85        Cottonw
ood    ID83522Craig      Rex      1012 VanGiesen
   Richland      WA99352Craft      Robert      3
87 Crest Dr    Eugene       OR97405Creagor
   Allen    3104 N 30th       Spokane       WA
99203Lockman    Don      4041 1/2 22nd Ave.     Se
attle     WA98105Dalke      David      2515 Briarw
ood Ct     Richland    WA99352
```

FIGURE 3-2.
Christmas list,
raw form

make your interpreting job even easier because you could start a new record on each line, as in Figure 3-3. Figure 3-3 presents the same data as Figure 3-2, but the data is just arranged differently.

When a computer program reads one of these sequential files (whether it is a DBMS program or a BASIC program), it must know in advance exactly what the record and field lengths are. It is an easy matter for the program

Last Name	First Name	Address	City	State/ZIP
Caplinger	Wayne	124 Sommerset	Richland	WA99352
Carlson	Kerry	8331 Washington St	Eugene	OR97401
Shoquist	Stephen	5170 SE Chestnut Ave	Beaverton	OR97005
Clark	Bob	1600 LK PK Dr #90	Tumwater	WA98502
Clauss	Scott	E 3204 Daisy Ave	Spokane	WA99208
Ramp	Henry	574 Locustfield Rd	Teaticket	MA02536
Coady	Elizabeth	480 NE Conifer Blvd	Corvallis	OR97330
Coleman	Tim	908 Queen Ave	Yakima	WA98902
Connoly	Janet	3428 SW 28th	Portland	OR97202
Conover	Bruce	4765 SW 3rd	Gresham	OR97030
Cook	Bob	2132 Nashua Circle	Englewood	CO80110
Cozby	Dave	P.O. Box 85	Cottonwood	ID83522
Craig	Rex	1012 VanGiesen	Richland	WA99352
Craft	Robert	387 Crest Dr	Eugene	OR97405
Creagor	Allen	3104 N 30th	Spokane	WA99203
Lockman	Don	4041 1/2 22nd Ave	Seattle	WA98105
Dalke	David	2515 Briarwood Ct	Richland	WA99352

FIGURE 3-3.
Christmas list,
one record per line

to read in 70 characters at once and to interpret the fields contained there. In fact, the program could start at the beginning of the file and read in 1000 records, one at a time, and print out all the records for last names beginning with "K." This is exactly what the DBMS does: It makes a sequential pass of the database. Most packages can do this quite quickly, but the speed depends on the record length; the shorter the record the faster the scan.

Direct Access

Sequential access is fine if you always start at the beginning of the file. But suppose you know that a certain name is stored in record number 537 and you want it quickly. It so happens that most disk operating systems, including CP/M, allow you to go directly to the record you want, bypassing the sequential scan and thus saving a great deal of time.

Direct access is fine as long as you know which record you are looking for and if the record length is the same for all records. You can use it in a payroll system, for instance, where the employee number is exactly the same as the record number. Imagine, for example, that you have just selected the employee number as the "key," that is, the field that uniquely identifies the record. You start out with a fixed number of employees, say 100. Perhaps 20 employees leave during the year and you replace them with 25 new employees. When the time comes to print W-2 forms, the maximum employee number is 125, so that there are 20 inactive slots for next year.

It is convenient to use the record number for the employee number, but for some other applications a direct correlation assignment does not always work. Let's use a customer file as an example. Most businesses assign customer numbers so that the customer file remains in alphabetical order. This requires the key to be both numerical and alphabetical. Since you are always adding new customers, you assign a six-digit number as the key and leave a lot of space between the numbers. As you acquire new customers, you just squeeze them into the holes. If you want to access the files directly, you need to allow space for 999,999 records. At only 100 characters per record, this requires ten megabytes. As disk storage densities increase in the future, this method may be practical. Clearly, however, direct access does not satisfy the customer file requirements.

If you needed to find particular entries in the customer file you could, of course, always do a sequential scan from the start of the file. If the customers were in order by number, you could stop if you went past the target number, knowing that the customer was not on file.

There is a better way to find customers though called the *binary search,* and it makes use of the direct access method. Assuming that the binary search program knows how many customer records there are, it divides that number in half and then reads the file at that point. If this test customer number is higher than the customer number you requested, the program knows that the target is in the first half of the file and divides that part of the file in half again. The program keeps dividing the interval in half until it finds the customer number you requested. The binary search may be made more efficient by building in a "memory" that stores certain file locations, providing easy reference points throughout the file.

Pointer Files

If you have ever written a BASIC program that handles disk files, you know that BASIC allows you to use both sequential and direct

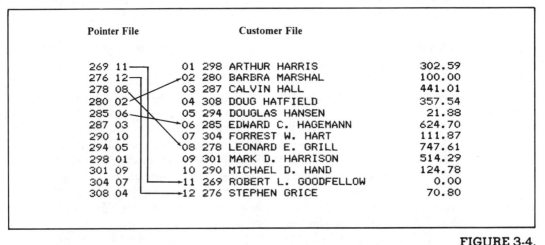

FIGURE 3-4.
Pointer file to customers

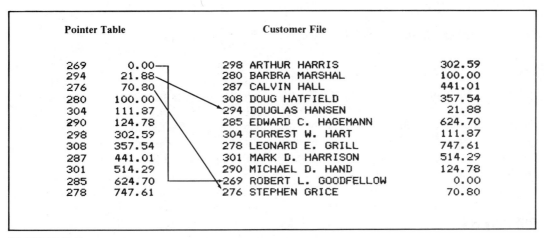

Pointer Table

269	0.00
294	21.88
276	70.80
280	100.00
304	111.87
290	124.78
298	302.59
308	357.54
287	441.01
301	514.29
285	624.70
278	747.61

Customer File

298	ARTHUR HARRIS	302.59
280	BARBRA MARSHAL	100.00
287	CALVIN HALL	441.01
308	DOUG HATFIELD	357.54
294	DOUGLAS HANSEN	21.88
285	EDWARD C. HAGEMANN	624.70
304	FORREST W. HART	111.87
278	LEONARD E. GRILL	747.61
301	MARK D. HARRISON	514.29
290	MICHAEL D. HAND	124.78
269	ROBERT L. GOODFELLOW	0.00
276	STEPHEN GRICE	70.80

FIGURE 3-5.
An alternate view of
a file sorted by sales

(sometimes called random) disk access. If your assignment is to write a program that looks up customers, you will probably define an array in memory consisting of pairs of numbers—the three-digit customer number (the *key*) and the direct record address, called a *pointer*—as shown in Figure 3-4. When your program first starts up, it reads the whole customer file sequentially and fills in the table. When you need to look up a customer, the program searches the array in memory, matching the customer number. When the match is made, the program finds the record number, then goes out to disk to get the customer information. Although this method is easy to program, it has two disadvantages: a delay on program startup while the whole customer file is read, and the need for memory space for all the customer numbers and record numbers.

The next logical step after the table-in-memory method is the use of a disk file for storing the pointer table. This permits tables to be larger than available memory, but you still need a way to search the pointer file. You can use either the sequential scan or the binary search, knowing that it is quicker to search the small pointer file than it is to search the main file.

A pointer file can also store the results of a sort. If your main customer file was in customer number order, and you wanted a list of customers organized by total sales in ascending order, you could leave the main file alone. A sort program could generate a pointer file in the proper order. A report program would make a sequential pass through this pointer file, thus having an alternate view of the main data file. See Figure 3-5.

ADDING AND DELETING DATA

Pointer files work very well for sequential access and adequately for random access, but they get messy if you need to add records to the main file. In fact, you might as well run the sort program over again and make a new pointer file. The following section introduces alternate methods for adding and deleting data.

The Update

All the techniques described so far, with the possible exception of the sort, can be programmed directly in standard disk BASIC. However, none of them allows you to add a record directly into what appears to be the middle of an existing file. This is a fundamental problem in programming. It used to be sidestepped by the update process in which you made a small, separate file of the records you wanted to add, then sorted that file, and finally merged the new file with the main file, which was always kept in sorted order. In this way the new records were interleaved with the old, forming a third file which replaced the original main file. See Figure 3-6 for a merge example. The update is an old data processing standby that doesn't even need direct access. In fact, it even works with tapes.

ISAM

ISAM stands for Indexed Sequential Access Method, but some people argue it stands for "incredibly slow access method." This is IBM's method of solving the fundamental problem of adding records into the middle of a file while allowing you to access individual records by key.

The ISAM file always appears to be in sequential order by key. How does it work? There is a very complicated system of track and cylinder indexes plus overflow areas, all very dependent on the disk hardware. The access method is, in effect, built right into the disk. It is also built into the operating system and the programming language, usually COBOL. Though many microcomputer software manufacturers advertise ISAM, IBM makes the genuine article. The real ISAM allows access to records of different lengths, but most imitations demand fixed-length records.

Index Files

The index file is the most popular ISAM substitute in the microcomputer world. It is very similar to the pointer file, except that it is more efficient for keyed access and it allows adds and deletes. Like the pointer file, the index file is separate from the main data file. The problem, however, is that the index file accessing is too complicated to code in BASIC. Either choose a language with the index capability built in, buy an add-on indexing package, or get a DBMS.

Multiple index files may be made from a single data file in order to view that file in different sort orders. You could add a new name to a mailing list, for example, and have the software link it into both the alphabetical and ZIP code indexes. You could then run a report in either sort order without having to sort the whole file.

Remember that an index (or pointer) file takes up disk space, calculated as key length multiplied by the number of keys, plus a little extra. The more indexes you have, the more disk space is used.

List of Names to Be Added

636   DONALD G. RADCLIFFE

647   LYLE and BETTE REYNOLDS
648   VERNE REYNOLDS INC.

657   R.M. RITA/ B.A. MILLER

681   SALT WATER TAVERN

Original List of Names

612   THOMAS I POTTER
618   D.R. & K. PRATT
622   THOMAS PRYOR

640   DANIEL A. RANNEY
643   R. RAYMOND & J. WOODARD
646   CHARLES REYNOLDS

652   DONALD C. RIEDEL

660   EARL E. ROBICHEAUX
665   ROBERT J. ROSS
670   DONALD E. ROSTRON
674   HAROLD J.RUNSTAD
675   JAMES M. RYAN

683   DR. LEE SANDERS
684   SUE ANN SANDERS
688   RICHARD G. SASS

Resulting List of Merged Names

612   THOMAS I POTTER
618   D.R. and K. PRATT
622   THOMAS PRYOR
636   DONALD G. RADCLIFFE
640   DANIEL A. RANNEY
643   R. RAYMOND and J. WOODARD
646   CHARLES REYNOLDS
647   LYLE and BETTE REYNOLDS
648   VERNE REYNOLDS INC.
652   DONALD C. RIEDEL
657   R.M. RITA/ B.A. MILLER
660   EARL E. ROBICHEAUX
665   ROBERT J. ROSS
670   DONALD E. ROSTRON
674   HAROLD J.RUNSTAD
675   JAMES M. RYAN
681   SALT WATER TAVERN
683   DR. LEE SANDERS
684   SUE ANN SANDERS
688   RICHARD G. SASS

FIGURE 3-6.
Merge example

Hashing

Hashing is a data access method. Hashing does roughly the same thing that an index file does but in an entirely different way. The index provides a complex path for finding a record from a key, but hashing does it in one easy step. The idea is to invent an algorithm for converting a key into a direct record address. As an example, consider the familiar customer file with six-digit keys. Suppose there are only 13 customers and thus a maximum of 13 records in which to store their information. Try a hashing algorithm in which the customer number is divided by 13 (which just happens to be a prime

number) and in which the remainder plus 1 is used as the record number. Figure 3-7 shows the results of this operation.

Looking at the hash codes in Figure 3-7, you notice that there are some duplicates, namely 6 and 11. These are called *synonyms,* and they always show up in hashing schemes. They are handled by overflow records at the bottom of the file, with pointers linking them to the original records. Consider the case of customers 488875 and 582215 both hashing to 11. The first one there, 488875, gets the slot, and the second goes into the overflow record. If the program needs the record for customer 488875, it goes right to it in one access. If it needs 582215, it

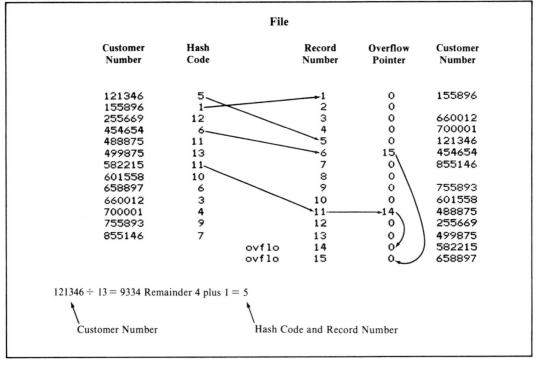

FIGURE 3-7.
Hashing

quickly finds out the record is not in 11 as it should be. The program then follows the pointer down to record 14.

Actual hashing schemes are usually more complicated, using different hashing algorithms and often grouping several records into a "bucket" to save references to the overflow area. If the key is alphanumeric, such as a last name, it can easily be converted into a number by using the ASCII codes for the letters. Hashing has the advantage of being fast, usually requiring only one disk access, but it depends on advance knowledge of the maximum number of records in the file. Also, there is no equivalent of multiple indexes. If you need to view the hashed file in a different order, you have to use an auxiliary index file or do a sort.

Trees

A brief review is in order here. You need a quick way to find records in a large disk file based on a key, such as customer number or part number. You need a separate disk file called an index, plus some software to read it. When you give the software a query key, it looks through the index to see if the key is there. If it is, the program gets the record number and then the actual record from the main file. In addition, the index program should allow adds and deletes as well as sequential access in key order.

Binary Search Tree

The B⁺-tree (the plus sign is intentional) is the most common way of setting up an index file. It has its roots in the work of R. Bayer and E. McCreight, done at Boeing Scientific Research Labs about 1972. The precursor of the B⁺-tree was the binary search tree, an early solution to the problem of file access. This method is not very efficient, but it is perhaps the easiest to understand. Starting out with the query key—the key you are trying to match in the main file—the index program goes to the root node and compares the key there against the query key. Each node, including the root, contains a key and two branches. If the query key is less than the node key, the program takes the left branch. If they are equal, it has found what it was looking for. If the query key is greater, the program takes the right branch. If the program gets to the bottom of the tree and still hasn't matched the key, it knows the key is not there.

Figure 3-8 shows a binary tree used to find a particular customer by number. If the program needs to find the record for customer 301, it goes through the following sequence:

1. Start at the root node. 301 is greater than 280, so take the right branch.

2. Go to the second-level node on the right. 301 is greater than 298, so take the right branch again.

3. Go to the rightmost third-level node. 301 is less than 304, so take the left branch.

4. Go to the fourth-level node that is second from the right. 301 is equal to the key there, so the desired record number is 9.

5. Use direct access to read record 9 from the main data file.

Notice that the tree is unbalanced, meaning that it is going to take longer to find customer 294 than to find 269. In fact, the tree becomes more unbalanced as more keys are added; adding key 295 requires another level. Also, since each node requires only a few bytes, there has to be a logical way of distributing these nodes over the records in a disk file.

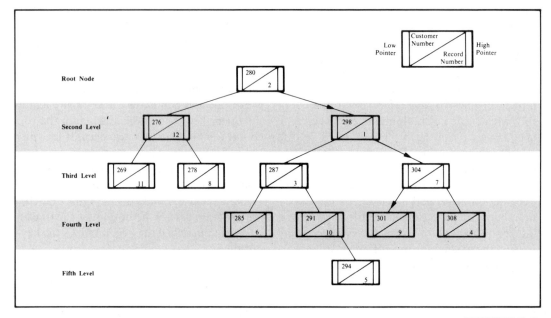

FIGURE 3-8.
Unbalanced binary tree path
highlighting customer 301

The B-Tree

The binary tree stores only one key at each node. Storing a number of keys at each node greatly reduces the number of levels in the tree and also lets the tree stay balanced after insert and delete operations. This balance is achieved by splitting a node in two after it contains a specified number of keys. The split may propagate up through the tree, even causing the root node to split, adding another level to the tree. This type of tree is called the B-tree and is illustrated in Figure 3-9.

Figures 3-10 and 3-11 show the results of adding records to the tree. Note that it takes longer to insert customer number 293 as shown in Figure 3-9 because the whole tree must be rearranged. Adding key 295 to the tree in Figure 3-10 causes the 287-290-293-294 node to split with 293 "promoted" to a higher node. If the root node had some room to spare, key 293 could have been accommodated. But since the root node was full too, it had to split, creating a new root node formed, as shown in Figure 3-11. In other words, when a fifth key is added to a node, a middle key is created. This middle key becomes a new root node, while the two smallest and the two largest form new, separate, second-level nodes.

Finding a key in a B-tree is similar to finding a key in the binary tree. The program sequentially searches the root node for the key. If it doesn't find it there, it gets a pointer to a lower-level node, and so on. To find the key 301 in the tree of Figure 3-9, the program uses the pointer

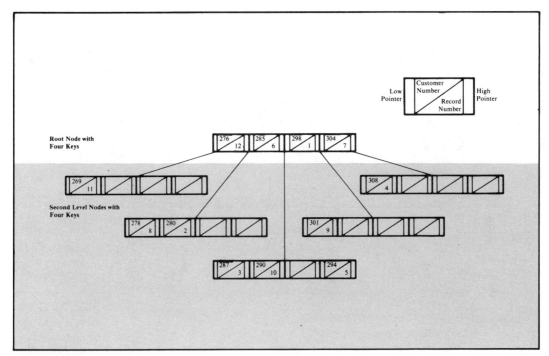

FIGURE 3-9.
B-tree before
insertion

between 298 and 304 in the root. This takes it to the node that is second from the right, where it finds 301 immediately. The nodes, larger than four entries in practice, are stored in individual fixed-length disk records. The "pointer" is just the disk record number. Try programming that in BASIC.

The B$^+$-Tree

In both the binary tree and the B-tree, the actual record numbers in the main file are coded into the tree so that the program doesn't always have to go to the bottom. This works very well if you need indexed access, that is, the ability to find individual records. If you need sequential access, however, you are in trouble because there is no path to the "next" record. This problem was solved with a step from the B-tree to the B$^+$-tree. The B$^+$-tree goes further by demanding that the actual references to main-file record numbers be in the leaves—the lowest level—of the tree, forcing the program to go all the way to the bottom of the tree for each access. Since the tree is still balanced, all these leaves "line up" as shown in Figure 3-12, and the record numbers are in sequential order according to the customer number key. For

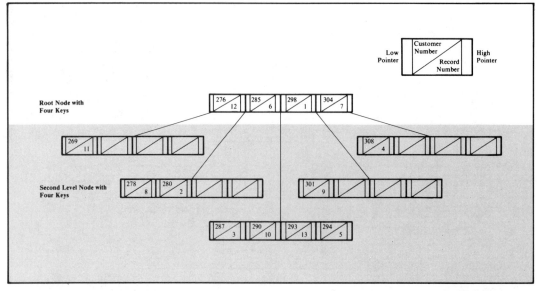

FIGURE 3-10.
B-tree after insertion
with no node splitting
(customer number 293 added)

sequential access, the program just "walks" along the bottom level, and it still has the indexed access capability of the plain B-tree.

All three tree systems delete keys using the reverse of the add process. A lot of software developers, however, don't include all the delete logic. Instead, they mark the main data record as deleted, and then pretend it doesn't exist. This is not advantageous for disk storage, but the space is recovered during the periodic "index rebuild," or garbage collection.

If the DBMS you choose uses B^+-trees (as many do) you must realize that it may take a long time to build an index. This is a very important part of the necessary reorganization process. The slowness results from the need to rearrange the index when a newly added key fills up certain nodes, as shown in Figure 3-9. Often the affected nodes are spread out over the disk, increasing execution time. If a large data file was out of order to start with, the index build could take many hours. Programmers often use an assembly language sort on the data file before indexing it in order to speed up the process.

Multiuser B^+-Trees

Imagine a combination of one index file and one data file serving two people using the computer simultaneously. If the two users are both reading the data file through the index, there is no problem. But suppose that one of the users adds a new record to the file. There is now a time window, which could be as long as several seconds, during which time the index file is being adjusted to accommodate the new entry. During that time, the index will be in a sufficient state of disarray to prevent the second user from finding the desired key. The problem gets worse if the two users try to update at the same time. Any DBMS that serves several users must be able to "lock out" some users from those parts of the tree being updated by other users. All of this is done with the help of the operating system and is completely invisible to the programmer and operator.

VIRTUAL MEMORY

A typical computer program views a disk file as a collection of records, each divided into fields. The program reads or writes one record at a time. If you think about it, the only reason

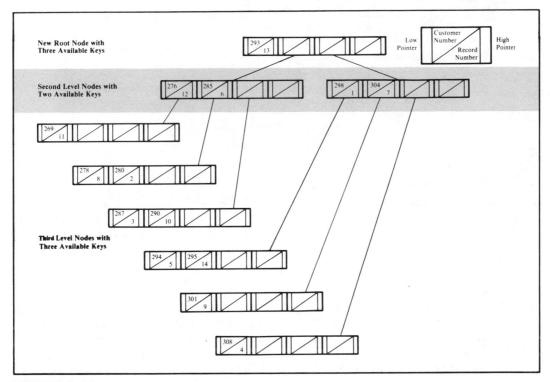

FIGURE 3-11.
B-tree after second insertion showing node splitting and level increase (record 295 added)

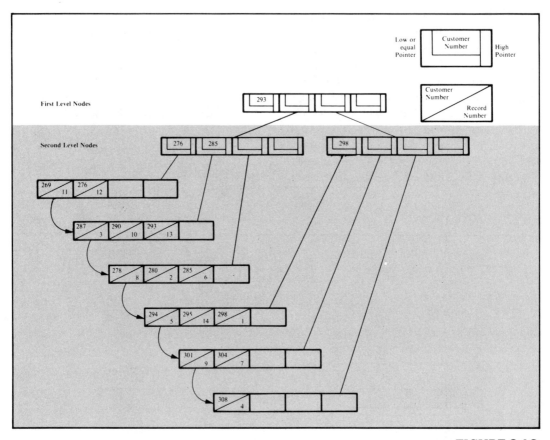

First Level Nodes

Second Level Nodes

FIGURE 3-12.
B$^+$-tree showing sequential
linking of keys

programmers use files in the first place is that there is not enough RAM (Random Access Memory) space to hold all the data a program uses. It would be much easier to define a huge array of data, read it in from disk at the start of program execution, and write it back at the end. Virtual memory makes the programmer think there is an infinitely large memory. He or she writes program statements like DIMENSION NAME$(30000) or ADDRESS$(30000) and doesn't

consider whether the computer is "out of memory." The software automatically reads and writes chunks of data as required.

Central to virtual memory implementations is the page, a fixed-length unit of memory, typically 1024 bytes, that is transferred to and from disk as necessary. A DBMS will have RAM space for a fixed number—maybe 20—of these pages, and a disk file may contain 200 or more pages. The DBMS calculates which pages are needed from disk and reads them into memory. When all RAM pages are full, the program writes the least recently accessed page back to disk if it has been changed, and then reads in a new page. If a needed page is in memory already, no disk read is necessary, and data access is almost instantaneous. The more page space there is in RAM, the faster the program runs.

Virtual memory may be used with record- or field-type data structures with one or more records per page. More complex data structures, as found in the NDBMS, can be built with pages. Individual pages can contain data dictionary and schema information, as well as pointers and data items.

4

Condor Series 20
A Relational Data Base
Management System

C ondor is an efficient, command-driven Relational Data Base Management System and a powerful report generator. Since its commands operate on *entire* databases, you must use the relational model totally. There is no programming language to access individual records, so if you are a programmer, you have to readjust your thinking.

Condor is best suited for unstructured, informational tasks. Perhaps your requirements are not firm and you need to design as you proceed. Business data processing is not excluded, but Condor systems are very batch-oriented, allowing rapid data entry but no on-line lookups. If you were entering general ledger journal vouchers, for example, you wouldn't know about invalid account numbers until after the batch was closed.

It takes some effort to learn Condor well enough to create your own applications, but HELP menus allow you to create simple systems for clerical personnel. Condor has its own file utilities and allows direct execution of programs other than Condor programs, thus reducing your involvement with CP/M.

Condor is sold in three levels. Level 1 is a file management system with some multifile capabilities. This enables you to get an inexpensive start with data bases. Level 2 adds the true relational operators JOIN and PROJECT, which make it a true RDBMS. Level 3 adds a superb on-screen report generator and an indexing scheme.

This chapter examines Condor through two examples. The first is an unstructured "word processing" situation where Condor answers questions about words. The second is a business inventory and sales analysis problem which leads to a discussion of the report generator. Together these examples explain most of the important Condor commands. Consider your own information processing needs as you read these examples.

The first example group does not show word processing in the text editing sense, but rather, it shows you how an RDBMS can manipulate a data base of words. The example shows you a spelling check. The check is slower than most commercially available programs but is more versatile. Also included is a crossword puzzle solving program, which may be an entertaining feature for some.

Data entry procedures are not covered until the inventory example. Don't worry about how the data gets into Condor; just concentrate on what Condor can do with it.

SYSTEM OVERVIEW

DBMS Checklist

☒ Data Dictionary
  Specifies type, length, limits, and default

☒ Query Facility
  Integral part of package

☒ Report Generator
  Produces on-screen report layout, multilevel subtotals, subheadings; permits computations

☒ File Compatibility
  Reads and writes to or from any file

☒ Restructure Capability
  Allows added, deleted, rearranged fields; changing field size requires ASCII dump or load

☒ Effective Error Handling
  Good

☒ Documentation and Support
  Documentation good, support fair

☒ Multiple Files
  Uses relational operators limited in Level 1

☒ Full-Screen Editing
  Uses the cursor to edit

☒ On-Screen Display Format

☐ Password Security

☐ Multiuser Capability

☒ Menu-driven
  Report generator only

☐ Program-driven

☒ Command-driven

☒ Built-in Language
  Limited to simple command procedures; no branching or individual record access

☐ Established Language

☐ Access Time
  Index option not available for test

☒ Processing Speed
  Maximum 23,000 records per minute on hard disk

☒ Data Access Method
  Sequential. (B-tree indexed-sequential method available soon)

Price (4/82)

Condor 20-1
  Basic file management system $295

Condor 20-2
  Relational database functions added $595

Condor 20-3
  Report generator and indexing functions added $995

Publisher

Condor Computer Corporation
2051 South State St.
Ann Arbor, MI 48104
(313) 769-3988

System Requirements

· Z-80 microprocessor system
· The CP/M operating system (MP/M acceptable)
· A minimum of 48K bytes of memory
· One or more disk drives
· A cursor-addressed 24 × 80-character video terminal
· Text printer

SYSTEM OVERVIEW (Continued)

Specifications			
		Characters per field	127 max
		Largest number	± 2,148,373,647
Data Types	Alphanumeric	Smallest number	± 0.01
	Alphabetic	Numeric accuracy	9 digits
	Fixed-point binary numeric	Index key length	127 bytes max
	Dollar	Terms in COMPUTE command	32 max
	Julian date	Sort keys	32 max
Records per database file	32,767 max	Sort file size	128K max
Bytes per record	1024 max	Logical conditions in SELECT	
Fields per record	127 max	command	32 max

Throughout the next chapters, operator input is underscored (for example, when you see ENTER FILENAME:PROPERTY, this will indicate that you must enter the word "PROPERTY"). Command names are written with capital letters (CREATE, EDIT, DISPLAY) and filenames, database names, and fields appear in small capital letters (TEXT, WORD, COUNT).

LEVEL 1—FILE MANAGEMENT

Example:

A Spelling Checker

Commands:

COMPARE, LIST, READ, SAVE, SORT, TABULATE

Look at the following 100-word paragraph from a popular novel.* You need to load it into a Condor database so you can "play" with the individual words.

There was a sudden roar of applause followed by the accelerated clangour of guitars deploying downwind; the bull had pulled away from the fence and once more the scene was becoming animated: Hugh and the bull tussled for a moment in the centre of a small fixed circle the others created by their exclusion from it within the arena; then the whole was veiled in dust; the pen gate to their left had broken open again, freeing all the other bulls, including the first one who was probably responsible; they were charging out amid cheers, snorting, scattering in every direction.

Your word processor program can eliminate the punctuation and globally replace all spaces with a quote comma quote pattern (","). After some minor cleanup, you have a CP/M file called TEXT.ASC which looks like the following:

```
"There","was","a","sudden,","roar",
"of","applause","followed","by",
"the","accelerated","clangour","of",
"guitars","deploying","downwind",
"the","bull","had"...
```

---

*From page 308 in *Under The Volcano* by Malcolm Lowry (J.B. Lippincott Co.). Copyright 1947 by Malcolm Lowry. Reprinted by permission of Harper & Row, Publishers, Inc.

Now you use Condor's DEFINE command to create a database called TEXT where each record contains only one field, WORD, of length 18. DEFINE, which is explained further in the inventory example, produces a data dictionary like the following:

Field	Type	Length
WORD:	Alpha	18 chars

The READ command reads data in almost any format and stores data items in a Condor database. The Condor database is named TEXT, and TEXT.ASC is the name of the ASCII file.

```
READ TEXT TEXT.ASC
```

Now all the words in the paragraph are loaded into the database, and you LIST them on the video screen. The database name is TEXT, and WORD is the field to be listed.

```
LIST TEXT BY WORD
WORD
There
was
a
sudden
roar
of
applause
followed
by
the
accelerated
clangour....
```

You're still in the "play with words" mode, but your goal is to do a spelling check on your text paragraph. The paragraph contains some repeated words such as "a" and "and," and you want to eliminate duplicates to speed up the spelling check. You start by SORTing the words alphabetically. The phrase BY WORD indicates that the WORD field is the sort key.

```
SORT TEXT BY WORD
LIST TEXT BY WORD
```

```
WORD
a
a
a
accelerated
again
all
amid
and
and
animated
applause
..........
```

Capital letters do not interfere with the SORT because Condor converts to upper-case letters for sorting and matching so "the" is equivalent to "The." Next you use the TABULATE command to make a new database with the original WORD field plus a new field, COUNT, showing the number of occurrences of each word in the TEXT database. This new 74-record database contains no duplicate words. Whenever Condor creates a new database, it arbitrarily names it RESULT. The SAVE command lets you rename RESULT as a permanent database named, in this case, TABTEXT. The [S] in the TABULATE command tells Condor to direct the output to a RESULT database instead of to the screen or the printer.

```
TABULATE TEXT BY WORD [S]
SAVE TABTEXT
LIST TABTEXT BY WORD COUNT
```

WORD	COUNT
a	3
accelerated	1
again	1
all	1
amid	1
and	2
animated	1
applause	1
arena	1
away	1
becoming	1

In order to have a spelling check, you need a "dictionary." (Don't confuse this dictionary with the DBMS data dictionary.) You may have already bought a good spelling check program to use with your text editing program. Although that program may have a dictionary of 20,000 words, you can only use that dictionary to check word spellings in your documents. However, if you convert the dictionary into a Condor database, you will have full control over the dictionary; you can check spelling, solve crossword puzzles, and play any word games you want. A competent programmer can convert a commercial spelling check dictionary into a delimited ASCII file which you can load into Condor. You READ it into a database called WORDS, structured like TEXT, with the addition of the LENGTH (in characters) of each word. The LENGTH will be used later in this chapter to help solve crossword puzzles.

```
LIST WORDS BY WORD
WORD            LENGTH
A               1
ABANDON         7
ABANDONED       9
ABATEMENT       9
ABBREVIATE      10
ABBREVIATED     11
ABBREVIATING    12
ABBREVIATION    12
ABBREVIATIONS   13
ABDUCT          6
ABDUCTION       9
..........
```

Remember that now you have two databases. One, TABTEXT, contains one record for each unique word in the paragraph; the other, WORDS, contains one record for each dictionary word. Let Condor COMPARE the databases, creating a new database, MISMATCH, with only those words from TABTEXT that don't match the dictionary. Condor does not distinguish lower- from upper-case words.

```
COMPARE TABTEXT WORDS NOT MATCHING WORD
SAVE MISMATCH
LIST MISMATCH BY WORD COUNT
WORD            COUNT
bulls           1
centre          1
clangour        1
deploying       1
Hugh            1
tussled         1
veiled          1
```

The 20,000 word dictionary had no match for the British spelling or the plural nouns or for the infrequently used words contained in the excerpt.

This job runs eight minutes with a hard disk. It takes so long because each of the 20,000 dictionary words has to be compared with the 100 TEXT words one at a time. Specialized spelling check programs are much faster because they take advantage of both the text buffer and the dictionary being sorted and execute a kind of "match-merge." It is possible that a second-generation RDBMS will be sophisticated enough to perform these functions.

LEVEL 2—RELATIONAL DATA BASE MANAGEMENT SYSTEM

Example 1:

Part of Speech Analysis

Commands:

JOIN, PROJECT, REORG, UPDATE

Suppose you want to know the frequency of usage of different parts of speech. First, make a list of all the parts of speech, giving each a one-character code. Put these in a database called SPEECH.

```
LIST SPEECH BY PART DESCRIPTION
PART  DESCRIPTION
A     Adjective
B     Adverb
R     Article
C     Conjunction
N     Noun
P     Preposition
U     Pronoun
V     Verb
```

Now you have to specify the part of speech for each word in TABTEXT. Some word dictionaries include parts of speech codes permitting Condor to use them directly. Using manual coding, you begin by REORGanizing the TAB-TEXT database to include a new field called PART, the one-character code for the part of speech. REORG demands that you define a new screen layout, NEWTEXT.FRM, which contains the new PART field. (The screen layout process will be explained in the inventory example.) UPDATE uses the video screen to step through all the words in TABTEXT, allowing you to key in the proper code.

```
REORG TABTEXT NEWTEXT.FRM
UPDATE TABTEXT
LIST TABTEXT BY WORD PART
WORD          PART
a             R
accelerated   A
again         B
all           A
amid          P
and           C
animated      A
applause      N
arena         N
away          B
becoming      V
broken        V
. . . . . . . . . .
```

You now have two databases, an expanded TABTEXT plus SPEECH, with the PART field in common. JOIN makes a new database similar to TABTEXT, but it has the additional fields COUNT and DESCRIPTION. Because you have DESCRIPTION, you no longer need PART or COUNT. Next you PROJECT this database, keeping the WORD and DESCRIPTION fields, while throwing away PART and COUNT. Notice that the temporary RESULT database was first defined as the output of JOIN, then rewritten as the output of PROJECT.

```
JOIN SPEECH TABTEXT BY PART
PROJECT RESULT BY WORD,DESCRIPTION
LIST RESULT BY WORD,DESCRIPTION
WORD          DESCRIPTION
a             Article
accelerated   Adjective
again         Adverb
all           Adjective
amid          Preposition
and           Conjunction
animated      Adjective
applause      Noun
arena         Noun
away          Adverb
becoming      Verb
broken        Verb
. . . . . . . . . .
```

Now you SORT the RESULT database by DESCRIPTION and SAVE it as BYDESCR.

```
SORT RESULT BY DESCRIPTION
SAVE BYDESCR
LIST BYDESCR BY WORD,DESCRIPTION
WORD          DESCRIPTION
veiled        Adjective
whole         Noun
. . . . . . . . . .
broken        Verb
animated      Adjective
sudden        Adjective
then          Adverb
. . . . . . . . . .
all           Adjective
again         Adverb
```

the	Article	Minimum	
a	Article		1
and	Conjunction	Maximum	
pen	Noun		22
scene	Noun	Average	
....			12

Using TABULATE again, you count the occurrences of the parts of speech. This time TABULATE outputs to the screen and shows a grand total.

```
TABULATE BYDESCR BY DESCRIPTION
DESCRIPTION     COUNT
Adjective       12
Adverb           9
Article         13
Conjunction      2
Noun            22
Preposition     14
Pronoun          6
Verb            14

Total           92
```

TABULATE again to a database instead of to the screen ([S] option), and SORT the result by COUNT, which is now the count of the parts of speech. The STAX parameter COMPUTEs the total, minimum, maximum, and average number of occurrences of each part of speech.

```
TABULATE BYDESCR BY DESCRIPTION [S]
SORT RESULT BY COUNT
LIST RESULT BY COUNT, DESCRIPTION AND
  COMPUTE STAX COUNT
COUNT       DESCRIPTION
22          Noun
14          Verb
9           Adverb
12          Adjective
14          Preposition
6           Pronoun
13          Article
2           Conjunction
Total
  92
```

LEVEL 2—RELATIONAL DATA BASE MANAGEMENT SYSTEM

Example 2:

Crossword Puzzle Solver

Commands:

RUN, SELECT

After you have the spelling dictionary in a database, you can consider new uses for it. If you've ever solved a crossword puzzle, you know the main problem is finding words when you only know a few letters. You will have a clue like "charge against property" and a space for four letters, the first an "L" and the third an "E." If you represent unknowns with a question mark, the word becomes "L?E?". How will Condor and the dictionary help? The SELECT command makes a new, smaller database, selecting only records meeting certain criteria. Condor recognizes the "?" as a "wild card identifier," and if you ask for all words that resemble "L?I?" with a length of four characters, four matching words emerge from the dictionary.

```
SELECT WORDS WHERE WORD EQ L?E? AND LENGTH
  EQ 4
LIST RESULT BY WORD
LIED
LIEN
LIES
LIEU
```

Which one is the "charge against property?"

You could use the same program to create crossword puzzles as well as solve them. If you need a six-letter word beginning with "S" and ending with "EN," "S???EN" will result in the following words:

```
SADDEN
SCREEN
SEAMEN
SHAKEN
SOFTEN
SPOKEN
STOLEN
SUDDEN
SULLEN
SUNKEN
SWEDEN
```

Can you think of clues which several of these words will satisfy? That should substantially increase the puzzle's challenge.

It is tedious to type in the entire SELECT and LIST commands each time you search for words. Condor lets you automate the process with a command file which prompts you for the key and word length. You write this command file, called CROSS.CMD, using a text editor, and then you let Condor execute it through the RUN command.

RUN CROSS

The command file is listed here. "$1" and "$2" are *variables* which hold the values you have entered for key and length. Semicolons indicate comments, and asterisks indicate special control commands not available from the keyboard.

Incidentally, Condor allows direct use of your text editor without returning to CP/M. If you use the CP/M editor, ED, typing "$ED" moves you to the text editor. You return directly to Condor when you have finished.

```
; -- CROSS.CMD --
; crossword puzzle solver for CONDOR
;
*MESSAGE **** CROSSWORD PUZZLE SOLVER
  ****
*MESSAGE Enter the word, ? for unknown
  letters - use double quotes
*GET $1
*MESSAGE Enter the length of the word
*GET $2
SELECT WORDS WHERE WORD EQ $1 AND LENGTH
  EQ $2
LIST RESULT BY WORD
*END
```

The crossword puzzle solver is useful as long as there are not clues like "a river in Russia" or "a Norwegian statesman." If this is the case, a much larger dictionary that includes geographical and biographical names would be helpful. Running on a hard disk, Condor scans the 20,000 word dictionary in about one minute.

LEVEL 2—RELATIONAL DATA BASE MANAGEMENT SYSTEM

Example 3:

Inventory

Commands:

DEFINE, DESTROY, ENTER, PRINT, TITLE

Suppose you want to take advantage of the recent small computer boom, and you open a store specializing in computer books. You decide you must "computerize" the store's business operations to impress the customers, but you don't like any of the "canned" inventory programs you've seen.

You decide you need the following inventory reports for proper management control:

1. Price List. A list of the publishers, catalog numbers, titles, and retail prices.

2. Daily Sales Report. A list of the volumes sold, the total sales dollars for each title, and the total daily sales.

3. Sales Analysis Report. A list of the year-to-date and period-to-date quantity sold and the sales amounts by title with a subtotal by publisher.

4. Reorder Report. A list of the books with quantities below their "reorder point," indicating they must be reordered from the distributor.

Defining the Inventory Database

The first required database is the Book Inventory Master, called BOOKS. It has a data dictionary as illustrated in Figure 4-1.

Most field labels are self-explanatory. The SALES.DOLLARS is year-to-date sales and

QUANTITY.SOLD is the quantity sold in the current period (day).

Condor now lets you DEFINE your BOOKS database. You type

DEFINE BOOKS

After a brief dialog, you get a blank screen. You begin defining a database by typing a *form,* indicating the screen position and length of each field. You can also embellish it with rows of asterisks and operator instructions. Condor provides a full-screen editor similar to a word processor's. Figure 4-2 shows the definition in process, and Figure 4-3 shows the completed form. The bottom line in Figure 4-2 shows the prompts Condor provides; they tell you how to insert and delete characters and lines. (You move the cursor around the screen with control characters.) The field names are enclosed in square brackets ([ ]), and the underscored areas represent input areas. Thirty underscores set the TITLE field at 30 characters.

After the form is completed, you type ^E, and Condor prompts you for extra field information. At this point Condor only knows the

Field	Type	Length	Low Limit	High Limit
PUBLISHER:	Alphanumeric	3 chars		
CATALOG.NUMBER:	Numeric	4 digits	0	9999
TITLE:	Alphanumeric	30 chars		
RETAIL.PRICE:	Dollars	5 places	0.00	99.99
REORDER.POINT:	Numeric	4 digits	0	9999
QUANTITY.ON.HAND:	Numeric	4 digits	0	9999
YTD.QUANTITY.SOLD:	Numeric	5 digits	0	99999
SALES.DOLLARS:	Dollars	8 places	0.00	99999.99
QUANTITY.SOLD:	Numeric	4 digits	0	9999

FIGURE 4-1.
Book Inventory Master

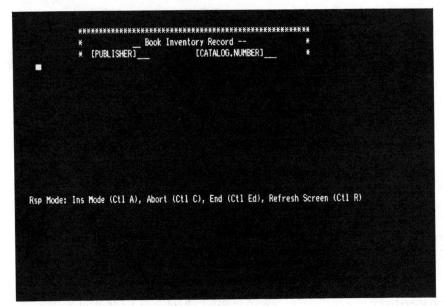

FIGURE 4-2.
Creating a form with
screen position and
length of field

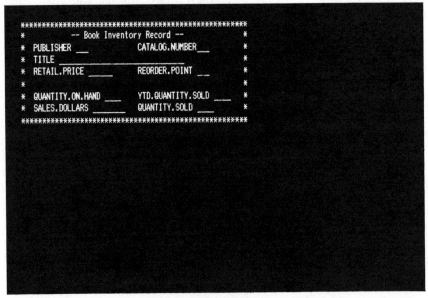

FIGURE 4-3.
Form definition
completed

length and position of the fields on the screen. You have to tell Condor whether they are alphabetic, alphanumeric, numeric, dollar, or date fields. You can also specify lower and upper limits and default values. If you specify the default value, it appears in quotes following the upper limit. If you do not specify a default value, a space enclosed by quotes appears. Numbers are entered as strings of digits but are stored on disk in binary and require less space. A four-digit number can be squeezed into two bytes.

A simple editing procedure permits you to fill in the missing field characteristics. Figure 4-4 shows this edit in progress. The following is a printout of the completed data dictionary:

```
Attribute summary of database BOOKS
1.PUBLISHER: A,3,0,3,"  "
2.CATALOG.NUMBER: N,2,0,32767,"  "
3.TITLE: AN,30,0,30,"  "
```

```
4.RETAIL.PRICE: $,3,.00,99.99,"  "
5.REORDER.POINT: N,2,0,9999,"50"
6.QUANTITY.ON.HAND: N,2,0,9999,"55"
7.YTD.QUANTITY.SOLD: N,3,0,99999,"0"
8.SALES.DOLLARS: $,4,.00,99999.99,"0.00"
9.QUANTITY.SOLD: N,2,0,9999,"0"
Record Size (Bytes) = 52
Total Records = 0
```

Look at line number 5 as an example. Decoding Condor's attributes yields the following table:

REORDER.POINT	Field name
N	Field is numeric
2	Two bytes of disk storage accommodating numbers in range ±32767
0	Lower limit is zero
9999	Upper limit is 9999
50	Default value is 50 units

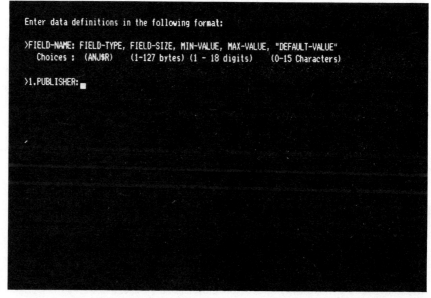

FIGURE 4-4.
Entering values to define fields

Once your BOOKS database has been defined, three CP/M files are involved. The file BOOKS.FRM contains the data-entry screen format, BOOKS.DEF contains the data dictionary, and BOOKS.DAT (now empty) contains the actual inventory data. These three files are linked together in Condor's dictionary file, DATA.DIC, which contains entries for all databases on a disk.

Entering the Data

Database data entry begins by typing

ENTER BOOKS

The screen in Figure 4-3 comes up, and you key in data as shown in Figure 4-5. Condor's full-screen editor allows you to move backward and forward within and among fields. If you enter a value out of range (greater than the upper limit, for instance) Condor tells you and prevents you from continuing. If a field has a default value, it is automatically skipped, although you can override this feature.

To make sure your database is sorted in order of the publisher and catalog number, type

SORT BOOKS BY PUBLISHER CATALOG.NUMBER

Printing the Data

After you enter data for two publishers' books, you can print out the price list. PRINT is just like LIST except the output is sent to the printer. Condor has an abbreviation feature, similar to CP/M's, that allows you to substitute "P*" for publisher. Since only the first field character is recognized by Condor, it's a good idea to start field names with unique first letters, as shown in Figure 4-6.

TITLE D, 'COMPUTER BOOK PRICE LIST, 'P
PRINT BOOKS BY P* C* T* RET*

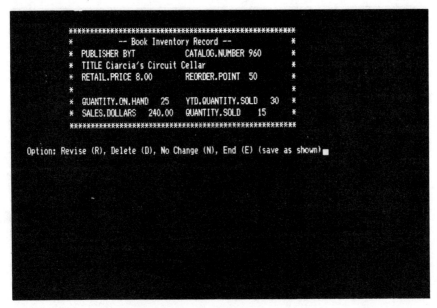

FIGURE 4-5.
Completed data entry form

```
   04/15/82       COMPUTER BOOK PRICE LIST      Page 1

   PUBLISHER CATALOG.NUMBER  TITLE                    RETAIL.PRICE

      BYT      960     Ciarcia's Circuit Cellar          8.00
      BYT     1040     Layman's Guide to SBC's          10.00
      BYT     4925     You Just Bought a Personl What   11.95
      BYT     6745     Beginner's Gde to UCSD Pascal    11.95
      BYT     8360     Threaded Interpreted Languages   18.95
      OSB     1988     PET/CBM Personal Compter Guide   15.00
      OSB     8806     Some Common BASIC Programs       14.99
      OSB     8821     Z80 Assembly Language Prgmng     16.99
      OSB     8828     Running Wild                      3.95
      OSB     8844     CP/M User Guide                  12.99
      OSB     8847     Business Systems Buyers Guide    15.00
```

FIGURE 4-6.
Printed book price
list

This report was automatically formatted by Condor. The column headings are the same as the field names. If you want a neater report, you must use the Report Generator, described later in this chapter.

Defining the Daily Sales Database

Now that you have the inventory file defined, you need another database to accumulate daily sales. The only information required is the publisher and catalog number plus the quantity sold, which you obtain from tags removed from purchased books or directly from the cash register. Using the same method you used to define BOOKS, you define a new database called DAILYSLS with the form shown in Figure 4-7. Condor prints the data dictionary of this database as follows:

```
Attribute summary of database DAILYSLS
1.PUBLISHER: A,3,0,3," "
2.CATALOG.NUMBER: N,2,0,9999," "
```

```
3.QUANTITY.SOLD: N,2,0,9999," "
Record Size (Bytes) = 8
Total Records = 0
```

Notice that the field names exactly match those in BOOKS. This is no accident, as you will see. The next step is to enter data into the form and print it out (see Figure 4-8).

```
ENTER DAILYSLS
PRINT DAILYSLS BY P* C* Q*
```

Producing the Daily Sales Report

You need a daily sales report showing not only PUBLISHER, CATALOG.NUMBER, and QUANTITY.SOLD, but also the categories TITLE and SALES.DOLLARS. The TITLE comes directly from the BOOKS database, and SALES.DOLLARS is computed from QUANTITY.SOLD and RETAIL. PRICE. How does Condor join it all in one place? Through JOIN, of course. But you can't JOIN BOOKS with DAILYSLS. The common field SALES.DOLLARS will cause problems

FIGURE 4-7.
DAILYSLS data entry
form

FIGURE 4-8.
Printed Daily Sales
Report

because it has different values in each database; in BOOKS it represents year-to-date sales. You must first eliminate the SALES.DOLLARS field from the BOOKS database, and you do that by PROJECTing BOOKS into a temporary database called BOOKPROJ. PROJECT also eliminates nuisance fields like QUANTITY.ON.HAND and YTD.QUANTITY.SOLD which are not needed for the Daily Sales Report.

```
PROJECT BOOKS BY P* C* T* RET* SALES*
SAVE BOOKPROJ
Attribute summary of Data Base BOOKPROJ
1.PUBLISHER: A,3,0,3," "
2.CATALOG.NUMBER: N,2,0,32767," "
```

```
3.TITLE: AN,30,0,30," "
4.RETAIL.PRICE: $,3,.00,99.99," "
5.SALES.DOLLARS:
  $,4,.00,99999.99,"0.00"
Record Size (Bytes) = 43
Total Records = 19
```

Now you are ready for JOIN. You are matching records on the PUBLISHER and CATALOG. NUMBER fields "P* and C*." Every occurrence of "P*" and "C*" in the DAILYSLS database is "hooked up" to the corresponding occurrence in BOOKPROJ. Because there are no duplicate PUBLISHER or CATALOG.NUMBER pairs in BOOKPROJ, you end up with exactly the same number of records you started with in DAILYSLS (see Figure 4-9 for an illustration of a JOINed report).

```
PROJECT BOOKS BY P* C* T* RET* SALES*
SAVE BOOKPROJ
Attribute summary of database POSTING
1.PUBLISHER: A,3,0,3," "
2.CATALOG.NUMBER: N,2,0,32767," "
3.TITLE: AN,30,0,30," "
4.RETAIL.PRICE: $,3,.00,99.99," "
5.SALES.DOLLARS:
  $,4,.00,99999.99,"0.00"
```

```
6.QUANTITY.SOLD: N,2,0,9999," "
Record Size (Bytes) = 45
Total Records = 11
LIST POSTING BY P* C* T* RET* Q*
```

Note that JOIN BOOKPROJ DAILYSLS is not the same as JOIN DAILYSLS BOOKPROJ. The latter JOIN produces a result set in the sort order of BOOKPROJ rather than in the sort order of DAILYSLS.

What if you make a mistake? Suppose you enter BTY for the publisher instead of BYT. In this system, that record gets lost in JOIN because it does not have a match in the BOOKS file. To guard against losing records, you can run a **COMPARE** NOT MATCHING on DAILYSLS and BOOKPROJ. The resulting database will show all transactions without books.

You now have all the necessary information except the extended amount sold. Condor lets you **COMPUTE** this with the result going into SALES.DOLLARS. This field was PROJECTed out of BOOKS especially for this purpose.

```
COMPUTE POSTING ST SALES.DOLLARS =
    QUANTITY.SOLD * RETAIL.PRICE
```

PUBLISHER	CATALOG NUMBER	TITLE	RETAIL PRICE	QUANTITY SOLD
BYT	6745	Beginner's Gde to UCSD Pascal	11.95	1
OSB	8828	Running Wild	3.95	2
OSB	8844	CP/M User Guide	12.99	4
OSB	8806	Some Common BASIC Programs	14.99	5
OSB	1988	PET/CBM Personal Compter Guide	15.00	5
BYT	1040	Layman's Guide to SBC's	10.00	6
BYT	4925	You Just Bought a Personl What	11.95	8
BYT	960	Ciarcia's Circuit Cellar	8.00	15
BYT	8821	Z80 Assembly Language Prgmng	16.99	18

FIGURE 4-9.
JOINed PUBLISHER and
CATALOG fields

All that remains is to have Condor print the final Daily Sales Report. This is accomplished by typing

```
TITLE D, 'DAILY SALES AMOUNT REPORT, ',P
PRINT POSTING BY P* C* T* Q* S*
    COMPUTE TOT Q* S*
```

Figure 4-10 shows you the resulting printout.

Producing the Sales Analysis And Reorder Reports

Now you must turn your attention to the basic functions of an inventory system. You need to know how many of each book you have sold this year, how much money you have made, and which books you need to reorder. Condor provides the POST command to add QUANTITY.SOLD from the daily transactions (POSTing database) to the QUANTITY.SOLD in the BOOKS database. First you use COMPUTE to make sure that all the BOOKS QUANTITY.- SOLD fields are zero, then you POST. The new report is shown in Figure 4-11.

```
COMPUTE BOOKS ST QUANTITY.SOLD = 0
```
(ST is Condor's abbreviation for "such that")
```
POST BOOKS POSTING MATCHING P* C*
    ADD QUANTITY.SOLD
LIST BOOKS BY P* C* T* QUANTITY.SOLD
```

Now that you know how many of each book were sold, it is a simple matter to deduct this amount from QUANTITY.ON.HAND and add it to YTD.QUANTITY.SOLD. Year-to-date sales dollars, called SALES.DOLLARS in the BOOKS database, are easily calculated.

```
COMPUTE BOOKS ST QUANTITY.ON.HAND =
    QUANTITY.ON.HAND = QUANTITY.SOLD
COMPUTE BOOKS ST YTD.QUANTITY.SOLD =
    YTD.QUANTITY.SOLD + QUANTITY.SOLD
COMPUTE BOOKS ST SALES.DOLLARS =
    QUANTITY.SOLD * RETAIL.PRICE +
    SALES.DOLLARS
```

Look at these COMPUTE statements for a moment. They really look like statements in a BASIC or COBOL program, but there's one difference. Here you are computing *all the*

```
 04/15/82          DAILY SALES AMOUNT REPORT        Page 1

PUBLISHER CATALOG.NUMBER TITLE                   QUANTITY.SOLD SALES.DOLLARS
    BYT    6745     Beginner's Gde to UCSD Pascal      1           11.95
    OSB    8828     Running Wild ,                      2            7.90
    OSB    8844     CP/M User Guide                     4           51.96
    OSB    8806     Some Common BASIC Programs          5           74.95
    OSB    1988     PET/CBM Personal Compter Guide      5           75.00
    BYT    1040     Layman's Guide to SBC's             6           60.00
    BYT    4925     You Just Bought a Personl What      8           95.60
    BYT     960     Ciarcia's Circuit Cellar           15          120.00
    OSB    8821     Z80 Assembly Language Prgmng       18          305.82

    Total                                             77          952.68
```

FIGURE 4-10.
Daily Sales Report

```
      PUBLISHER CATALOG.NUMBER      TITLE                QUANTITY.SOLD

        BYT        960      Ciarcia's Circuit Cellar        15
        BYT       1040      Layman's Guide to SBC's           9
        BYT       4925      You Just Bought a Personl What    8
        BYT       6745      Beginner's Gde to UCSD Pascal    11
        BYT       8360      Threaded Interpreted Languages    0
        OSB       1988      PET/CBM Personal Compter Guide    5
        OSB       8806      Some Common BASIC Programs         5
        OSB       8821      Z80 Assembly Language Prgmng     18
        OSB       8828      Running Wild                       2
        OSB       8844      CP/M User Guide                    4
        OSB       8847      Business Systems Buyers Guide      0
```

FIGURE 4-11.
POSTed book list

records in the database; COBOL computes only *one data item* at a time. Condor forces three complete passes of the database, but it's faster than you might think.

Suppose your distributor sent you 55 copies of each book when you opened the store, and this was the default value for QUANTITY.ON.HAND when you first set up the BOOKS database. To look at the new quantity after daily sales have been deducted, type

```
LIST BOOKS BY P* C* QUANTITY.ON*
   YTD* SALES*
```

The new report is illustrated in Figure 4-12.

At last you have enough information to produce a Sales Analysis Report (Figure 4-13). Condor lets you SUBTOTal during a PRINT in order to show quantity and dollar subtotals for each publisher. Grand totals are automatic.

```
TITLE D,'   SALES ANALYSIS REPORT BY
   PUBLISHER,   ',P
PRINT BOOKS P* C* T* Y* SALES* COMPUTE TOT Y*
   SALES* SUBTOT USING P*
```

Now you can produce the last report, the Reorder Report as shown in Figure 4-14. This

is a list of all books with QUANTITY.ON.HAND less than or equal to the REORDER.POINT. This is done with Condor's SELECT command, which creates a new database containing only those records meeting certain criteria. (@ is Condor's symbol for indicating the contents of the field.)

```
SELECT BOOKS ST Q* = @ REORDER.POINT
TITLE D,   'REORDER LIST,   'P
PRINT RESULT BY P* C* T* Q*
```

Creating a HELP Menu

All this data entry and reporting takes a long time to produce, and you wouldn't want to try to remember every step involved. Condor lets you automate the whole process with a HELP menu which you create using the same full-screen editor you used to define the data-entry screens. Figure 4-15 shows the HELP menu in use. Each number the user enters (1 through 7) links to one of the command sequences shown below. These command files are similar to those in the crossword puzzle example.

```
PUBLISHER CATALOG.NUMBER QUANTITY.ON.HAND YTD. QUANTITY.SOLD SALES.DOLLARS

   BYT        960              40                   15           120.00
   BYT        1040             46                    9            90.00
   BYT        4925             47                    8            95.60
   BYT        6745             44                   11           131.45
   BYT        8360             55                    0             0.00
   OSB        1988             50                    5            75.00
   OSB        8806             50                    5            74.95
   OSB        8821             37                   18           305.82
   OSB        8828             53                    2             7.90
   OSB        8844             51                    4            51.96
   OSB        8847             55                    0             0.00
```

FIGURE 4-12.
Book list with
year-to-date sales

```
04/15/82        SALES ANALYSIS REPORT BY PUBLISHER        Page 1

PUBLISHER CATALOG.NUMBER      TITLE           YTD.QUANTITY.SOLD   SALES.DOLLARS

   BYT        960      Ciarcia's Circuit Cellar        15           120.00
   BYT        1040     Layman's Guide to SBC's          9            90.00
   BYT        4925     You Just Bought a Personl What   8            95.60
   BYT        6745     Beginner's Gde to UCSD Pascal   11           131.45
   BYT        8360     Threaded Interpreted Languages   0             0.00
   Subtotal                                            43           437.05

   OSB        1988     PET/CBM Personal Compter Guide   5            75.00
   OSB        8806     Some Common BASIC Programs        5            74.95
   OSB        8821     Z80 Assembly Language Prgmng     18           305.82
   OSB        8828     Running Wild                      2             7.90
   OSB        8844     CP/M User Guide                   4            51.96
   OSB        8847     Business Systems Buyers Guide     0             0.00
   Subtotal                                            34           515.63

   Total                                               77           952.68
```

FIGURE 4-13.
Sales Analysis
Report

```
04/15/82        REORDER LIST        Page 1

PUBLISHER CATALOG.NUMBER      TITLE              QUANTITY.ON.HAND
    BYT        960      Ciarcia's Circuit Cellar        40
    BYT       1040      Layman's Guide to SBC's          46
    BYT       4925      You Just Bought a Personl What   47
    BYT       6745      Beginner's Gde to UCSD Pascal    44
    OSB       1988      PET/CBM Personal Compter Guide   50
    OSB       8806      Some Common BASIC Programs       50
    OSB       8821      Z80 Assembly Language Prgmng     37
```

FIGURE 4-14.
Reorder Report

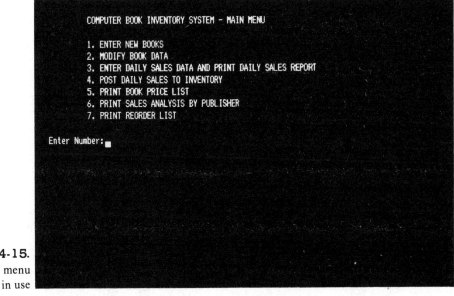

FIGURE 4-15.
The HELP menu
in use

Perhaps you've seen all the conventions of command files before, but you may need the following short review:

1. The semicolon indicates a comment line, making the sequence more readable.

2. Single quotes delimit character strings as used in the TITLE command.

3. Asterisks are "wild cards," allowing shorthand referencing of fields. "P*" is short for "PUBLISHER," "RET*" represents "RETAIL.SALES," and so on.

4. Blanks normally separate command line elements, but commas may be used instead.

Some command sequences are displayed in Figure 4-16.

```
; ENTERBKS.CMD - Enter new records to BOOKS database
ENTER BOOKS
SORT BOOKS BY P* C*
HELP MENU

; MODIBKS.CMD - Modify existing records in the BOOKS database
UPDATE BOOKS
SORT BOOKS BY P* C*
HELP MENU

; ENTERDLY.CMD - Enter daily sales to DAILYSLS and print a
report
EMPTY DAILYSLS
ENTER DAILYSLS
PROJECT BOOKS BY P* C* T* RET* SALES*
DESTROY BOOKPROJ
SAVE BOOKPROJ
JOIN BOOKPROJ DAILYSLS BY P* C*
DESTROY POSTING
SAVE POSTING
COMPUTE POSTING ST SALES.DOLLARS = QUANTITY.SOLD * RETAIL.PRICE
TITLE D,'        DAILY SALES AMOUNT REPORT        ',P
PRINT POSTING BY P* C* T* Q* COMPUTE TOT Q* S*
HELP MENU

; POSTDLY.CMD - Post daily transactions to BOOKS database
COMPUTE BOOKS ST QUANTITY.SOLD = 0
POST BOOKS POSTING MATCHING P* C* ADD QUANTITY.SOLD
COMPUTE BOOKS ST QUANTITY.ON.HAND = QUANTITY.ON.HAND -
QUANTITY.SOLD
COMPUTE BOOKS ST YTD.QUANTITY.SOLD = YTD.QUANTITY.SOLD +
QUANTITY.SOLD
COMPUTE BOOKS ST SALES.DOLLARS = QUANTITY.SOLD *
RETAIL.PRICE + SALES.DOLLARS
HELP MENU

; PRICELST.CMD - Print the price list report
TITLE D,'        COMPUTER BOOK PRICE LIST        ',P
PRINT BOOKS BY P* C* T* RET*
HELP MENU

; SLSANAL.CMD - Print the sales analysis report
TITLE D,'        SALES ANALYSIS REPORT BY PUBLISHER        ',P
PRINT BOOKS BY P* C* T* Y* SALES* COMPUTE TOT Y* SALES*
SUBTOT USING P*
HELP MENU

; REORDLST.CMD - Print reorder list report
SELECT BOOKS ST Q* <= @ REORDER.POINT
TITLE D,'        REORDER LIST        ',P
PRINT RESULT BY P* C* T* Q*
```

FIGURE 4-16.
Command sequences

The inventory system now works smoothly, but the operator must still approve the EMPTY-ing or DESTROYing of a file. This can be automated by adding "OK" when entering EMPTY and DESTROY.

LEVEL 3—REPORT GENERATOR PLUS INDEXING

Example:

Sales Analysis Report

Command:

COMPUTE

Look at the Sales Analysis Report by Publisher on the previous pages. It was automatically formatted by Condor through a one-line PRINT command (plus the TITLE statement). The PRINT command gives you no control of column positions or headings, nor does it allow more than one level of subtotals. Any calculations must be done by COMPUTE commands prior to the PRINT, using fields specially created for the purpose.

If you want fancier reports, you'll have to use Condor's REPORT subsystem, available only with Condor 20-3. Suppose you redesign the Sales Analysis by Publisher report as shown in Figure 4-17. You've added two new fields, squeezed the columns together, and moved PUBLISHER from each detail line to a section header position.

```
DATE 04/20/82          COMPUTER BOOK SALES ANALYSIS REPORT
                                BY PUBLISHER

CATALOG                              RETAIL  CURRENT   YTD    YTD
  NUMBER          TITLE              PRICE  QTY SOLD QTY SOLD SALES

PUBLISHER  BYT
0960       Ciarcia's Circuit Cellar   8.00     15      30    240.00
1040       Layman's Guide to SBC's   10.00      9      18    180.00
4925       You Just Bought a Personl What 11.95   8    16    191.20
6745       Beginner's Gde to UCSD Pascal 11.95  11     22    262.90
8360       Threaded Interpreted Languages 18.95  0      0      0.00
                            Totals           135     178   1930.10

PUBLISHER  OSB
1988       PET/CBM Personal Compter Guide 15.00   5    10    150.00
8806       Some Common BASIC Programs 14.99      5      10    149.90
8821       Z80 Assembly Language Prgmng 16.99   18     36    611.64
8828       Running Wild               3.95      2       4     15.80
8844       CP/M User Guide           12.99      4       8    103.92
8847       Business Systems Buyers Guide 15.00   0      0      0.00
                            Totals            44      78   1231.26
                       Grand Totals          179     256   3161.36
```

FIGURE 4-17.
Sales analysis by publisher using Report Generator

How can you tell Condor what the report looks like? You actually design the report directly on the screen the same way you designed the data entry forms. After typing

REPORT BOOKS

you see the screen of Figure 4-18. This is a menu, a departure from Condor's usual command-driven mode. Choosing "C," Create New Report Specification, gives you a blank screen on which you type an image of your report as shown in Figure 4-19.The headings "$TODAY" and "$PAGE" list the current date and page number; the expressions in square brackets, such as [TITLE], extract fields from the BOOKS database, and everything else results in printed text. You have all the full-screen editing commands you had when entering data-entry forms, plus you can fill the screen with a grid as shown in Figure 4-20.

After you type the report image on the screen, Condor asks you questions about the report. The first screen after formatting is shown in Figure 4-21. Here you enter house-keeping data such as page length and margins. Next, Condor moves through each line as defined on the image screen (blank lines are ignored), displaying it on the top of a new screen. Figure 4-22 shows line 6, the detail line. Condor asks you when you want the line printed and how you want it spaced. Entering a number in "Line number to skip to BEFORE printing line" or "Line number to skip to AFTER printing line" causes absolute positioning on the page. You can use this feature to position report headings or print checks and invoices. Entering a number in "Number of blank lines to insert BEFORE printing line" or "Number of blank lines to insert AFTER printing line" causes conventional single- or double-spaced reporting.

After you define the general specifications of the print line, you are prompted to specify each field in the line. Figure 4-23 shows the leftmost field, C* or CATALOG.NUMBER, being defined. The starting column number and print width come from the form and definition files, respectively, but you can override them. This is useful if your report is more than 80 columns wide (the width of the screen). As you can see from the figure, you have a choice of eight different field print formats.

Condor steps you through all the lines and through all the fields in each line. When you're done, you can print out the report (Figure 4-17), and for a record of your work, you can print (describe, in Condor's language) the specification as shown in Figure 4-24. If you're not satisfied with the report, you can go back to the menu of Figure 4-18, choosing "R" to revise an existing report specification. You can't get back to the format screen, but you can change line spacing, column positions, and field print formats. Neither can you substitute fields or change the text. To do so you must recreate the report.

When you are satisfied with the report, you may save its specifications to disk for future use. You provide a name which is entered into Condor's database dictionary for the current disk. The report may be invoked with a *selection* specification. You could, for instance, run the Sales Analysis report for a particular publisher or for books with prices over $10.00.

You may also compute values from existing database fields. If you did not already have year-to-date sales stored in the database, you could have calculated it from YTD.QUANTITY. SOLD and RETAIL.PRICE.

The Condor Report Generator works well as long as your report is not wider than 80 columns. When you try to design a 132-column report on an 80-column screen, you have a

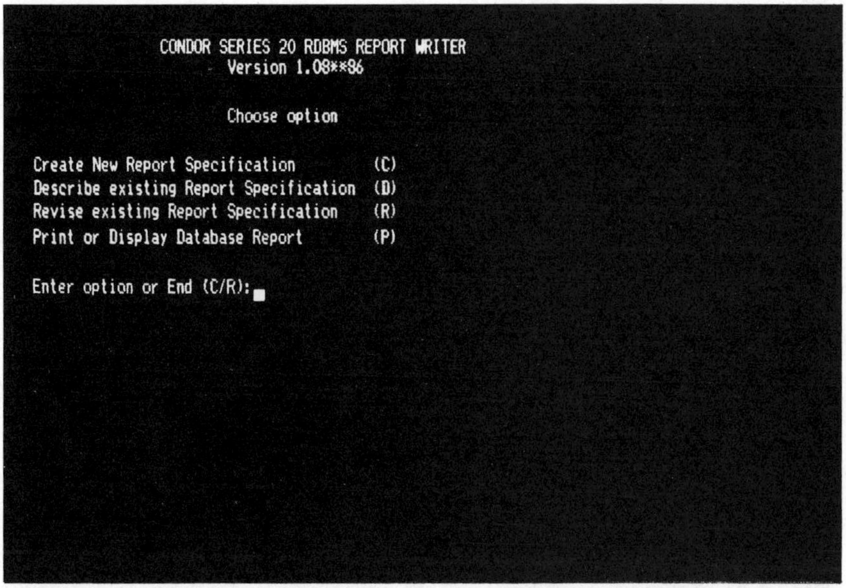

FIGURE 4-18.
The REPORT
WRITER menu

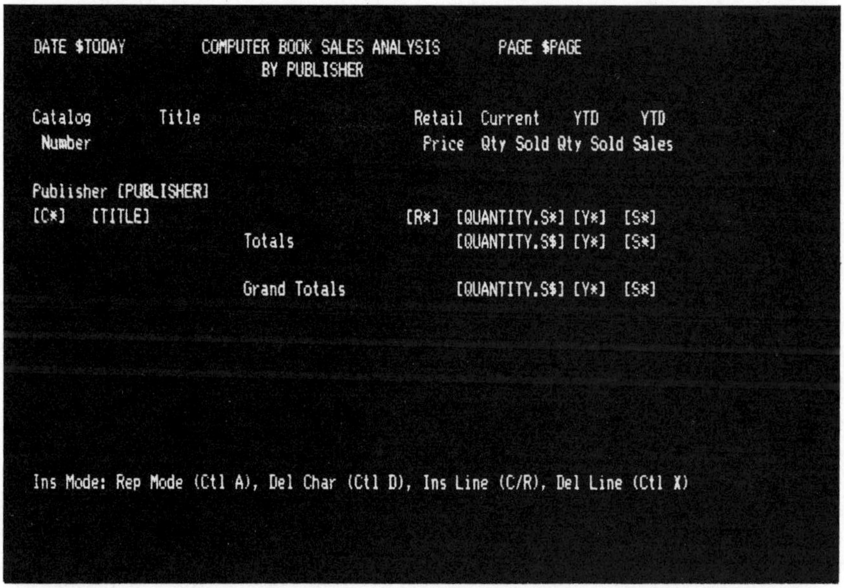

```
        CONDOR SERIES 20 RDBMS REPORT WRITER
                Version 1.08**86

                Choose option

Create New Report Specification      (C)
Describe existing Report Specification  (D)
Revise existing Report Specification   (R)
Print or Display Database Report      (P)

Enter option or End (C/R):
```

FIGURE 4-19.
Type an image
of the REPORT
on the screen

```
DATE $TODAY          COMPUTER BOOK SALES ANALYSIS       PAGE $PAGE
                          BY PUBLISHER

Catalog       Title                    Retail  Current   YTD    YTD
 Number                                 Price  Qty Sold Qty Sold Sales

Publisher [PUBLISHER]
[C*]   [TITLE]                         [R*] [QUANTITY.S*] [Y*]  [S*]
                        Totals             [QUANTITY.S$] [Y*]  [S*]

                        Grand Totals       [QUANTITY.S$] [Y*]  [S*]




Ins Mode: Rep Mode (Ctl A), Del Char (Ctl D), Ins Line (C/R), Del Line (Ctl X)
```

```
DATE:$TODAY...:....2..COMPUTER.BOOK.SALES.ANALYSIS....:...6....:....7PAGE:SPACE
....:....:....1....:....2....:....BY PUBLISHER...:....5....:....6....:....7....:....8
....:....:....1....:....2....:....3....:....4....:....5....:....6....:....7....:....8

Catalog..1....:....Title:....3....:....4....:......Retail:..Current:...YTD...:.YTD8
.Number..1....:....2....:....3....:....4....:......Price:.Qty.Sold.Qty7Sold:Sales
....:....:....1....:....2....:....3....:....4....:....5....:....6....:....7....:....8
Publisher1[PUBLISHER]...:....3....:....4....:....5....:....6....:....7....:....8
[C*]:...[TITLE]....2....:....3....:....4....:..[R*]..[QUANTITY.S*]..[Y*].:.[S*]
....:....:....1....:....2....:....Totals:....4....:....5..[QUANTITY.S$]..[Y*].:.[S*]
....:....:....1....:....2....:....3....:....4....:....5....:....6....:....7....:....
....:....:....1....:....2....:...Grand.Totals....:....5..[QUANTITY.S$]..[Y*].:.[S*]
....:....:....1....:....2....:....3....:....4....:....5....:....6....:....7....:....8
....:....:....1....:....2....:....3....:....4....:....5....:....6....:....7....:....8
....:....:....1....:....2....:....3....:....4....:....5....:....6....:....7....:....8
....:....:....1....:....2....:....3....:....4....:....5....:....6....:....7....:....8
....:....:....1....:....2....:....3....:....4....:....5....:....6....:....7....:....8
....:....:....1....:....2....:....3....:....4....:....5....:....6....:....7....:....8
....:....:....1....:....2....:....3....:....4....:....5....:....6....:....7....:....8
....:....:....1....:....2....:....3....:....4....:....5....:....6....:....7....:....8
....:....:....1....:....2....:....3....:....4....:....5....:....6....:....7....:....8
....:....:....1....:....2....:....3....:....4....:....5....:....6....:....7....:....8
Ins Mode: Rep Mode (Ctl A), Del Char (Ctl D), Ins Line (C/R), Del Line (Ctl X)
```

FIGURE 4-20.
The REPORT with optional grid

```
INSTRUCTIONS:

Define report specification

Prompts will be displayed as required

Parentheses () indicate the codes or the range expected.
Brackets [] indicate the existing default values.
Entering only a (C/R) causes the default velues to be used.

Describe Page Format:

Page Length - physical lines per page (1-127) [ 66 ]:
Left margin - Enter column number (1-127) [ 1 ]:
Right margin - Enter column number (1-132) [ 80 ]:
Top margin - Enter line number (1-127) [ 1 ]:
Bottom margin - Enter line number (127) [ 60 ]:

OK (Y/N)?
```

FIGURE 4-21.
Enter data to describe page format

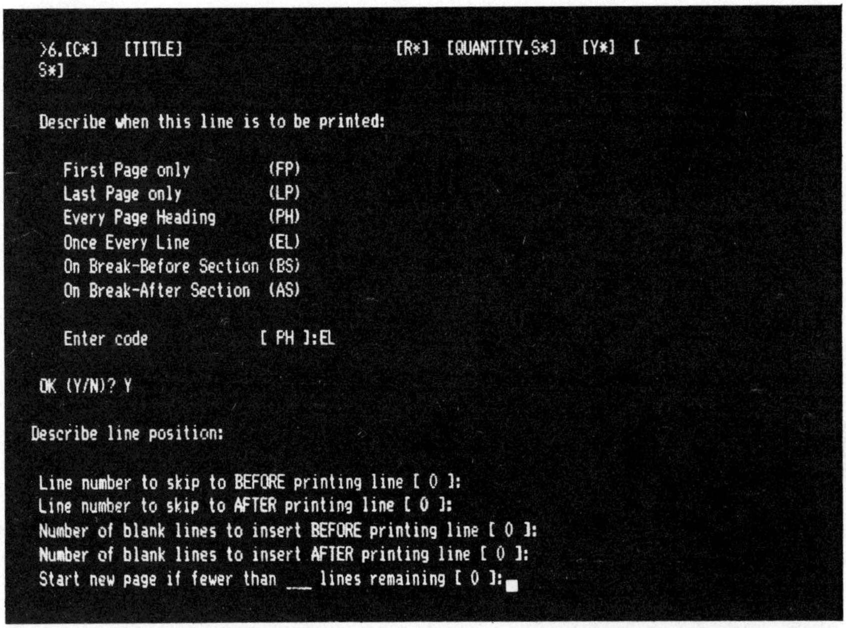

```
>6.[C*]   [TITLE]                          [R*] [QUANTITY.S*]  [Y*] [
S*]

Describe when this line is to be printed:


    First Page only         (FP)
    Last Page only          (LP)
    Every Page Heading       (PH)
    Once Every Line          (EL)
    On Break-Before Section  (BS)
    On Break-After Section   (AS)


    Enter code              [ PH ]:EL

OK (Y/N)? Y

Describe line position:

Line number to skip to BEFORE printing line [ 0 ]:
Line number to skip to AFTER printing line [ 0 ]:
Number of blank lines to insert BEFORE printing line [ 0 ]:
Number of blank lines to insert AFTER printing line [ 0 ]:
Start new page if fewer than ___ lines remaining [ 0 ]:
```

FIGURE 4-22.
Choose options
on printing a
specific line

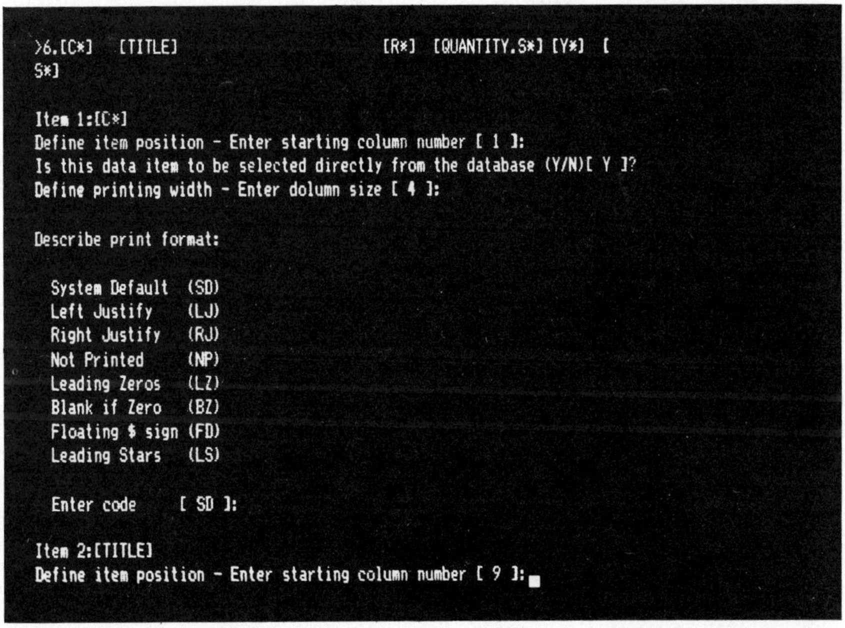

```
>6.[C*]   [TITLE]                          [R*] [QUANTITY.S*] [Y*] [
S*]

Item 1:[C*]
Define item position - Enter starting column number [ 1 ]:
Is this data item to be selected directly from the database (Y/N)[ Y ]?
Define printing width - Enter dolumn size [ 4 ]:

Describe print format:

    System Default   (SD)
    Left Justify     (LJ)
    Right Justify    (RJ)
    Not Printed      (NP)
    Leading Zeros    (LZ)
    Blank if Zero    (BZ)
    Floating $ sign  (FD)
    Leading Stars    (LS)


    Enter code       [ SD ]:

Item 2:[TITLE]
Define item position - Enter starting column number [ 9 ]:
```

FIGURE 4-23.
Defining the print
format for each
field in a line

```
\NP
Report Specification for SLSANAL

    Page Format

        Physl    Left     Right    Top      Bottom
        Lines    Margin   Margin   Margin   Margin

         66        1        90       1        60
```

>1.DATE $TODAY COMPUTER BOOK SALES ANALYSIS REPORT PAGE $PAGE

```
Print on
(PH) - Every Page Heading

        Line #  Line #  Space   Space   Look
        Before  After   Before  After   Ahead

           1       0       0       0       0

    Item                    Type  Format   Column  Length  Print
    DATE                    TEXT  SD            1       4   VAL
    $TODAY                  TEXT  SD            6       8   VAL
    COMPUTER                TEXT  SD           23       8   VAL
    BOOK                    TEXT  SD           32       4   VAL
    SALES                   TEXT  SD           37       5   VAL
    ANALYSIS                TEXT  SD           43       8   VAL
    REPORT                  TEXT  SD           52       6   VAL
    PAGE                    TEXT  SD           78       4   VAL
    $PAGE                   TEXT  SD           83       5   VAL
```

>2.BY PUBLISHER

```
Print on
(PH) - Every Page Heading

        Line #  Line #  Space   Space   Look
        Before  After   Before  After   Ahead

           2       0       0       0       0

    Item                    Type  Format   Column  Length  Print
    BY                      TEXT  SD           33       2   VAL
    PUBLISHER               TEXT  SD           36       9   VAL
```

>3.Catalog Title Retail Current YTD YTD

```
Print on
(PH) - Every Page Heading
```

(continued)

FIGURE 4-24.
Report specification for
Sales Analysis Report

Line # Before	Line # After	Space Before	Space After	Look Ahead
4	0	0	0	0

Item		Type	Format	Column	Length	Print
Catalog		TEXT	SD	1	7	VAL
Title		TEXT	SD	20	5	VAL
Retail		TEXT	SD	49	6	VAL
Current		TEXT	SD	58	7	VAL
YTD		TEXT	SD	69	3	VAL
YTD		TEXT	SD	81	3	VAL

>4.Number Price Qty Sold Qty Sold Sales

Print on
(PH) - Every Page Heading

Line # Before	Line # After	Space Before	Space After	Look Ahead
5	0	0	1	0

Item		Type	Format	Column	Length	Print
Number		TEXT	SD	2	6	VAL
Price		TEXT	SD	50	5	VAL
Qty		TEXT	SD	58	3	VAL
Sold		TEXT	SD	62	4	VAL
Qty		TEXT	SD	67	3	VAL
Sold		TEXT	SD	71	4	VAL
Sales		TEXT	SD	80	5	VAL

>5.Publisher [P*]

Print on
(BS) - Break Before Section
Control Items
PUBLISHER

Line # Before	Line # After	Space Before	Space After	Look Ahead
0	0	0	0	2

Item		Type	Format	Column	Length	Print
Publisher		TEXT	SD	1	9	VAL
P*		DATA	SD	12	3	VAL

>6.[C*] [TITLE] [RET*] [QUANTITY.S*] [Y*] [S*]

Print on
(EL) - Every Line

(continued)

FIGURE 4-24.
Report specification for
Sales Analysis Report (continued)

```
        Line #  Line #  Space    Space   Look
        Before  After   Before   After   Ahead

          0       0       0        0       2

    Item                    Type  Format   Column  Length  Print
    C*                      DATA  LZ          1       4     VAL
    TITLE                   DATA  SD         10      30     VAL
    RET*                    DATA  SD         49       6     VAL
    QUANTITY.S*             DATA  SD         56       5     VAL
    Y*                      DATA  SD         67       5     VAL
    S*                      DATA  SD         77       8     VAL
```

>7.Totals [QUANTITY.S*] [Y*] [S*]

```
Print on
(AS) - Break After Section
Control Items
PUBLISHER
```

```
        Line #  Line #  Space    Space   Look
        Before  After   Before   After   Ahead

          0       0       0        1       0

    Item                    Type  Format   Column  Length  Print
    Totals                  TEXT  SD         30       6     VAL
    QUANTITY.S*             DATA  SD         56       5     SUB
    Y*                      DATA  SD         67       5     SUB
    S*                      DATA  SD         77       8     SUB
```

>8.Grand Totals [QUANTITY.S*] [Y*] [S*]

```
Print on
(LP) - Last Page Only
```

```
        Line #  Line #  Space    Space   Look
        Before  After   Before   After   Ahead

          0       0       4        0       0

    Item                    Type  Format   Column  Length  Print
    Grand                   TEXT  SD         30       5     VAL
    Totals                  TEXT  SD         36       6     VAL
    QUANTITY.S*             DATA  SD         56       5     TOT
    Y*                      DATA  SD         67       5     TOT
    S*                      DATA  SD         77       8     TOT
*   COMPUTED DATA-ITEMS
```

FIGURE 4-24.
Report specification for
Sales Analysis Report (continued)

problem. Since there is no horizontal scroll or "pan" capability, you must squeeze the headings and field names into 80 columns and expand them later in the "question and answer" phase. Likewise, you may wrap around the headings and indicate the end of line by typing a double back slash (\\).

INDEXING

Condor has recently added an indexing capability which was not available for testing at the time of this writing. From the documentation, it appears that full B$^+$-tree indexing is supported as described in Chapter 3.

To index the BOOKS database, you type

`INDEX BOOKS USING P* C*`

This sets up both PUBLISHER and CATALOG. NUMBER jointly as the key so that all newly added books are listed in the proper sequences for LISTs and PRINTs. You no longer have to sort the database each time you add a new book. Since you cannot sort a database that is larger than 128K, this comes in handy.

Multiple indexes are allowed, but only the primary index is updated by ENTER and UPDATE operations. You may specify that an index allow or not allow duplicate keys. In the book example, you would certainly not allow them because you need a unique identifier for each book.

Condor makes good use of its indexes. If you DISPLAY, DELETE, SELECT, or UPDATE an indexed database, Condor will try to use the index for faster access. If you selected all books for PUBLISHER = OSB, Condor would start processing, not at the first record in the database, but at the first record for OSB.

Additional Condor Command Features

A few other useful Condor commands, COMBINE, DELETE, DISPLAY, and

UPDATE, have not been covered in the examples so far.

COMBINE attaches records of two databases with identical data dictionaries. One database is tacked onto the end of the other; there is no merge. DELETE eliminates records meeting specified conditions. Using the BOOKS database as an example, you could have deleted all records for a publisher whose books were no longer stocked. The records aren't really purged from the file, but are made invisible. A subsequent SORT will get rid of them.

Both DISPLAY and UPDATE let you step through the records in a database, using the form to show the record on the screen. UPDATE differs from DISPLAY only in that it permits changes to the data. Both these commands accommodate selection criteria made up of "equal to," "greater than," or "less than" expressions linked by several ANDs or ORs; ANDs and ORs cannot appear in the same expression. You could, for instance, step through only those books from publisher BYT with retail prices over $15.00. The records failing the selection are still "processed" because Condor does a sequential pass of the database. Indexing is a considerable shortcut, however.

All printing so far has been in tabular form. If you need to, you can print a screen image as defined by a form, allowing production of mailing labels.

Transfer to or from Non-Condor Programs

Condor can read and write ASCII sequential files in the following four different formats:

[ ]   Fixed-length, continuous ASCII stream, no delimiters among data items. Numeric data items are right-justified.

[A]   Abridged—variable length—data items separated by a tab (ASCII 09), records demarcated by <CR> or <LF>. All trailing blanks are truncated.

[B] Basic—variable—data items enclosed in quotes (") and delimited by commas, records optionally demarcated by <CR> or <LF>.

[R] RPG—Fixed length—no delimiters between data items, records are demarcated by <CR> or <LF>. Numeric fields are right-justified.

These file types cover most microcomputer formats, including those used by various BASICs and COBOL. Condor uses the READ and WRITE commands for file conversion. READ automatically determines how to read a file, and WRITE requires an option. Needless to say, the field lengths in fixed-length files must correspond to the data dictionary for the database.

Documentation

The *Condor Series 20 User's Manual* is a 160-page document produced by a word processor of typesetting quality. As is quite common in software manuals, the first half of the Condor manual is a tutorial (14 chapters) that introduces you to various data base features. Following this tutorial is an appendix of almost equal length that describes each command in alphabetical order. Concluding the manual are more appendixes that describe terminal configuration and present some sample data dictionaries.

Tutorial

Chapter 1 of the Condor manual describes specifications and conventions, and Chapter 2 explains the CP/M interface. Also included is a very useful "warm-up" that lets you define, enter, sort, and print a simple database for birthdays.

The manual's remaining chapters familiarize you with various Condor command-related features. Chapter 3, for instance, only deals with DEFINE, FORMAT, LIST, and PRINT. There are some examples that are expanded through several chapters, namely, a general ledger with journal, an employee/task/department problem, a mailing list, and a system to track parts ordered by a customer. All have explicit step-by-step instructions with explanations of what is happening. This system works well except for some references to later chapters. You must understand Chapter 9, FORMAT Command Details, in order to start the general ledger problem in Chapter 3.

Command Descriptions

Each command is listed alphabetically, starting at the top of a page, with one to three pages of explanation. The following is an example of this format:

TABULATE

PURPOSE:	Summarize and print specified data items
SYNTAX:	**TABULATE database BY d1, d2,...** {AND COMPUTE statistic d3, d4,..., d32} [option]
	Where statistic can be one of the following words: TOTAL (TOT, ADD, SUM), MIN, MAX, AVERAGE (AVE, AVG) The word compute may be abbreviated with "{"
OPTIONS:	[A] Means accumulate subtotals [P] Means print results on printer [S] Means create result set

RESULT SET: $DAT, $DEF, $FRM
(if option chosen)

EXAMPLES: TABULATE CLIENTS
BY STATE
TABULATE CLIENTS
BY STATE AND
COMPUTE TOTAL
WAGE [P]
TABULATE CLIENTS
BY STATE @ TOT
WAGE, AVERAGE
HOURS

USAGE:

The database must by sorted by the tabulating key ....

Excerpted with permission from Condor Series 20 User Manual, 1981, 1982, Condor Computer Corporation.

Support

Telephone support is provided from Ann Arbor during regular business hours. During testing of the package for the book, a small problem required an answer from Condor's technical support staff. Although the support person acknowledged a possible bug and promised to research further, no other response was received.

Configuration

Condor does full-screen editing, and this means you must specify your terminal. There are eight modules available for configuring to the following terminals:

ADDS Regent 20 25 40 60 100 20
Beehive Micro-BI Micro-B2
  B100 B150 B550
Hazeltine 1500 1510 1520
Infoton (GTC) 100 101 200 400
Lear Seigler ADM-1A ADM-2
  ADM-3A ADM-31 ADM-42

Soroc IQ - 120 IQ - 140
Pickles & Trout CP/M for
TRS-80 II

If your terminal is not one of these, Condor lets you define your own module, but you must know the cursor addressing sequences. Perhaps your dealer can help.

If your terminal is a Hazeltine, for instance, you have to type in TERM HAZL every time you start Condor. This is a tedious task, and you can avoid it by establishing a CP/M SUBMIT file. Condor also requires a six-digit *license number* every time you start. The SUBMIT file can contain the license number and the terminal type.

Error Handling

Condor makes extensive error checks when executing each command. Errors are described in plain English, making a list of error messages unnecessary. For example, if you try to compare two fields of different sizes in a SELECT statement, Condor issues the following message:

```
ERROR - Comparing Variables with Different
    Field Sizes.
```

A disk full condition returns the following message:

```
ERROR - Disk Overflow.
```

Most operations may be aborted with a ^C. Condor asks for verification with FORMAT, ENTER, UPDATE, and DISPLAY.

Technical Information

File Usage

Condor stores the actual data for a database in its own CP/M disk file with a .DAT extension. A .FRM file contains the screen form, and a .DEF file contains the field parameters (type, length, default, and so on). Together the .FRM and .DEF files make up the data dictionary. Report specifications are stored in .RPT files, and indexes in .IDX files. Another file, DATA.DIC, is a catalog of all Condor databases on a disk. A database dictionary (do not confuse this with the data dictionary) entry for BOOKS looks something like the following:

```
1   Records
Title  Data   Form   Definition  Index  Report
BOOKS  BOOKS  BOOKS  BOOKS              BOOKS
```

It is possible to use the same .FRM, .DEF, and .RPT files for different databases. This allows you to keep inventories of two stores on one disk, using the same data dictionary and report specification. Consider the following example:

```
2   Records
Title   Data    Form   Definition Index  Report
BOOKS1  BOOKS1  BOOKS  BOOKS             BOOKS1
BOOKS2  BOOKS2  BOOKS  BOOKS             BOOKS2
```

Condor provides the commands COPY, DESTROY, and RENAME to manipulate DATA.DIC. DESTROYing a database, for instance, erases not only the dictionary entry, but also the .DAT, .FRM, .DEF, .RPT, and .IDX files. Anyone who tries to use CP/M to copy and rename Condor files will regret it; you may never untie all the knots. Erasing DATA.DIC is equivalent to erasing a disk.

Data Record Length

A data file's record is equal to the sum of its field lengths plus one byte. The length is printed when you use the DESCRIBE option in the DEFINE command, and the extra byte is reserved for flagging deleted records. Note again that Condor stores numbers in a compact binary form. Its unique Julian date format stores a date in three bytes. Dates are entered in standard "mmddyy" or "ddmmyy" format and converted to a number, allowing you to subtract two dates to find the difference in days.

The Shell

One unique feature of Condor is its use of the *shell.* A conventional CP/M program is loaded into memory starting at location 100H and continues to location 3000H. It may have some *overlays,* pieces of code that are temporarily read in from disk to do special jobs. Figure 4-25 shows a memory map of such a system. This serves well unless you need to execute another program such as BASIC or a text editor. In that case the CP/M program must exit, and you call up the next program by name. This can be automated by using the first program to set up a CP/M SUBMIT file, but that is a crude way to do things.

When Condor is initiated by typing "DBMS," a program DBMS.COM loads at location 100H as usual, but then immediately relocates itself to high memory as shown in Figure 4-26. The lower half of memory is now free for Condor's modules, each of which executes a command. This same memory can also be used by non-Condor programs. The high memory part of Condor, called the shell, accepts keyboard input, acting just like CP/M's console command processor (CCP).

Performance

The following are specifications on performance of Condor systems. Important information about the applicability of hard and soft disks is noted, as well as sort and data access method ratios.

Benchmark 1

1635 records, 150 characters each, 5-digit key

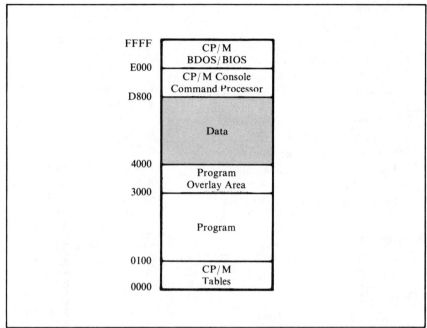

FIGURE 4-25.
Conventional
memory
utilization

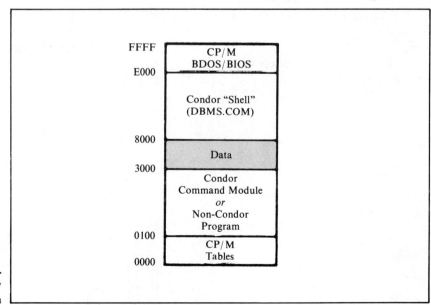

FIGURE 4-26.
Condor's memory
utilization

Floppy disk:

Index build (not available)
Sort index (not applicable)
Index setup (not applicable)
Indexed access (not available)
Sequential pass (0:45 nonindexed)

Hard disk:

Index build (not available)
Sort index (not applicable)
Index setup (not applicable)
Indexed access (not available)
Sequential pass (0:20 nonindexed)

Benchmark 2:

20,210 records, 21 characters each, 18-character key

Hard disk:

Index build (not available)
Sort index (not applicable)
Index setup (not applicable)
Indexed access (not available)
Sequential pass (0:52 nonindexed)

Sort:

300 records, 93 characters each
Floppy disk (1:02)

Restrictions

Condor has no internal programming language or interface to an established language. The best you can do is WRITE out a file, run a BASIC program, then READ the file back in. There's no way to validate data on entry, short of checking the type and the upper and lower limits.

The sort restriction of 128K maximum file size is difficult to live with. The manual says break a large file up, sort each section, then COMBINE the results. You might, for instance, first SELECT all names with first letter "A" through "K," then select "L" through "Z." Condor claims it is working to eliminate the sort restriction.

It is annoying that LIST and PRINT commands, for instance, don't allow both field and record selection. It would be convenient to PRINT all records meeting certain criteria, but you must do a SELECT first.

Security

Condor is not a secure system. Even if you build a HELP menu, the program's operator can abort any command, return to Condor, and modify data at will.

COMMAND SUMMARY

ABORT [1]
   Stops a RUN command

APPEND [1]
   Attach records of one database to another

CHANGE [2]
   Change data item values in a database

COMBINE [2]
   Attach records of two databases, creating a
   RESULT database

COMPARE [1]
   Compare data item values in two databases and
   create a RESULT database

COMPUTE [1]
   Compute data item values in a database

COPY [1]
   Copy a database or a file

DATE [1]
   View or enter date

DEFINE [1]
   Create a new database, redefine or describe a
   database

DELETE [2]
   Delete records of a database meeting specified
   conditions

DESTROY [1]
   Eliminate a database or file

DIC [1]
   View entries in the data dictionary

DIR [1]
   View the list of files in the disk directory

DISPLAY [2]
   View selected records of a database

EMPTY [1]
   Eliminate all records in a database

ENTER [1]
   Insert new records into a database

FORMAT [1]
   Create or revise a form or HELP screen

HELP [1]
   Assist operator in selecting procedures (menu)

INDEX [3]
   Create or rebuild a database index

JOIN [2]
   Attach data items of two databases by matching
   data item values

LIST [1]
   View records of a database in sequential order

LOG [1]
   Log a new disk in the computer

POST [1]
   Update data item values in one database with
   those from another

PRINT [1]
   Print records of a database in sequential order

PROJECT [2]
   Create a RESULT database from selected data items
   of a database

READ [1]
   Transfer records from an ASCII file to an existing
   database

RENAME [1]
   Change the name of a database or file

REORG [1]
   Reorganize the structure of a database, adding or
   deleting data items

REPORT [3]
   Create, revise, or describe a report specification;
   print or view a report

RESTART [1]
   Continue processing an interrupted command
   procedure

RUN [1]
   Start processing a command procedure with
   directives

COMMAND SUMMARY (Continued)

SAVE [1]

Save a RESULT database

SELECT [1]

Select database records meeting specified conditions, creating a RESULT database

SET [1]

Set Condor operating parameters

SORT [1]

Sort database records by data item values

STAX [1]

View or print statistics of data item values

SYS [1]

Exit from Condor

TABULATE [1]

Summarize and print specified data items

TERM [1]

Define system video terminal

TITLE [1]

Print report headings

UPDATE [1]

Change data item values in a database meeting specified conditions

WRITE [1]

Transfer records from a database to an ASCII sequential file

NOTE: The number following each command indicates the lowest level of Condor in which the command is available. The commands are also included in subsequently higher levels of the system.

5

dBASE II from Ashton-Tate

One of the most heavily advertised data base packages is the dBASE II, a relational database management system. Some of the early ads generated more than a few complaints. However, it seems that the more outrageous the ad is, the more the product name sticks in people's minds and the more people buy it. In the microcomputer software world, this popularity motivates the publisher to fix all the bugs and to produce new enhanced versions. Other companies write compatible applications and related programs, causing the original package to become a "standard."

The dBASE II is a good and useful package, and at least one support package has appeared. Ashton-Tate offers a full refund if you are not satisfied with its product. You might be tempted just to make a copy and send back the original saying you didn't like it. The catch is that two disks are provided. One disk is unsealed and allows creation of databases of not more than 15 records; the other is the full-capability program and is securely sealed. You only get your money back if you don't break the seal. The abbreviated disk lets you learn everything about using the package but does not tell you about performance with large files.

There can be no doubt that dBASE II is a Relational Data Base Management System (RDBMS). Since Chapter 2 established the differences between relational and network data bases, you can evaluate Ashton-Tate's preference for relational over network/hierarchical methods. dBASE II is a true relational data base management system with all the advantages and disadvantages that are described in Chapter 2.

The key to appreciating dBASE II is to consider it a *two-level* system. On the first level you have an interactive *data storage and retrieval package* suitable for a microcomputer owner who needs a simple personal or business data processing tool. This first level is *more* than a file management system because of its powerful commands, which work on entire files and multiple files.

On the second level, dBASE II is a *system development package* containing its own programming language. A skilled programmer can use it to create a system for inventory, sales order processing, and so on—problems formerly solved with a collection of BASIC or COBOL programs. Because of this built-in language, you are never "boxed in," as with a low-level FMS. dBASE II lets you develop

SYSTEM OVERVIEW

DBMS Checklist

☒ Data Dictionary

    Defines type, size, and number of decimal places; identifies fields by name

☒ Query Facility

    Integral part of package

☒ Report Generator

    Produces one level of subtotals with subheadings; permits multifield computation

☒ File Compatibility

    Reads and writes to or from any file

☒ Restructure Capability

    Adds, changes, deletes fields, matches on field names, allows change of field size

☒ Effective Error Handling

    Excellent

☒ Documentation and Support

    Good

☒ Multiple Files

    Uses relational operators; accesses individual record via language

☒ Full-Screen Editing

    Move-the-cursor style

☐ On-Screen Display Format

☐ Password Security

☐ Multiuser Capability

☐ Menu-driven

☒ Program-driven

    With built-in language

☒ Command-driven

    Commands are subset of language

☒ Built-in Language

    Interpreted and structured

☐ Established Language

☒ Access Time

    One-half second indexed access (hard disk); two seconds on diskette

☒ Processing Speed

    10,580 records per minute (hard disk)

☒ Data Access Methods

    Sequential, indexed-sequential, direct

Price (4/82)

$700

Publisher

Ashton-Tate
9929 West Jefferson Boulevard
Culver City, CA 90230
(213) 204-5570

System Requirements

· 8080, 8085, or Z-80 microprocessor system

· The CP/M operating system (MP/M and CDOS acceptable)

· A minimum of 48K bytes of memory

· One or more disk drives

· A cursor-addressed 24 × 80-character video terminal

· Optional text printer

SYSTEM OVERVIEW (Continued)

Specifications		Largest number	$\pm 1.8 \times 10^{63}$
		Smallest number	$\pm 1.0 \times 10^{-63}$
Data types	Character	Numeric accuracy	10 digits
	1-digit-per-byte numeric	Character string length	254 characters max
	Logical	Command line length	254 characters max
Records per database file	65,535 max	Report header length	254 characters max
Characters per record	1000 max	Index key length	100 characters max
Fields per record	32 max	Expressions in SUM command	5 max
Characters per field	254 max	Number of memory variables	64 max

multifile business applications, thus already entering NDBMS territory. A good rule of thumb is to use dBASE for three-file or simpler applications, but use an NDBMS for more complex systems such as fully integrated accounting packages.

STORING AND RETRIEVING DATA

Example:

Personal Property Inventory

Commands:

BROWSE, DISPLAY, EDIT, INDEX, REPORT, SORT

Let's say you are looking for a new and practical function for your microcomputer. A glib salesperson persuades you to pay $700 for dBASE II. By coincidence your insurance agent calls, begging you to make a list of your personal property. What a good chance to make the computer do what might otherwise be so unpleasant a task that you would never get around to doing it.

Entering the Data Dictionary

Assuming the dealer configured the program to your terminal (if not, configuration information appears later in this chapter), and you know how to insert the disk into the computer, you bravely type in DBASE<CR> and wait for your problems to be solved. What happens? dBASE asks for the date and comes back with a dot (.)—nothing but a dot. You are on your own. Maybe it's time to look at the manual, where you find that you may enter any of 64 commands. Remember that these command names are written in large capital letters in this text, field names are written in small capital letters, and all operator input is underscored. Study the following dialog:

```
. CREATE
ENTER FILENAME: PROPERTY
ENTER RECORD STRUCTURE AS FOLLOWS:
    DECIMAL PLACES,FIELD NAME,TYPE,WIDTH
```

Perhaps it's time to think about the problem a little more. For each piece of property you own, you may want to specify CLASS (furniture, camera, hi-fi, and so on), DESCRIPTION, VALUE, and DATE ACQUIRED. These four items are *fields,* and each group of four fields makes up a *record.* Going back to dBASE, you define the STRUCTURE as follows:

```
001 CLASS,C,10     "C" indicates a character field
002 DESCRIP,C,30   The description field is 30
                   characters long
003 VALUE,N,8,2    Value is a numeric field eight
                   digits long with two decimal
                   places
004 DT:ACQRD,N,6
005
```

You have just entered the *data dictionary,* a step common to all data base packages. The words CLASS, DESCRIP, VALUE, DT:ACQRD, along with type and length information, are now permanently associated with your database.

Entering the Data

Getting back to the job at hand, dBASE asks "INPUT DATA NOW?" A "Y" allows you to just type in the data. When you fill up one field, you automatically move on to the next; if you make a mistake, you can move back to the previous field with a ^E. (Throughout this book, the control key is represented by a caret [^].) In fact, you can insert or delete characters and move around, within, and between fields by using control keys. Finishing the last field of the record moves you on to the next. dBASE uses the same "ESDX diamond" certain word processing programs use for moving the cursor. These may be mapped to the "arrow" keys on some terminals. This is an example of *full-screen editing,* one of the outstanding features of dBASE II, and it would be difficult to think of an easier, more efficient way to enter data.

Figure 5-1 shows the screen after one record has been entered. While the reverse video and screen layout are automatically supplied by dBASE II, this capability depends on the terminal you use. Figure 5-1 was taken from a TRS-80 Model II microcomputer with a built-in terminal.

You have little choice as to what your screen will look like—dBASE formats it automatically. Fields are laid out one per line, continuing on a second screen if necessary, and you can't have more than 32 fields.

Entering the Command

Now is a good time to explain the syntax of commands like DISPLAY, an often used dBASE command. According to the *dBASE II System User Manual,* the display command is described as follows:

DISP(LAY) [<scope>] [FOR <exp>] [<exp list>][OFF]

DISPLAY (and any other command) can be referenced by the first four letters. In the previous command

scope may be ALL, RECORD n, or NEXT n records (default is the current record)

exp is the selection criterion such as VALUE> 500 (default is all)

exp list is a list of the fields to be displayed (default is all)

OFF suppresses the record number on the left.

Complex logical expressions are allowed, such as

```
. DISPLAY FOR VALUE>500.AND.(CLASS=
  'COMPUTER'.OR.CLASS='HIFI')
```

Here all records with value in excess of $500 and classified as computer or hi-fi are displayed.

```
RECORD # 00001
CLASS    :COMPUTER :
DESCRIP  :Tandy Model II CPU, 64K    :
VALUE    : 3899.00:
DT:ACORD :810220:
```

FIGURE 5-1.
One record entered
on the screen

The next few examples will give you a good idea of command usage. In most cases, the syntax is very logical and much like English syntax.

Displaying, Sorting, and Editing Data

Suppose you have been able to successfully enter a number of property items and you want to see what you have. The key command here is DISPLAY, which you use in a number of ways. Here you will see every field of every record.

```
. DISPLAY ALL
00001  COMPUTER  Tandy II    3899.00 810220
00002  HIFI      Receiver     479.00 760101
00003  HIFI      Turntable    350.00 791031
00004  SPORTS    Skis         199.00 750101
00005  SPORTS    Kayak        500.00 760101
00006  HIFI      Speakers    1000.00 740101
00007  SPORTS    Ski Boots    100.00 790101
00008  COMPUTER  Printer     1999.00 810101
```

Another try with DISPLAY yields an abbreviated listing. Only two of the fields, DESCRIP and VALUE, are shown, and the word OFF suppresses the record number. Remember that DISP is shorthand for DISPLAY.

```
. DISP ALL DESCRIP VALUE OFF
Tandy II      3899.00
Receiver       479.00
Turntable      350.00
Skis           199.00
Kayak          500.00
Speakers      1000.00
Ski Boots      100.00
Printer       1999.00
```

Incidentally, the record number, displayed to the left of the data in the first listing of this section, is the key to finding a particular record. To change a field for the "printer," the eighth record, just type

```
. EDIT 8
```

and you return to the screen in Figure 5-1. From this point on, record 8 is the current record, and a simple reference brings up data only for the current record.

```
. DISPLAY
00008  COMPUTER  Printer  1999.00  810101
```

While EDIT allows you to change existing records, you can add new records with the INSERT command. This causes all the following records to be moved down, so it may be more efficient to use the APPEND command to add records onto the end of the database.

DISPLAY (and some of the other commands) can make logical selections on the data.

```
. DISPLAY FOR VALUE > 500
00001  COMPUTER  Tandy II  3899.00   810220
00006  HIFI      Speakers  1000.00   740101
00008  COMPUTER  Printer   1999.00   810101
```

Until now, the records have been listed in the order in which you entered them. If you would like to see them by class, you may SORT them on that field. You make a new database called PROP1 (the original one is PROPERTY) and switch to it with the USE command.

```
. SORT ON CLASS TO PROP1
SORT COMPLETE
. USE PROP1
. DISPLAY ALL CLASS DESCRIP VALUE DT:ACQRD
  OFF
COMPUTER  Tandy II            3899.00  810220
COMPUTER  Printer             1999.00  810101
HIFI      Receiver             479.00  760101
HIFI      Turntable            350.00  791031
HIFI      Speakers            1000.00  740101
SPORTS    Skis                 199.00  750101
SPORTS    Kayak                500.00  760101
SPORTS    Ski Boots            100.00  790101
```

Shown here are a few more examples of DISPLAY in action. Notice that you only need the first few *unique* characters of a field to get a match—HI is good enough to get you HIFI and anything else beginning with HI.

```
. DISPLAY ALL FOR CLASS = 'HI'
00003  HIFI    Receiver     479.00   760101
00004  HIFI    Turntable    350.00   791031
00005  HIFI    Speakers    1000.00   740101
. DISPLAY ALL FOR DESCRIP = 'S'
00005  HIFI    Speakers    1000.00   740101
00006  SPORTS  Skis         199.00   750101
00008  SPORTS  Ski Boots    100.00   790101
```

BROWSE

So far you have seen how the EDIT command allows you to change one record at a time and how the DISPLAY command lets you show multiple records on the screen. But perhaps you want to display *and* update a whole screen. That's exactly what the BROWSE command allows, as you can see in Figure 5-2. You can *scroll* up and down through all the records in the database, and you can *pan* left and right if your records take up more than the 80-column screen width. You can also move the cursor anywhere on the screen to edit the data.

REPORT

The DISPLAY command is good for quick database inquiries and can output to the video screen or to the printer. The REPORT command takes this one step further, allowing more presentable output with page headings, totals, and subtotals. Here's how it works with the PROPERTY example. First there is a long dialog between the user and the dBASE II program, and then the report appears on the screen.

```
. USE PROP1
. REPORT
ENTER REPORT FORM NAME: SAMPLE1
ENTER OPTIONS, M = LEFT MARGIN, L =
  LINES/PAGE, W = PAGE WIDTH
PAGE HEADING? (Y/N) y
```

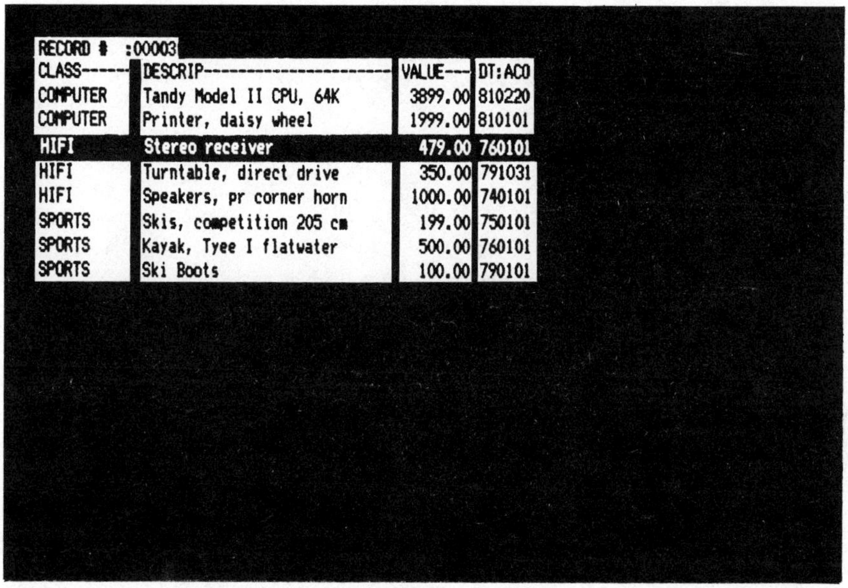

FIGURE 5-2.
BROWSE scrolls
through or pans
across the screen

```
ENTER PAGE HEADING:                          Description            Value        Date
  Sample Property Report 1                                                    Acquired
DOUBLE SPACE REPORT? (Y/N) n                                                  (yymmdd)
ARE TOTALS REQUIRED? (Y/N) y                 * Property in class COMPUTER
SUBTOTALS IN REPORT? (Y/N) y                 Tandy II            3899.00     810220
ENTER SUBTOTALS FIELD: CLASS                 Printer             1999.00     811110
SUMMARY REPORT ONLY? (Y/N) n                 ** SUBTOTAL **
EJECT PAGE AFTER SUBTOTALS? (Y/N) n                              5898.00
ENTER SUBTOTAL HEADING:
  Property in class                          * Property in class HIFI
COL   WIDTH,CONTENTS                         Receiver             479.00     740101
001   30,DESCRIP                             Turntable            350.00     791031
ENTER HEADING: Description                   Speakers            1000.00     740101
002   10,VALUE                               ** SUBTOTAL **
ENTER HEADING: Value                                             1829.00
ARE TOTALS REQUIRED? (Y/N) y
003   10,DT:ACQRD                            * Property in class SPORTS
ENTER HEADING: Date Acquired (yymmdd)        Skis                 199.00     750101
ARE TOTALS REQUIRED? (Y/N) n                 Kayak                500.00     760101
004                                          Ski Boots            100.00     790101
PAGE NO. 00001                               ** SUBTOTAL **
11/16/81                                                          799.00
Sample Property Report 1                     ** TOTAL **
                                                                 8526.00
```

Notice the total, subtotal, and subheading lines which dBASE identifies with asterisks. You may only have *one level* of subtotals, enough for most everyday reports.

The specifications for the report printed above are safely stored on a disk file called SAMPLE1. You can run the report again, and perhaps print it with some selection criteria the same way you did with DISPLAY.

```
. SET HEADING TO HIFI Only
. REPORT FORM SAMPLE1 FOR CLASS='HIFI'
PAGE NO. 00001   HIFI Only
11/16/81
Sample Property Report 1

Description          Value         Date
                                   Acquired
                                   (yymmdd)

* Property in class HIFI
Receiver           479.00         740101
Turntable          350.00         791031
Speakers          1000.00         740101
** SUBTOTAL **
                   1829.00

** TOTAL **
                   1829.00
```

Let's try another report, this time with a summary of all the records.

```
.REPORT
ENTER REPORT FORM NAME: SAMPLE2
ENTER OPTIONS, M = LEFT MARGIN,
  L = LINES/PAGE, W = PAGE WIDTH
PAGE HEADING? (Y/N) y
ENTER PAGE HEADING:
  Property Summary Report
DOUBLE SPACE REPORT? (Y/N) n
ARE TOTALS REQUIRED? (Y/N) y
SUBTOTALS IN REPORT? (Y/N) y
ENTER SUBTOTALS FIELD: CLASS
SUMMARY REPORT ONLY? (Y/N) y
EJECT PAGE AFTER SUBTOTALS? (Y/N) n
ENTER SUBTOTAL HEADING:
  Property in class
```

```
COL  WIDTH,CONTENTS
001  10,VALUE
ENTER HEADING:
ARE TOTALS REQUIRED? (Y/N) y
002
PAGE NO. 00001
11/16/81
Property Summary Report
*  Property in class COMPUTER
** SUBTOTAL **
   5898.00

*  Property in class HIFI
** SUBTOTAL **
   1829.00

*  Property in class SPORTS
** SUBTOTAL **
   799.00

** TOTAL **
   8526.00
```

These examples show most of the power of the REPORT command. Additionally, you can print an *expression* involving fields and constants such as UNIT:PRICE * QUANTITY. If you need fancier reports, dBASE will do them, but you have to write a program as described later in this chapter.

OPERATING ON ENTIRE DATABASES

Example:

Personal Property Inventory

Commands:

Commands:
COPY, COUNT, SUM, TOTAL

There are some useful features in dBASE that go along with the relational data model. These are commands which operate on a whole database. Two such commands are SUM and COUNT, which work well with the property database. You can check the results against the reports above.

```
. SUM VALUE
28526.00
. SUM VALUE FOR CLASS='HIFI'
1829.00
. COUNT FOR CLASS='HIFI'
3
```

Another command, TOTAL, works a lot like the *summary* capability in the REPORT command. Instead of printing a report, it makes a new database called PSUMMARY, the number of decimal places held by a field. Here's how it works with the PROPERTY database.

```
. USE PROP1
. TOTAL ON CLASS TO PSUMMARY FIELD
     CLASS,VALUE
00003 RECORDS COPIED
. USE PSUMMARY
. DISPLAY STRU
STRUCTURE FOR FILE: PSUMMARY.DBF
NUMBER OF RECORDS:00003
DATE OF LAST UPDATE: 00/00/00
PRIMARY USE DATABASE
FLD NAME      TYPE    WIDTH    DEC
001 CLASS      C       010
002 DESCRIP    C       030
003 VALUE      N       008     002
004 DT:ACQRD   N       006
**TOTAL **             00055
. DISP ALL
00001 COMPUTER Tandy II 5898.00 810220
00002 HIFI     Receiver 1829.00 760101
00003 SPORTS   Skis      799.00 750101
```

There is only one thing wrong here. The description and data fields are meaningless because the HIFI record reflects the total value for *all* hi-fi equipment, which includes three items. The receiver is only the first item in the original list. The dBASE documentation

implies that only those fields listed in the FIELD clause should be included in the new database, but as you can see, this is not the case. You could easily eliminate the unwanted fields with the COPY command.

```
. COPY TO NEWSUM FIELD CLASS,VALUE
. USE NEWSUM
. DISP ALL
00001     COMPUTER     5898.00
00002     HIFI         1887.00
00003     SPORTS        849.00
```

NONSEQUENTIAL ACCESSING

Example:
Inventory

Commands:
INDEX

Everything you have done until now has used a *sequential* record-by-record pass through the database. dBASE is quick about this, keeping a lot of data in memory at a time. But as your database grows, the sequential passes become slower. To give you an example, a pass through an inventory database of 1600 records, each containing about 140 characters, takes two minutes on a system with a floppy disk and one minute with a hard disk. If you know the record number, you can get the data in a fraction of a second, but if you know only a part number, for instance, you could be waiting as long as two minutes.

One solution dBASE provides for this access problem is the *index*. You choose a field which uniquely identifies the record and declare it to be the *key*. Keys do not make much sense in the personal property database, so let's take a look at an inventory system where each part is identified by a unique 5-digit number.

```
. DISPLAY STRUCTURE
STRUCTURE FOR FILE: PARTS.DBF
NUMBER OF RECORDS:00100
DATE OF LAST UPDATE: 11/16/81
PRIMARY USE DATABASE
FLD       NAME       TYPE  WIDTH     DEC
001       PARTNUM    C     005
002       DESCRI     C     030
003       PRICE      N     007       002
** TOTAL **                00043
```

As described in Chapter 3, the index gives you a new logical view of the data but at the expense of maintaining a separate file. Each index—and there can be many—is given its own name. The first step is to build the index, specifying the key, PARTNUM, and the index name, PART-INDEX.

```
. INDEX ON PARTNUM TO PART-INDEX
00100   RECORDS   INDEXED
```

This could take a number of minutes for a large file, but it doesn't have to be done often. When you APPEND a record, the index is automatically updated. Once the index is built, you get started by typing

```
. USE PARTS INDEX PART-INDEX
```

Even though the records may be in random order, DISPLAY or REPORT will organize them in order of part and number. The command FIND will bring up any part in less than two seconds. The found record becomes the current record, and you can DISPLAY or BROWSE to your heart's content.

```
. FIND '13000'
. DISPLAY
00038 13000 HEADSETS************* 0000000
. DISPLAY NEXT 10
00038 13000 HEADSETS************* 0000000
```

```
00039 13110 RECORD  HDSET...1039    0000046
00040 13120 RECORD  ROAD            0000063
00041 13130 GRAN  SPORT             00031.2
00042 13140 RECORD  TRACK..1040     0000040
00043 13220 SEALED  HEADSET         00062.5
00044 13225 MOD III SEALED          0059.95
00045 13250 ALLOY                   0000047
00046 13270 ALLOY                   00047.5
00047 13290 TANDEM                  00017.5
```

Notice that the current record is number 38, containing part number 13000. You could also index on description, in which case the key would be *nonunique,* so that a FIND would bring up the *first* occurrence of a match, as follows:

```
. INDEX ON DESCRI TO DESC:INDEX
00100 RECORDS INDEXED
. FIND 'AL'
. DISPLAY
00013  10035     ALL MODELS    00020.5
. DISPLAY NEXT 10 PARTNUM DESCRI
00013  10035     ALL MODELS
00070  21640     ALL-ROUND
00045  13250     ALLOY
00046  13270     ALLOY
00095  22305     ALLOY EXTRA LONG
00088  22213     ALLOY STEM KIT
00090  22230     ALLOY TRACK STEM
00093  22301     ANODIZED
00057  92225     B-50
00065  21325     BARS
```

Part number 10035 is the first part beginning with "AL," and there is a total of eight such parts. dBASE gives you a choice when FINDing through an index: You can either match the way "AL" brought up "ALL MODELS," or you could match *exactly,* in which case you would have to type "ALL MODELS" to find that part. One last possibility is to index a database on a *combination* of fields. For example, you could use a supplier plus a part number as a key if the same part came from different sources at different prices.

Suppose you wanted to look at parts in order of part and number *and* in description order. dBASE lets you maintain up to seven indexes simultaneously on any database. This means that APPENDing a new part links that record into *both* the part and number and description indexes—a feature normally associated with the NDBMS.

RESTRUCTURING THE DATABASE

Example:

Inventory Plus Cost

Commands:

APPEND, MODIFY, REPLACE

Suppose you have been using the parts inventory system for a while and you decide to keep track of cost in addition to price. There is no place to put cost, so you have to make room. The idea here is to make a new, empty database with a cost field added, then move the data from the old to the new database. Last, you have to set all costs to zero in preparation for entry of the real costs.

The steps are as follows:

```
. COPY TO NEWPARTS STRUCTURE
. USE NEWPARTS
. MODIFY STRUCTURE
MODIFY ERASES ALL DATA RECORDS ...
   PROCEED? (Y/N) y
```

Now you have made a new database called NEWPARTS and you need to MODIFY its structure to include cost. Here you begin full-screen editing again, and you are able to change field information or delete or add fields anywhere, all by use of the control keys. See Figure 5-3 for

a look at the structure screen. You don't use a specific *command* to add COST to the structure; rather you position the cursor to the place you need COST inserted, type the insert key, then type in COST with type, length, and number of decimal places. After adding the COST field, the new structure looks like the following:

```
. DISPLAY STRUCTURE
STRUCTURE FOR FILE: NEWPARTS.DBF
NUMBER OF RECORDS:00000
DATE OF LAST UPDATE: 11/16/81
PRIMARY USE DATABASE
FLD   NAME      TYPE    WIDTH    DEC
001   PARTNUM   C       005
002   DESCRI    C       030
003   PRICE     N       007      002
004   COST      N       007      002
** TOTAL **              00050
```

To continue, you load the data from the old database to the new database, replacing all the new blank COST fields with zero.

```
. APPEND FROM PARTS
00100 RECORDS ADDED
. REPLACE ALL COST WITH 0
00100   REPLACEMENT(S)
. DISPLAY NEXT 10
00001  10000  FRAMES *******  0000000  0.00
00002  10009  MIXTE FRAME     0000450  0.00
00003  10010  TRACK           0000295  0.00
00004  10011  TOUR/COMMUTE    0000425  0.00
00005  10012  CUSTOM          0000495  0.00
00006  10013  RACING          0000445  0.00
00007  10014  CUSTOM          0000495  0.00
00008  10020  SAN CRIST       0000495  0.00
00009  10021  SAN CRIST       0000525  0.00
              W/STAYS
00010  10025  SUPER           0000550  0.00
```

An important thing to notice is that dBASE matches *field names* when APPENDing or doing other operations. If the "from" database had fields that didn't appear in the "to" database, these fields would be ignored.

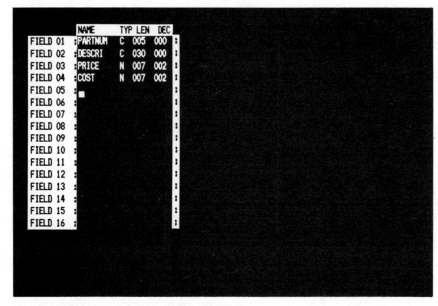

FIGURE 5-3.
Use INSERT key to
add the new field,
COST

CHANGING DATA

Example:

Parts Inventory

Commands:

CHANGE, REPLACE

You have already seen one use of REPLACE when you replaced all the blank COST fields with zeros. You can just as easily use it to raise up all the prices by an inflation adjustment of ten percent with

. <u>REPLACE ALL PRICE WITH PRICE * 1.1</u>

CHANGE performs the functions of REPLACE and provides the option of changing each field individually. A control key allows you to keep the original value.

```
. DISPLAY NEXT 6
00038   13000   HEADSETS************   0000000
00039   13110   RECORD HDSET...1039    0000046
00040   13120   SUPER RECORD ROAD      0000063
00041   13130   GRAN SPORT             00031.2
00042   13140   RECORD TRACK..1040     0000040
00043   13220   SEALED HEADSET         00062.5
. CHANGE NEXT 5 FIELD PRICE
RECORD: 00038
PRICE: 0000000
TO:

RECORD: 00039
PRICE: 0000046
TO:     47.50

RECORD: 00040
PRICE: 0000063
TO:     65

RECORD: 00041
PRICE: 00031.2
TO:     35

RECORD: 00042
```

```
PRICE: 0000040
TO:      42

. DISPLAY NEXT 6
00038  13000  HEADSETS*********  0000000
00039  13110  RECORD HDSET...1039    47.50
00040  13120  SUPER RECORD ROAD      65.00
00041  13130  GRAN SPORT            35.00
00042  13140  RECORD TRACK..1040     42.00
00043  13220  SEALED HEADSET       00062.5
```

be done more efficiently with indexes and programming.

UPDATE, on the other hand, has more potential. Begin with two databases, each sorted by the same key. Call one the master, the other the transaction file. Transactions are matched to the master by key, and specified fields from the transaction record are either added to, or substituted for, those corresponding fields in the master record.

OPERATING ON MULTIPLE DATABASES

Commands:

JOIN, UPDATE

CREATING MENU-DRIVEN SYSTEMS

Example 1:

A Data Retrieval System

One relational data base standard, PROJECT, is *missing* from dBASE II, but this does not cause any problem. Since PROJECT only selects certain fields from the main database, you can achieve the same effect by COPYing selected fields to a new database. Technically, however, the PROJECT operator isn't supposed to leave you with any duplicate records, so you will have to SORT and TOTAL to get rid of any of these duplicates.

dBASE does provide the JOIN command, though. It is advertised as being one of the most powerful commands present, but that is a matter of opinion. JOIN takes each record of the first database and compares it individually to each record of the second database. If the specified keys match, a record is written to a third database containing a list of fields from both source databases. You could use this command if you wanted to add part description information to customers' orders for those parts. The operation would take a long time with any reasonably sized database, and a lot of redundant data would be generated. The same thing could

Previously, you have seen dBASE used as an "electronic file" operated with simple commands from the keyboard. This is fine for a computer operator who has taken the time to become familiar with the program. However, many people have limited time to perform specific tasks. They work best with menu-driven systems with limited choices. You can use dBASE to create these systems, setting up procedures for nearly foolproof day-to-day procedures, while retaining the ability to examine any piece of data instantly and to create new reports at will.

In order for you to get an idea of what dBASE will do, study the following two examples. The programming behind these examples is described later in the *language* section.

The data retrieval system is not a business application, but it may be useful to you. Suppose you have a library of books and magazine articles (in this case, pertaining to bicycles and cycling) and you want to know which items meet certain criteria. For example, you want to know which books were published after 1969 on the subject of safety. This question could be answered very easily with techniques you have seen already.

```
. DISPLAY ALL FOR YR:PUB >= 69 .AND.
    SUBJECT = 'safe'
```

Any file management system could answer this question easily. But there is another question: Which books contain references to "safety," "standards," *and* "the Western United States?" And suppose you wish to impose the condition that the resulting system will be so easy to use that you only have to remember the word "books" to use it. What you need is a system which associates a number of keywords with book records and retrieves any record for which *all* the *entered* keywords match. If more than one person needs to use the system, it's a good idea to limit the keywords so that someone doesn't classify a book under "law" instead of "legal."

You are going to need *two* databases, one for the keywords and one for the book records.

```
. USE KEYWORDS
STRUCTURE FOR FILE: KEYWORDS.DBF
FLD    NAME        TYPE      WIDTH    DEC
001    KW:CODE     C         002
002    KW:WORD     C         010
. DISP NEXT 10 KW:CODE KW:WORD
00010  CL   CLOTHING
00011  CN   CHAINS
00012  CO   COMMUTING
00013  CP   COMPONENTS
00014  CR   CRANKS
00015  DE   DERAILLEUR
00016  EN   ENGINEERNG
00017  EU   EUROPE
00018  FA   FRAMES
00019  FE   FREEWHEELS
. USE BOOKS
STRUCTURE FOR FILE: BOOKS.DBF
```

```
FLD    NAME        TYPE      WIDTH    DEC
001    BK:KEYS     C         024
002    BK:SOURCE   C         020
003    BK:DATE     C         020
004    BK:ABSTRAC  C         060
005    BK:TITLE    C         040
006    BK:AUTHOR   C         030
. DISP NEXT 10 BK:KEYS BK:TITLE
00001  TA.           Show Bike for Two
00002  GE.           Gearing to Suit You
00003  MO.           Back Country Cycling
00004  HP.FU.AE.     No Brakes on Human Power
00005  AE.HP.TR.     Mech. Drives/Human Power
       EN.FU.
00006  TA.CH.        Kid-back Tandems
00007  SA.           The ISO's Intl. Bicycle
00008  TA.           A Bicycle Built for Two
00009  TU.WE.        55 Oregon Bicycle Trips
00010  TU.WE.WA.     Explore by Bicycle
```

From looking at the keyword file, you may notice that keywords are identified by a two-letter code. You enter these codes whenever you do a retrieval or add a book, so you really need a list by your side at the terminal. Up to eight codes are stored in the first field of each book record, and each code is separated by dots (see above). Don't worry about how they get in there, the program takes care of that.

To start the system, you just type

```
. DO BOOKS
```

and you see the *main menu* shown in Figure 5-4. Figure 5-5 shows the inquiry screen without your data entry, and Figure 5-6 shows it after the data has been entered. Notice that the system automatically looked up the codes you entered and displayed the keywords to the right. Look at Figure 5-6 to see the records selected. If you were adding a record instead of inquiring, everything would be the same except that you would key in source, date, abstract, title, and author on the lower part of the screen, as shown in Figure 5-7.

FIGURE 5-4.
Main menu (data
retrieval system)

FIGURE 5-5.
Blank inquiry screen

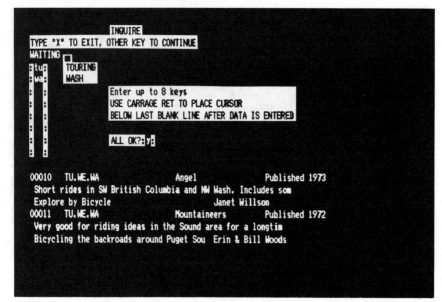

FIGURE 5-6.
Inquire screen with data entered

```
              INQUIRE
TYPE "X" TO EXIT, OTHER KEY TO CONTINUE
WAITING
:tu:    TOURING
:wa:    WASH
              Enter up to 8 keys
              USE CARRAGE RET TO PLACE CURSOR
              BELOW LAST BLANK LINE AFTER DATA IS ENTERED

              ALL OK?: y:


00010   TU.WE.WA             Angel          Published 1973
Short rides in SW British Columbia and NW Wash. Includes som
Explore by Bicycle                  Janet Willson
00011   TU.WE.WA             Mountaineers   Published 1972
Very good for riding ideas in the Sound area for a longtim
Bicycling the backroads around Puget Sou  Erin & Bill Woods
```

```
              ADD
ENTER "X" TO EXIT, OTHER KEY TO CONTINUE
WAITING
:tu:    TOURING
:eu:    EUROPE
              Enter up to 8 keys
              USE CARRAGE RET TO PLACE CURSOR
              BELOW LAST BLANK LINE AFTER DATA IS ENTERED

              ALL OK?: y:


SOURCE:home library        :
DATE:September 1981      :
ABSTRACT:Touring routes in England, Wales, Scotland and Ireland    :
TITLE:CTC Route guide to Britain & Ireland    :
AUTHOR:Cycle Touring Club of Britain :
```

FIGURE 5-7.
Adding a record

Five *command* files, or programs, are used in this example:

    BOOKS.CMD
    INQUIRE.CMD
    ADD.CMD
    GETKEYS.CMD
    DISPBOOKS.CMD

They are briefly described in the dBASE II language section of this chapter and completely listed in Figure A-1 of Appendix A for review.

If you wanted to extend this example, you could SELECT on the keywords as above *and* SELECT on some other criteria, such as date and author. To do this you simply use COPY to make a new, smaller database, then feed this database to the keyword program in place of the full database. In case you were wondering how to *change* the content of a field and how to *delete* a record, wonder no more. Just reference the record by number, then use dBASE's EDIT and DELETE commands.

CREATING MENU-DRIVEN SYSTEMS

Example 2:

Sales Order Entry

This example pushes dBASE II to the limits with a business application previously only possible on a minicomputer. What you see here is by no means the entire system, but enough to show you what dBASE can and cannot do.

Consider a wholesaling company that sells to its customers on credit. The sales staff takes orders over the phone, the warehouse ships the orders and accepts incoming merchandise, and the accounts receivable department records the customer payments. What is needed is a system that allows sales orders, receipts, and cash to be entered into the computer, then prints invoices, tracks inventory, and produces all the necessary reports.

A further requirement on the system is that it must be on-line. Customers often ask the questions "Is that product in stock?", "Can you get me some by next week?", and "How much more credit do I have?" The controller always asks "What's our sales figure for the month?" or "What's our accounts receivable balance?" The purchasing agent needs to know what products need to be ordered as soon as a vendor's representative calls. If the system is on-line it means that if an order is entered at 3:00 P.M., an inquiry at 3:01 will reflect that fact. Since dBASE II isn't at this point multiuser, everyone must share the same terminal.

In this example, only the sales order entry, product inquiry, and on-order report will be shown. The following are five files needed for the system:

· The Customer File (CU)
· The Inventory File (IT)
· Sales Order Headers (RH)
· Sales Order Details (RD)
· Invoices (IC).

Structures for the RH and RD files are shown in Figure 5-8. If you've worked with an order entry system before, you will recognize this as a "sophisticated" system.

Taking command of your imaginary computer, you type in "DO MAIN" and see the main menu shown in Figure 5-9. Now suppose the telephone rings and a customer asks if she can get 50 units of product 210000. You're sure you don't have any in the warehouse now, but you think there might be a shipment arriving tomorrow. However, you don't know who else has ordered the same product and when you

```
FLD   NAME        TYPE   WIDTH   DEC
001   RH:ORDER     N     006          * Sales order no.
002   RH:CUST      N     006          * Customer no.
003   RH:DTORD     N     006          * Date ordered
004   RH:DTDELV    N     006          * Est. delivery date
005   RH:CUSTPO    C     015          * Customer PO
006   RH:FREIGHT   N     001          * Freight code
007   RH:DELVIA    C     010          * Delivery via
008   RH:SLSMAN    N     002          * Salesman
009   RH:TERR      N     002          * Sales territory
010   RH:TERMS     N     002          * Credit terms
011   RH:TAXREGN   N     002          * Sales tax region
012   RH:TAXABLE   L     001          * Sales taxable
013   RH:PRINTED   L     001          * Sales order printed
014   RH:IVCPRN    L     001          * Invoice printed
015   RH:INVOICE   N     006          * Invoice no.
016   RH:CARRIER   C     010          * Carrier
017   RH:BLNBR     N     006          * Bill of lading no.
018   RH:DTSHIP    N     006          * Date shipped
019   RH:NAME      C     025          * Billing name
020   RH:ADDR1     C     038          * Billing address
021   RH:ADDR2     C     038
022   RH:SNAME     C     025          * Shipping name
023   RH:SADDR1    C     038          * Shipping address
024   RH:SADDR2    C     038
025   RH:AMOUNT    N     009    002   * Total amount
026   RH:COST      N     009    002   * Total cost
027   RH:WEIGHT    N     007    001   * Total weight
028   RH:PRICED    L     001          * All details priced
029   RH:TAX       N     007    002   * Sales tax
030   RH:FRT       N     007    002   * Freight charges
031   RH:MISC      N     007    002   * Misc. charges
STRUCTURE FOR FILE:RD-FILE.DBF
FLD   NAME        TYPE   WIDTH   DEC
001   RD:ORDER     N     006          * Sales order no.
002   RD:SEQUNCE   N     002          * Sequence within order
003   RD:CUST      N     006          * Customer no.
004   RD:PRODUCT   N     006          * Product no.
005   RD:QORDRD    N     004          * Qty. ordered
006   RD:QBKORD    N     004          * Qty. backordered
007   RD:QSHIPD    N     004          * Qty. shipped
008   RD:DESC      C     040          * Product description
009   RD:UWEIGHT   N     007    001   * Unit weight
010   RD:UPRICE    N     007    002   * Unit price
011   RD:UCOST     N     007    002   * Unit cost
012   RD:DISC      N     002          * Trade discount
013   RD:AMOUNT    N     009    002   * Extended amount
014   RD:WEIGHT    N     007    001   * Extended weight
015   RD:COST      N     009    002   * Extended cost
016   RD:DTDELV    N     006          * Est. delivery date
```

(continued)

FIGURE 5-8.
Structure for
sales order headers
and details

FIGURE 5-8.
Structure for
sales order headers
and details
(continued)

```
017   RD:LINE      N    002    * Product line
018   RD:INVOICE   N    006    * Invoice no.
019   RD:SLSMAN    N    002    * Salesman
020   RD:TOINVTY   L    001    * Processed to inventory
021   RD:DTIVC     N    006    * Date invoiced
```

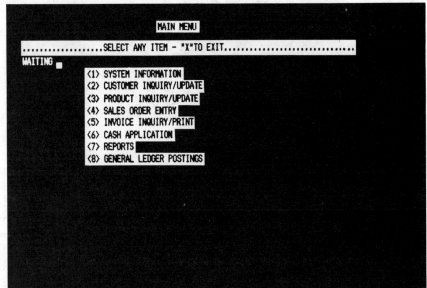

FIGURE 5-9.
Main menu
(sales order entry)

promised to deliver it. To find out what's going on, you select PRODUCT INQUIRY, enter the product code 210000, and get the screen shown in Figure 5-10. You can see that there is nothing in inventory, but you are expecting 500 units to arrive in the next 10 days. However, you've promised to ship 300 in the next 10 days and another 300 in the next 30 days, leaving you 100 short. You can now make the decision of whether to promise the 50, depending on who

has the second order for 300 and also depending on whether your supplier can speed up the next shipment. If you need to look at sales details individually, you can do so. It is important to note that if you shipped the last 150 units *one minute ago,* that would be reflected in the screen totals. This is on-line data processing, and you can do it with dBASE II.

You decide that you can ship 50 units next week, and the customer places the order for

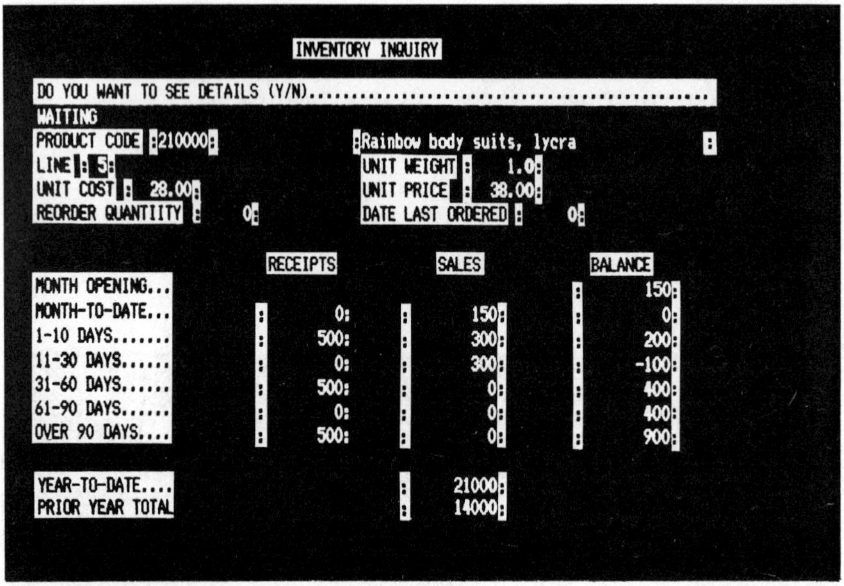

FIGURE 5-10. Select product inquiry for on-line data processing

that product and two other products, both in stock. From the main menu of Figure 5-9 you select SALES ORDER ENTRY and are prompted for a sales order number and customer number. When you enter the sales order number, the computer checks for a sales order by that number already in the file, and when you enter the customer number, the computer looks up that number in the customer master. If the customer is found, the screen looks like the one in Figure 5-11. Note that information such as salesperson code, billing names and addresses, and shipping names and addresses is automatically filled in from the customer file. What you are doing is entering the sales order *header*— that information which will be printed on top of the shipping document and invoice. By using the RETURN key you can step from field to field, entering or overriding information; other keys will let you back up if you make a mistake. Figure 5-12 shows the sales order header after you enter the rest of the information.

When you are finished with the header, you are ready for the sales order *details,* one per product ordered. As you can see in Figure 5-13, you enter details one at a time, with the information coming from the inventory file just as the header information came from the customer file. The unit price is extended by the quantity, and the details appear on the lower half of the screen as you complete them. Each detail has a sequence number so you can add more details anywhere or change them later. Information is added to the details for later sorting and reporting.

At this point you may wonder how fast this all is. On 8-inch floppy disks there is usually a one-second delay in looking up customers and products and a seven-second delay after the header and after the last detail. The longer delays are there because dBASE II supports only two files open at one time, and it takes time to close one and open another. In this example, the customer file is the secondary

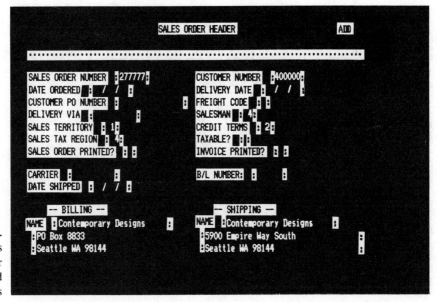

FIGURE 5-11.
Enter the sales
order header
for invoice and
shipping documents

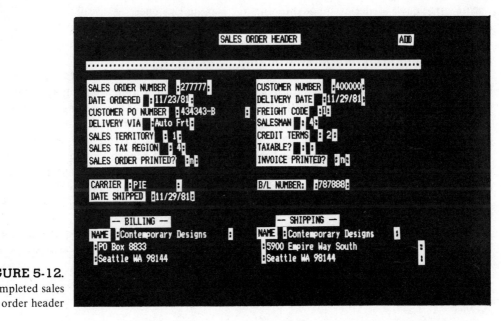

FIGURE 5-12.
Completed sales
order header

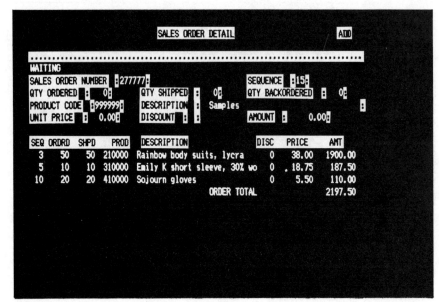

```
                      SALES ORDER DETAIL                              ADD

....................................................................................
WAITING
SALES ORDER NUMBER  :277777:              SEQUENCE   :15:
QTY ORDERED    :     0:       QTY SHIPPED    :     0:    QTY BACKORDERED   :    0:
PRODUCT CODE   :9999999:      DESCRIPTION    :  Samples                           :
UNIT PRICE     :   0.00:      DISCOUNT    :  :         AMOUNT  :      0.00:


SEQ ORDRD  SHPD   PROD   DESCRIPTION                   DISC   PRICE      AMT
  3    50    50  210000  Rainbow body suits, lycra       0    38.00   1900.00
  5    10    10  310000  Emily K short sleeve, 30% wo     0  . 18.75    187.50
 10    20    20  410000  Sojourn gloves                  0     5.50    110.00
                                          ORDER TOTAL            2197.50
```

FIGURE 5-13.
Enter sales order details

database when you are entering the header, but the product file is active when you are entering details.

After the day's ordering and shipping is complete, you can print invoices and other reports. A sample report, On-Order Details by Product, is shown in Figure 5-14. Note that this report did not come via the REPORT command in dBASE but rather was programmed in dBASE's internal language. REPORT would have worked except the customer name was needed in the detail lines, and that was only available in the sales order header. Even though this is a two-database report, it still is produced at almost full printer speed.

THE dBASE II LANGUAGE

The examples above show what dBASE II can do. Now you will see how it does it. If you are familiar with BASIC, you know what a language is; and if you have studied Pascal or C you know what a *structured* language is. The dBASE language is a structured programming language. There is absolutely no GOTO as found in most BASIC languages. If you don't like structured programming, don't buy dBASE II.

In Chapter 2 you saw the trade-offs between built-in and established languages. The built-in language of dBASE has commands which tie right into the database—words like SKIP, CONTINUE, FIND, and APPEND. When you access a record from a database, you can use all the field names just as you defined them in the data dictionary. There is no need to translate them into BASIC variables such as R2, D2, and so on.

Another strong point of the dBASE language is its ability to use the video screen. dBASE uses

```
@ 4,10 SAY 'DOLLARS' GET amount
   PICTURE '999.99'
```

to display the prompt "DOLLARS" (starting at row 4, column 10) and to accept data into the variable "amount."

The main structured programming constructs are DO WHILE, ENDDO; IF, ELSE, ENDIF; and DO CASE, ENDCASE. When you combine good structure with the special data handling and screen access commands, you get programs which are readable and easy to modify.

Appendix A contains *all* the programs in the Data Retrieval Example. The comments to the right were added later because the language syntax doesn't always allow them. You can contrast this code with the equivalent 621-line BASIC program found in an article by J.J. Sanger, M.D., in the November 1979 issue of *Kilobaud Microcomputing* magazine. Note that this original program was limited by the number of file keys fitting in memory to

```
                      On-Order  Detail  Report                    Page 1

CUSTOMER              ORDER #  SEQ  Q      PRICE   AMOUNT   DT ORDRD   DELVY DT
                                    ORDRD

PRODUCT 110000     Redwood short sleeve. wool

Panther Tree. the    666666   15   10     22.50    225.00  11/26/81   11/28/81
          PRODUCT  TOTAL            10

PRODUCT 210000     Rainbow body suits. lycra

Panther Tree. the    111111    5   10     38.00    380.00  11/22/81   11/28/81
Panther Tree. the    111111    5   10     38.00    380.00  11/22/81   11/28/81
Panther Tree. the    333333    5   50     38.00   1900.00  11/21/81   11/25/81
Contemporary Designs 444444    5   50     38.00   1900.00  11/20/81   11/29/81
Panther Tree. the    666666   10   36     38.00   1368.00  11/26/81   11/28/81
          PRODUCT  TOTAL           156

PRODUCT 310000     Emily K short sleeve. 30% wool. poly

Contemporary Designs 222222    5   20     18.75    375.00  11/20/81   11/25/81
Contemporary Designs 444444   10   25     18.75    468.75  11/20/81   11/29/81
Panther Tree. the    666666    5   24     18.75    450.00  11/26/81   11/28/81
          PRODUCT  TOTAL            69

PRODUCT 410000     Sojourn gloves

Comtemporary Designs 444444   15   20      5.50    110.00  11/20/81   11/29/81
Panther Tree. the    555555    5   10      5.50     55.00  11/24/81   11/26/81
          PRODUCT  TOTAL            30

      GRAND  TOTAL                 255
```

FIGURE 5-14.
On-order detail report

roughly 500 books. Also, the BASIC program was not nearly so sophisticated in its screen input and output. As far as performance goes, dBASE II uses the sequential pass; this could take several minutes for 1000 titles. The BASIC program, on the other hand, did its searching in memory and was faster.

Command Files

dBASE doesn't compile your programs, it *interprets* them, just like most BASICs. You write *command files* (programs) using your word processor program or with dBASE's own built-in full-screen editor, creating CP/M files with a .CMD extension. In the example, BOOKS.CMD is the "mainline" program containing the menu shown in Figure 5-4, plus calls (DOs) to ADD and to INQUIRE. There is one important operational consideration: Every time dBASE encounters a DO, it goes out to disk to get the module. If you have a program which processes each record in a database and you have one or more DOs in the record loop, your program will run slowly because of the extra disk reads. To avoid this, you have to "inline" the code that would logically go into a subroutine, making the program longer and less readable.

Primary and Secondary Databases

Most of your programs will step through a database record-by-record, using an index in most cases. You have access to two different databases, each indexed, one called the PRIMARY and the other the SECONDARY. You have to SELECT one or the other in order to move to a different record or to APPEND a record,

but you can use the fields in both current records. When you APPEND a new record, the index is automatically updated to include that record according to the key formula you have set up, but only the one index will be updated.

Screen Addressing

The GET and SAY commands which you use for video input and output are convenient but take some getting used to. After a whole screenful of SAYs or GETs, nothing happens until you do a READ. At that point, all the prompts appear on the screen, the input fields are laid out, and the cursor appears at the first GET. You can move the cursor around as you want between fields, but you stay in input mode until you finish the last field or key ^C.

Reports and Macros

Printing also uses the SAY command. You can position to any row or column on the paper, allowing easy printing on forms such as checks and invoices. You may wish to produce a report, which is superior to what the REPORT command can produce. The sample program in Figure A-1 of Appendix A (modules REPORT.CMD and NEWPAGE.CMD) prints the On-Order Detail Report in the Sales Order Entry example. Look closely at the use of the *macro* "&print" which is really a disguised SAY command that automatically increments the row number. With macros you can string together any commands you want, then execute them. The macro was used above in the GETKEYS module to simulate subscripted variables, something not normally allowed in the language. If the variable "isub" contains the string "5," then "k&isub" is really a new variable called "k5."

Conventions

The sample programs in Appendix A use a few conventions worth studying. The indentation helps line up DOs with ENDDOs, and IFs with ENDIFs, making the program a lot easier to read but, unfortunately, slower to run. The *variable* names are all in lower-case so that they stand out from the rest of the language. The data dictionary variables all have a two-letter prefix followed by a colon (rd:product, rh:name, and so on). This tells you immediately what file they are in, and it distinguishes them from *local* variables (line, page, and so on).

Variables

You can have up to 64 local variables which can be either numbers, character strings, or logicals. You don't define the variables at the top of the program as in COBOL or Pascal, nor do you specify a string by a dollar sign as in BASIC. A variable's type is determined by what you store there—a confusing concept at first. All variables are *global* and thus accessible to all modules.

Numeric variables are ten digits and have a provision for an exponent. The digits are stored individually so you don't have the same problems rounding off that you have with binary numbers. For example, $333.01 * 1000 = 333010.00$ instead of the 333010.01 that some BASICs give you.

Strings can be up to 254 characters long and you can manipulate them with a variety of string functions, including a *substring* operator which tells you if a string is equal to or contained in another. See the DISPLIB BOOKS.CMD module in Figure A-1 for an example.

Network Data Structures

The Sales Order Entry example described earlier in this chapter is an application normally reserved for network/hierarchical data base management systems. How does dBASE II handle this application? By *redundant data* and clever use of the *index*. Consider the problem of linking a sales order header with the corresponding sales details. If you look at the data dictionaries you can see that the sales order number is common to both header and detail and that the detail has a field called "rd:sequnce." The main *key* for the detail file is the sales order number *plus* the sequence number. dBASE allows you to FIND on just the order number, retrieving the *first* detail for that order. Using the SKIP command, you bring up each succeeding detail, stopping only when you find you are into the next order. The DISPDETS.CMD module, listed in Figure A-1, shows how all the order details are displayed on the screen.

Additional dBASE II Features

There is little reason to leave the dBASE environment. You have a powerful, full-screen editor which serves for all but serious program development for which you might want the block moves and search-and-replaces you're used to in your word processor. dBASE also gives you replacements for the CP/M PIP, REName, ERAse, and DIRectory functions. You can see your command filenames listed, for example, by typing

```
. DISPLAY FILES LIKE *.CMD
```

There is also a way to enter the data dictionary (STRUCTURE).

```
. USE PROP1
. COPY STRUCTURE EXTENDED TO PROPSTR
00004 RECORDS COPIED
. USE PROPSTR
. DISP STRUCTURE
STRUCTURE FOR FILE: PROPSTR.DBF
FLD     NAME          TYPE     WIDTH   DEC
001     FIELD:NAME    C        010
002     FIELD:TYPE    C        001
003     FIELD:LEN     N        003
004     FIELD:DEC     N        003
. DISP ALL
00001   CLASS         C        10      0
00002   DESCRIP       C        30      0
00003   VALUE         N        8       2
00004   DT:ACQRD      N        6       0
```

This also works the opposite way—you can CREATE a database from the structure stored in another. Many programming possibilities are created; one is the orderly *documentation* of the database. You simply add a new field FIELD:DESC where you store a complete description of the field. Then you use this dictionary database as the "source" of the structure of the real database.

Transfer to or from Non-dBASE Files

Computer programs written in BASIC or any other language cannot interface directly with dBASE files. This is not a problem, however, because dBASE can use the APPEND command to convert a file from another program *into* a database, and it can use COPY to write a file *from* a database. To get involved in this you have to know something about the structure of the "foreign" files, and this comes only with some programming experience. For reference dBASE can work with delimited files such as those BASIC uses and nondelimited

ASCII files such as those COBOL uses. It cannot, however, use Microsoft BASIC fielded direct access files.

Documentation

dBASE II comes with a 350-page user's manual. This manual is divided into two parts: a *tutorial* written for a first-time user learning the system, and a *reference guide* written by the author of dBASE II, Wayne Ratliff. The second part came along with the package's metamorphosis from VULCUN, and the first part has been subject to changes since the first edition.

The tutorial is divided into six sections. They explain all the steps involved from installation to the creation of a working accounting system. Each section forms a logical lesson which could be completed in one session at the computer. You must realize that you will need some time to learn the system, but the tutorial is the best way to learn it.

Once you are able to use the system, you can start using the reference section, which is organized alphabetically by command. Each command is described and documented with examples and there's an index. An excerpt from the reference section follows.

[<**scope**>] FIELD <**list**> [FOR <**exp**>]

CHANGE is a command that allows the user to make a number of alterations to a database with minimum effort. All database fields that are referenced in the list are presented to the user in the order given by <list>. The user has the opportunity of entering new data, modifying the data or skipping to the next field. When the <list> has been exhausted, CHANGE will proceed to the next record as specified in the <scope>. The default scope is the current record.

A field can be deleted in its entirety by typing a ^Y (followed by a return) in response to the CHANGE? message. The CHANGE command can be aborted by typing an ESCAPE character.
Example:
. **USE CARDS**
. **CHANGE FIELD DATE**
RECORD: 00001
DATE: 08/19/82
CHANGE? **81**
TO   **82**
DATE: 08/19/82
CHANGE? <cr>

Excerpted with permission from dBASE II System User Manual, Part B Section 2, p. 48, 1981 by Ashton-Tate.

The distribution disk contains some sample databases with programs. You can have fun playing with these and learn some programming tricks in the process. These examples are described only in a disk file called CONTENTS and include

- An enhanced checkbook balancing and reporting system with full-screen operations
- A simple accounts payable system which prints checks and ties into the checkbook system
- A mailing list with full-screen editing and form letter capability
- Calendar conversions.

Support

Telephone support is good. When you phone with a question, someone returns your call and answers your question.

Configuration

dBASE II does full-screen editing and you have to describe your video terminal. A program called INSTALL is provided, enabling you to select your terminal from a menu. If your terminal is not listed, you have to go through a long procedure, a job for your dealer.

While dBASE allows for different video output codes, it doesn't permit customization for the keyboard. If you have "arrow" keys you may not be able to use them for moving between fields and characters, but instead will have to use ^E to move up, ^X to move down, ^S for left, and ^D for right movement.

The ease with which you can configure dBASE means that you can develop machine-independent software with full-screen editing. You don't have to buy or borrow one of each kind of terminal; you only have to assume dBASE works with all the terminals in its installation menu.

Error Handling

In general, dBASE's error handling is quite good. When you are in the *direct command* mode, invalid commands and syntax errors are handled as in the following dialog:

```
. DIPSLAY ALL CU:NUMBER CU:NAME
*** UNKNOWN COMMAND
DIPSLAY ALL CU:NUMBER CU:NAME
CORRECT AND RETRY (Y/N)? Y
CHANGE FROM :DIPS
CHANGE TO   :DISP
DISPLAY ALL CU:NUMBER CU:NAME
MORE CORRECTIONS (Y/N)? N
*** SYNTAX ERROR ***
               ?
DISPLAY ALL CU:NUMBER CU:NAME
CORRECT AND RETRY (Y/N)? Y
CHANGE FROM :NUMBER
CHANGE TO    :CUST
DISPLAY ALL CU:CUST CU:NAME
MORE CORRECTIONS (Y/N)? N
00001   300000  Panther Tree, the
00002   400000  Contemporary Designs
```

In the *program* mode the same thing happens, and if you correct the command the program will continue to execute. With large networks of command files you might not know exactly where the offending command is located because you know neither the module name nor line number. It is always possible to program yourself into a loop, but if you SET TALK ON, you can get some idea of where you are in the program.

You can break out of almost any program or multirecord command with the ESC key. If you were printing at the time, the printer would be stuck in the echo mode, but the SET PRINT OFF command gets you out. Using the ESC key is good for debugging, but you might not always want the operator to have full access to dBASE commands. In that case you can set ESCAPE off so that the RESET switch is the only way out to CP/M except for your programmed exits.

If you accidentally reference a disk drive that is not in your system, you will be sent directly to CP/M. Your open databases are ruined. The same thing happens if you don't initialize the system after a disk swap. However, you can program around this with the RESET command.

If you should be so careless as to COPY or SORT to the file in USE, that file will be scrambled with no warning. Also, if you have the same file open as PRIMARY and SECONDARY and you APPEND to it, you could be in trouble again.

Technical Information

No attempt has been made to disassemble and analyze the dBASE program itself. The following conclusions are drawn from experiments, from dumps of the actual database files, and from a brief chat with the author.

Each database is one CP/M file with fixed-length records delimited by blanks. There are no delimiters between fields, no quote marks, no carriage returns, no line feeds. Each database file has some space at the beginning (typically 520 bytes) where the data dictionary (STRUCTURE) is stored. This "header" contains the date of the file's last update plus the exact record count. You can easily estimate the disk space required for a database by the following formula:

bytes required = (sum of all field lengths +1) * number of records + 520

Because of the way CP/M allocates disk space, a file *never gets smaller*. If you delete records and repack the data base, you won't regain any space unless you later COPY or APPEND. Incidentally, the dBASE program plus overlays take about 60K bytes on the disk.

dBASE achieves a good measure of speed in sequential processing. Some large *disk buffers* permit dBASE to remember what records it previously read to disk so it doesn't have to go out to disk for those records. CP/M files are only closed when a QUIT returns to CP/M or when another database is USEd. Ashton-Tate claims dBASE II uses B*-tree indexing, but this is really the B$^+$-tree indexing described in Chapter 3. There is one CP/M file for each index which contains the actual index plus the key formula. Thus, if an index uses "customer number" + "part number" as the key, the field names and relationships are encoded into the index so that APPENDs can link in new entries. Up to seven indexes can be maintained simultaneously, meaning that a newly entered sales order detail can be linked into the sales order number index *and* into the part number index. If a key field is changed, the record is automatically relinked into the index in the correct place. These are all features which give dBASE II a little of the flavor of an NDBMS.

Indexing can be quick if the sort keys are short and the file is nearly in order. If you have sixteen hundred 140-byte records, a 30-byte key, and the data very much out of order, an index or sort can take as long as an hour, and dBASE sorts lasting over seven hours have been heard of. If you run into this problem, you can COPY your database into a non-dBASE file, pass that file to a machine-language sort, and then APPEND the result. This could save you considerable time.

SORTing is done with an algorithm chosen to minimize disk space usage. It is generally slower than indexing, but it does allow descending order. If you need to do serious sorting, use a commercial sort package.

Performance

The following are specifications on performance of dBASE II systems. Important information about the applicability of hard and soft disks is noted, as well as sort and data access method ratios.

Benchmark 1

1635 records, 150 characters each, 5-digit key

Floppy disk:

- Index build (5:13)
- Sort index (not applicable)
- Index setup (not applicable)
- Indexed access (1-2 seconds)
- Sequential pass (1:38 nonindexed, 4:15 indexed)

Hard disk:

- Index build (2:40)
- Sort index (not applicable)
- Index setup (not applicable)
- Indexed access (1/2 second)
- Sequential pass (0:25 nonindexed)

Benchmark 2

20,210 records, 21 characters each, 18-character key

Hard disk:

- Index build (30:00)
- Sort index (not applicable)
- Index setup (not applicable)
- Indexed access (1/2 second)
- Sequential pass (1:55 nonindexed)

Restrictions

There are some arbitrary limits in dBASE II which limit the package's usefulness in large-scale business applications. Perhaps it would be pushing the available memory space in an 8-bit microprocessor to raise these limits, but a 64K version of dBASE II (instead of the existing 48K version) might be the answer.

The 32-field maximum, together with the 1000-character limit, creates some problems for applications like payroll. It would be possible to solve this problem with multiple databases except for the limit of only two databases open at once. If multiple databases are used in sequence, the execution time becomes a problem.

Security

You may have noticed that there has been no mention of *security*. That's because there is none. At best you can disable the ESCAPE to the dBASE commands. This will help deter someone from entering the dBASE command mode. Your only *recovery* option is to use the last copy of the data disk.

Additional Packages

Ashton-Tate has released a *run-time* package designed for software developers wanting to protect their source code. The end-user doesn't have to buy dBASE II, but he or she can run the "compiled" applications programs. The resulting system is much more secure without the standard commands such as REPLACE, BROWSE, and so on.

Various entrepreneurs have exploited dBASE II's weak points with some interesting add-on packages. The most ambitious of these is the QUICKCODE program by Fox & Geller of Teaneck, N.J., a dBASE II program generator. This is briefly described in Chapter 8.

COMMAND SUMMARY

Creating Files

CREATE
    Sets up new structured databases

COPY
    Copies databases, their structures, or their data to a new file

REPORT
    Generates information to your specifications, selecting only the information you want, with or without totals and subtotals

SAVE
    Copies memory variables to a file for later use

INDEX
    Creates an index file for faster data location

Adding Data

APPEND
    Adds records onto the end of a database

CREATE
    Allows data entry when the file is created

INSERT
    Puts records into a file

Editing Data

EDIT
    Alters specific database records and fields

REPLACE
    Changes the contents of specified fields

CHANGE
    Edits specified fields in the database

DELETE
    Marks records for deletion

RECALL
    Erases the deletion mark

PACK
    Deletes the marked records

BROWSE
    Edits up to 19 records on the screen at once

Displaying Data

DISPLAY and LIST
    Show records, fields, and expressions

?
    Shows the value of variables or expressions

REPORT
    Formats and displays data according to specifications, with or without totals

READ
    Shows prompting information and data

SUM
    Totals the fields you specify in a database

TOTAL
    Totals specified fields to a new database

COMMAND SUMMARY (Continued)

File Manipulation

DO
Starts execution of a command file sequence

APPEND
Adds data from other files (even non-dBASE II)

SELECT
Switches between two databases in use

SORT
Organizes the database sorted on a field

Memory Variable Commands

ACCEPT
Stores character data for later use

INPUT
Accepts character, numeric, or logical data

WAIT
Accepts a single-character input

GET
Works like the INPUT command, used in the interactive, full-screen mode

SUM
Saves the totals to memory variables

SAVE
Stores memory variables to a disk file

RESTORE
Retrieves the stored memory variables

Other Commands

FIND
Locates an indexed record, typically in less than two seconds

LOCATE
Finds records that meet specified conditions

SKIP
Moves you forward or backward in the database

DO WHILE
Allows repetitive operations

IF-ELSE
Allows you to make choices

DO CASE
Allows you to select options

6

FMS-80 from
DJR Associates, Inc.

FMS-80 from DJR Associates, Inc., is a File Management System. While the user manual denies that FMS-80 is a data base management system, it reflects the old-fashioned belief that a DBMS requires intensive programming. However, according to the definitions in Chapter 3, FMS-80 is a DBMS and will be referred to as such throughout this chapter.

FMS-80 is *not* an RDBMS because it lacks the commands necessary to manipulate entire files and combinations of files. You can't use the relational PROJECT or JOIN operations with FMS-80. However, do not think the system is lacking, as you can perform similar tasks with the FMS-80. A programming language handling 19 files plus a sophisticated report generator compensate for the difficulty with which FMS-80 manipulates data, something you may feel is a shortcoming of the system.

FMS-80 is best suited for simple, well-defined business and information processing problems. Since FMS-80 works best with only one file, tasks such as validating a customer number on invoice entry and posting inventory transactions to a master file are good FMS-80 applications. When you need easy, simple programs that add, change, or delete records, select data, and print reports, then FMS-80 is ideal. Be careful, however, to keep file sizes below 5000 records since larger files slow operations significantly.

You may be wondering *who* can use FMS-80. As with any DBMS, by selecting options from the menu and keying in data, anyone can use an application which has already been set up. Setting up simple FMS-80 applications, however, demands systematic thinking and an adaptation to the computer's method of doing things. While it is not clear that a computer novice could learn to use FMS-80 without help, it is clear that a professional programmer is unnecessary.

FMS-80 is a two-level package, and DJR Associates has just begun selling it that way. You may start with FMS-81, a menu-driven, single-file system, at a reasonable cost, then expand to FMS-82 with multifile capability and a built-in programming language called EFM (Extended File Management). Any references to FMS-80 in this chapter extend to both FMS-81 and FMS-82.

SYSTEM OVERVIEW

DBMS Checklist

☒ Data Dictionary

   Defines type, size, picture (edit mask), and prompt/header; fields are identified by number

☒ Query Facility

   One record at a time

☒ Report Generator

   Multilevel subtotals; multifield computation permitted

☒ File Compatibility

   FMS files may be read or written to directly, but not easily with BASIC

☒ Restructure Capability

   EFM language (FMS-82) only

☒ Effective Error Handling

   Good

☒ Documentation and Support

   Good

☒ Multiple Files

   EFM language (FMS-82) only

☒ Full-Screen Editing

   By the numbers

☒ On-Screen Display Format

   With Quickscreen, a separate product from Fox & Geller (see Chapter 8)

☒ Password Security

   Through EFM language only

☐ Multiuser Capability

☒ Menu-driven

   Four system menus plus user menus

☒ Program-driven

   FMS-82 only

☐ Command-driven

☒ Built-in Language

   EFM language (FMS-82) only

☐ Established Language

☒ Access Time

   One to twenty seconds, depending on file size

☒ Processing Speed

   2500 records per minute maximum

☒ Data Access Method

   Sequential, pointer file

Price (4/82)

FMS-81	$495
FMS-82	$495
FMS-80 (FMS-81 and FMS-82 combined)	$995

Publisher

DJR Associates
2 Highland Lane
North Tarrytown, New York 10591

System Requirements

· 8080, 8085, or Z-80 microprocessor system
· The CP/M operating system (MP/M, CDOS, or Turbodos acceptable)
· A minimum of 48K bytes of memory
· One or more disk drives
· A cursor-addressed 24 × 80-character video terminal
· Optional text printer

Specifications

Data Types	Decimal
	Alphanumeric
	Variable length
Records per file	65,535 max
Characters per record	Approximately 10,000 max
Fields per record	255 max
Characters per field	254 max
Largest number	$\pm 10^{40} - 1$
Numeric accuracy	40 digits
Index key length	250 characters max

FMS-81

FMS-81 is a menu-driven system. It begins with four menus, as shown in Figure 6-1. The menus may look mysterious at first, but you will quickly learn how to use them. Since they are linked to one another, you don't have to return to the main menu every time you perform a different task.

From the File Definitions Menu you can

choose to input the data dictionary, set up CRT screens, decide how you will select and sort, define reports, and create your own menus. These activities are associated with *system development*—the initial definition and subsequent modification of your application.

The File Maintenance Menu and the File Reports Menu control the day to day operations of your system—entering data, changing data, and printing reports. You may only use

```
    Main Menu                       File Definitions Menu

 1. FILE DEFINITIONS MENU            1. DEFINE FD
 2. FILE MAINTENANCE MENU            2. GLOSSARY
 3. FILE REPORTS MENU                3. DEFINE KEYS
 4. UTILTIY                          4. PRINT KEY DEFINITIONS
 5. HELP                             5. SELECT
 6. BATCH                            6. PRINT SELECTION
 7. USER MENU                        7. DEFINE SCREEN
 8. EXIT FMS-80                      8. PRINT SCREEN DEFINITION
                                     9. DEFINE REPORT
                                    10. PRINT REPORT DEFINITION
                                    11. COMPILE EFM PROGRAM
                                    12. UTILITY
                                    13. DEFINE MENU
                                    14. PRINT MENU DEFINITION
                                    15. FILE MAINTENANCE MENU
                                    16. FILE REPORTS MENU
                                    17. FMS-80 MAIN MENU
                                    18. EXIT FMS-80

    File Maintenance Menu           File Reports Menu

 1. UPDATE                           1. PRINT FILE
 2. SUBFILE & AUTO FD                2. COUNT HITS
 3. SORT FILE                        3. REPORT
 4. RUN EFM PROGRAM                  4. DIRECT QUERY/UPDATE
 5. BUILD INDEX                      5. UTILITY
 6. UTILTIY                          6. FILE DEFINITIONS MENU
 7. FILE DEFINITIONS MENU            7. FILE MAINTENANCE MENU
 8. FILE REPORTS MENU                8. FMS-80 MAIN MENU
 9. FMS-80 MAIN MENU                 9. EXIT FMS-80
10. EXIT FMS-80
```

FIGURE 6-1.
The four main FMS-80 menus

these menus during the testing phase since you will create your own menus later.

Example:
Job Costing

Imagine you are a building contractor and that you need detailed cost records on each job. This widely used job cost application is usually part of a larger data processing system. Normally, job cost data is automatically generated from payroll and accounts payable systems, but in this simple example it's entered directly.

Each job has a number of phases. If you were building homes, you would start with phase 1, land acquisition, move to phase 2, building permits, continue with another phase, excavation, until you finally finished with carpet installation. You would want to keep track of all expense items by phase for each job so that you could know exactly what labor was spent and materials used.

In this job cost system each record contains the following fields:

Job number
Phase number
Labor code (1 = non-labor, 0 = labor)
Date (yymmdd)
Description
Vendor name or employee name
Dollar cost amount

Your goal is to enter data into the system and to print it out with phase subtotals and job totals.

Setting Up the Data Dictionary (FD)

FMS-80 calls its data dictionary a File Definition and refers to it as the FD. Select DEFINE FD from the File Definition Menu (Figure 6-1) and the screen shown in Figure 6-2 appears.

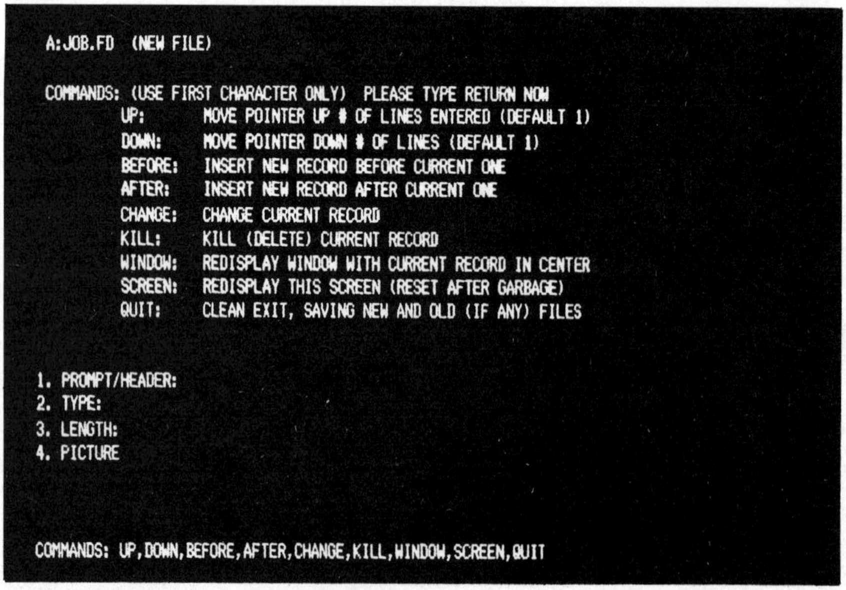

```
A:JOB.FD  (NEW FILE)


COMMANDS: (USE FIRST CHARACTER ONLY)  PLEASE TYPE RETURN NOW
       UP:       MOVE POINTER UP # OF LINES ENTERED (DEFAULT 1)
       DOWN:     MOVE POINTER DOWN # OF LINES (DEFAULT 1)
       BEFORE:   INSERT NEW RECORD BEFORE CURRENT ONE
       AFTER:    INSERT NEW RECORD AFTER CURRENT ONE
       CHANGE:   CHANGE CURRENT RECORD
       KILL:     KILL (DELETE) CURRENT RECORD
       WINDOW:   REDISPLAY WINDOW WITH CURRENT RECORD IN CENTER
       SCREEN:   REDISPLAY THIS SCREEN (RESET AFTER GARBAGE)
       QUIT:     CLEAN EXIT, SAVING NEW AND OLD (IF ANY) FILES




1. PROMPT/HEADER:
2. TYPE:
3. LENGTH:
4. PICTURE



COMMANDS: UP,DOWN,BEFORE,AFTER,CHANGE,KILL,WINDOW,SCREEN,QUIT
```

FIGURE 6-2.
DEFINE FD screen

You're about to enter the definition of the first field. Because FMS-80 expects each record to have a key, usually unique, you need one additional field called *transaction number* which you enter first. Figure 6-3 shows the screen after one field has been entered, and Figure 6-4 shows the screen with all the fields defined. The PROMPT/HEADER specifies the field *name* as it will appear later on both the screen and in report headings. The field TYPE is classified by either "A" for alphanumeric or "D" for decimal, and LENGTH is simply the number of characters or digits in the field. The PICTURE field determines how a number looks when printed or entered; you can insert dollar signs, commas, and decimals, plus other characters.

Figure 6-4 typifies how you interact with FMS-80. After entering all fields you can edit them. The asterisk on the left of the list of field definitions (in this example number 1) points to the current field you are editing. Move this pointer using the UP and DOWN commands to record to the lower area of the screen and change individual items by number. All input is alphanumeric characters or numbers, so there are no complicated CONTROL key sequences. In FMS-80, all field data entry must terminate with a RETURN; the cursor does not automatically move to the next field. Often you are asked "ARE YOU SURE?" and you must reply with a "Y" or "N" followed by RETURN.

You may print the completed FD either on the screen or on the printer by selecting GLOSSARY from the File Definitions Menu. Figure 6-5 shows this printed dictionary. Any time you refer to an FD you must use its name, a sequence of up to eight letters and numbers to which FMS-80 adds .FD to form a CP/M filename. The FD in this example was named JOB and appears in the directory as JOB.FD. You're

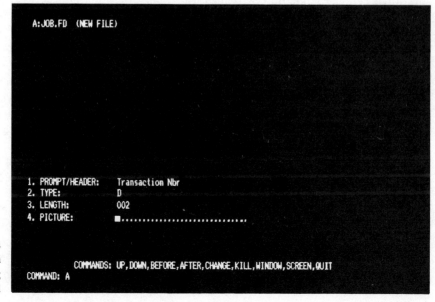

FIGURE 6-3.
DEFINE FD screen after defining one field

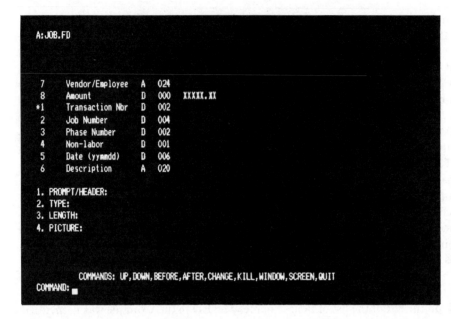

```
A:JOB.FD


    7      Vendor/Employee    A   024
    8      Amount             D   000    XXXXX.XX
   *1      Transaction Nbr    D   002
    2      Job Number         D   004
    3      Phase Number       D   002
    4      Non-labor          D   001
    5      Date (yymmdd)      D   006
    6      Description        A   020

   1. PROMPT/HEADER:
   2. TYPE:
   3. LENGTH:
   4. PICTURE:



           COMMANDS: UP,DOWN,BEFORE,AFTER,CHANGE,KILL,WINDOW,SCREEN,QUIT
   COMMAND: ▮
```

FIGURE 6-4.
DEFINE FD screen
after defining all
fields

going to be defining a data file, also called JOB, but you needn't make it match the FD name. In fact, you could have hundreds of data files all with the same layout and all using the FD name JOB.

Although you would probably rather ignore this CP/M file shuffle, you can't. You will have to keep track of numerous small files while developing a system because the program keeps asking for their names. Once the system is complete and you've set up your own menus, another operator won't be aware of individual data files.

Defining the Control File

After finishing the FD, one housekeeping job remains to be done before you enter data. You must define the key, the unique record

identifier. In this case, it is field 1, the Transaction Number. Selecting DEFINE KEYS from the File Definitions Menu lets you specify field 1, and PRINT KEY DEFINITIONS lets you print out the short report shown in Figure 6-6. According to the printout you have made another CP/M file called JOB.CTL which is tied to your FD, JOB.FD. You could have used two fields together to form a key, but one is sufficient for this example.

When you specified field 1 as the key, you referred to the Transaction Number field by its number. The field number is very important in FMS-80, especially when you write programs in the EFM language. Fields are always referenced by number, not by name, as they are in the RDBMS. The field name is incidental here and is printed on screens and reports only for convenience.

```
04/18/82               F M S - 8 0                      PAGE 1

                   FILE GLOSSARY FOR JOB.FD

--PROMPT/HEAD---      TYPE   LEN   ------------PICTURE-------------

1. Transaction Nbr    D     002
2. Job Number         D     004
3. Phase Number       D     002
4. Non-labor          D     001
5. Date (yymmdd)      D     006
6. Description        A     020
7. Vendor/Employee    A     024
8. Amount             D     008      XXXXX.XX
```

FIGURE 6-5.
Printed FD data dictionary
or glossary

```
04/18/82                F M S - 8 0                     PAGE 1
                   SORT CONTROL DEFINITION
   FILE: JOB.CTL          FD: JOB.FD         SELECT: (NONE)
      KEYS ARE LISTED IN DECREASING ORDER OF SIGNIFICANCE

          1.    Transaction Nbr    D
```

FIGURE 6-6.
Key definition report

Entering Data

Now that the preliminaries are over, you are ready to enter job cost data. FMS-80 demands a more rigorous data entry approach than many RDBMS and FMS systems. In other systems you can casually add new records where and when you want to, but FMS-80 uses the update method shown in Figure 3-6. You create a separate transaction file of adds, changes, and deletes which are sorted and merged with the existing file. While this appears to be more difficult than the direct method, it offers better data control. A printed report, or audit trail, shows all file changes, and you can print out your transactions to obtain totals. For financial applications, such as general ledger, these data control methods are necessities, but could be nuisances if you're just adding a new customer or vendor to the files.

If you had some job cost records on file already, you would be merging your new transactions with them. Since you are starting with a clean slate, things are simpler. The first step is the actual entry of the data. After selecting UPDATE in the File Maintenance Menu, you enter JOB when prompted for the FD name and you see the screen shown in Figure 6-7. Of course, all your transactions are adds, so you don't have the option to change or delete information.

Notice that the screen in Figure 6-7 shows the same field descriptions that you previously entered for File Definition. Simply type in your data; the system makes sure that alphanumeric characters don't go into numeric fields and that you don't enter too many characters or digits into a field. After entering the last item, in this case cost amount, you may change to any field by typing the corresponding field number or you may move to the next transaction.

When you are done, FMS-80 sorts the transactions by key (Transaction Number) and prints a list of all transactions as shown in Figure 6-8. Notice that two transactions have the Transaction Number 3. This mistake will demonstrate how the system handles duplicates.

After the transactions are sorted and printed, the system automatically applies the transactions. In this case there is no file to apply to, so all the transactions stored in the file JOB.TRX are written to a new data file called JOB.DAT. The duplicate transaction now causes problems. Unless you configure FMS-80 to accept duplicate keys, the data file won't accept two records with the same key; the first transaction is written to JOB.DAT, but the second is written to the reject file, JOB.REJ. Later you must either delete this transaction or change its number to prevent a conflict with the main data file.

Completing the update requires one last step.

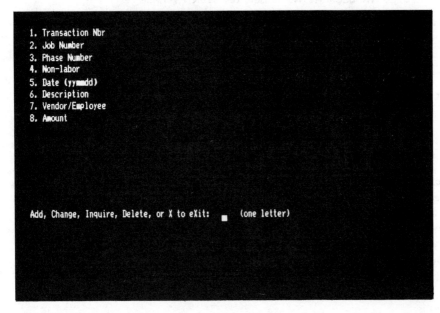

```
1. Transaction Nbr
2. Job Number
3. Phase Number
4. Non-labor
5. Date (yymmdd)
6. Description
7. Vendor/Employee
8. Amount




Add, Change, Inquire, Delete, or X to eXit: ▄   (one letter)
```

FIGURE 6-7.
Job transaction
entry screen

```
04/18/82              F M S - 8 0                    PAGE 1
FD: JOB.FD              SELECT:              FILE: JOB.TRX
------------------------------------------------------------------
Transaction    Job    Phase   Non-labor   Date (yy    Description
  Number      Number  Number                mmdd )

         Vendor/     Amount
         Employee
------------------------------------------------------------------

*** ADD
    01        8166      05                 0       811212   Payroll
Monty G. Butler             433.60
*** ADD
    02        8166      05                 1       811130   DEC PICKUP
George A. Pirrie, Jr.       155.00
*** ADD
    03        8166      07                 1       811130   NOVEM
Evergreen Septic Tank        15.80
*** ADD
    03        8166      07                 1       811130   NOVEM
Evergreen Septic Tank        15.80
*** ADD
    04        8166      07                 1       811130   NOVEMBER - JOBS
Pacific Northwest Bell      195.56
```

FIGURE 6-8.

List of transactions sorted by
key (transaction number)

FMS-80 now builds an index on the data file which is stored in yet another file called JOB.IDX.

If you began with several job records instead of an empty data file, your procedure would be almost the same except you could change and delete records as well as add them. If you try to change or delete a nonexistent record (determined by no matching keys), FMS-80 tells you immediately and prevents you from continuing until you enter the correct record. However, if you try to add a record with a key duplicated in the main data file, FMS-80 won't alert you until after the update when you find the DUPLICATE record in the reject file. If your original data file is large, the entire update process could take a long time, even if you requested only one transaction. However, this ensures a good audit trail.

There are some variations allowed in the update process. You can append new records onto the end of a file instead of merging them in, and you can use a program (only in FMS-82) for special processing such as adding a posting amount. You can make all this invisible to the operator by "customizing" the whole update procedure, or you can make up your own menu with different prompts.

Whichever update method you use, each record in your file must have a unique key. This is why you have Transaction Number in all your job records. If you don't have this unique

```
          04/18/82                F M S  -  8 0                           PAGE 1
          FD: JOB.FD              SELECT: (NONE)              FILE: JOB.DAT
```

Transaction Number	Job Number	Phase Number	Non-labor	Date (yy mmdd)	Description	Vendor/ Employee	Amount
01	8166	05	0	811212	Payroll	Monty G. Butler	4336.00
02	8166	05	1	811130	DEC PICKUP	George A. Pirrie, Jr	1550.00
03	8166	07	1	811130	NOVEM	Evergreen Septic Tan	158.00
04	8166	07	1	811130	NOVEMBER - JOBS	Pacific Northwest Be	1955.60
05	8166	08	1	811130	NOVEMBER	ABC Rentals	1152.50
06	8166	09	1	811130	NOV RETAINAGE	Powell Northwest Con	7000.00
07	8166	14	0	811212	Payroll	Bruce R. Corey	1634.40
08	8166	26	0	811212	Payroll	Monty G. Butler	4336.00
09	8166	26	0	811212	Payroll	James C. Lynch	7010.90
10	8166	26	1	811130	Gasoline, etc.	Chevron USA	825.00
11	8166	26	1	811130	NOVEMBER	Lumbermen's, Inc.	2740.10
12	8166	37	1	811130	NOVEMBER	Olympic Glass Co., I	5584.20
13	8166	40	1	811130	NOVEMBER	David Bryan Contract	554.40
14	8166	62	1	811130	Nov Retainage	Nelson's Htg & Air C	5310.90
15	8166	62	1	811130	November (90%)	Nelson's Htg & Air C	987.40
17	8169	05	0	811212	Payroll	Glen Sunderlin	6529.20
18	8169	05	1	811130	NOVEMBER - JOBS	Texaco	890.00
22	8169	08	1	811130	NOVEMBER	Star Rentals, Inc.	1719.10
23	8169	09	1	811130	NOVEMBER	ABC Rentals	3293.30
24	8169	10	0	811205	Payroll	Robert L. Stewart	3810.00
25	8169	10	1	811130	NOVEM	Bremerton Concrete P	7336.90
26	8169	10	1	811130	NOVEMBER	Kitsap Mechanical Co	4412.50
27	8169	15	0	811212	Payroll	James D. Young	4165.70
28	8169	15	0	811212	Payroll	Douglas M. Seals	4165.70
29	8169	15	0	811212	Payroll	Bruce R. Corey	1225.80
30	8169	15	0	811130	NOVEMBER	Oxygen Sales & Servi	138.00
31	8169	16	0	811205	Payroll	Glen Sunderlin	2292.70
32	8169	16	0	811212	Payroll	Glen Sunderlin	2176.40
33	8169	16	0	811212	Payroll	Floyd E. Amos	8518.00

FIGURE 6-9.

A 132-column printed report

identifier, the update will reject all adds for duplicate keys. If one of your jobs is complete and you want to purge those records, a "hole" in the transaction number sequence will appear. To be safe, all new transactions must have an increasingly higher transaction number. A later FMS-80 version does allow duplicate keys.

Printing Data

To print, simply select PRINT from the File Maintenance Menu. You have no control over the format of the print, but the results are acceptable if your paper is wide enough. Figure 6-9 shows a 132-column report and Figure 6-10 shows an 80-column version which fits on the video screen. If you had a file with 100 fields, the printout would be a disaster. There are other ways to print information that we will discuss later.

DIRECT QUERY/UPDATE

Suppose you just want to examine records individually and change one or two fields directly in the data file. The query option displays a record as shown in Figure 6-11. This looks like the screen in the update step, but you can't add or delete records. (In fact you can disable the change capability entirely if you want to be safe.) You may wonder how FMS-80 finds the record. Remember the last part of the update was an index build, which was based on the key Transaction Number. The query program checks the JOB.CTL file for the key, and asks you for it. Two seconds later you see the rest of the record. The query module lets you retrieve data with "wild cards" the same way CP/M selects files. Pressing "S*" will display everything beginning with the letter "S," and "Sm?th" will display "Smith" and "Smyth." Pressing RETURN produces the next

sequential record according to the index.

Alternate Indexes

You used Transaction Number in the update and query modes because that was the only unique key. To produce reports by job and phase you need the records in Job Number and Phase Number order. You could sort down the entire data file by Job Number and Phase Number, but this would waste time and disk space. Recall that the pointer file gives another view of the data (see Chapter 3). FMS-80 allows this, but calls it an index. A true index allows new entries to be inserted. FMS-80 rebuilds and sorts the index every time a record is added.

To create a new index on Job Number or Phase Number

- Create another control file specifying the two fields to make up the key
- Select the INDEX option in the File Maintenance Menu
- Sort by selecting SORT FILE from the same menu.

Later in this chapter the Report Generator will use this index, called JOB/PHAS.IDX.

Generating Reports

The Report Generator is one of the strong selling points of the FMS-80. You can use it to create sophisticated reports, but you must invest some time in learning it. Here is a preview of the process: Figure 6-12 shows what you must write, with the help of FMS-80, to produce the report in Figure 6-13. The detail records are printed with job totals and page breaks, but without phase subtotals. That's the next step.

The Report Definition (RD) is really a mini-program logically divided into five divisions (only four are used here). The first division,

```
04/18/82                  F M S - 8 0                        PAGE  1

FD: JOB.FD           SELECT: (NONE)            FILE: JOB.DAT
-----------------------------------------------------------------------
Transaction    Job     Phase    Non-labor    Date (yy    Description
  Number      Number   Number                  mmdd)
-----------------------------------------------------------------------
           Vendor/            Amount
           Employee
-----------------------------------------------------------------------

    01         8166      05          0         811212    Payroll
Monty G. Butler            4336.00
    02         8166      05          1         811130    DEC PICKUP
George A. Pirrie, Jr       1550.00
    03         8166      07          1         811130    NOVEM
Evergreen Septic Tan        158.00
    04         8166      07          1         811130    NOVEMBER - JOBS
Pacific Northwest Be       1955.60
    05         8166      08          1         811130    NOVEMBER
ABC Rentals                1152.50
    06         8166      09          1         811130    NOV RETAINAGE
Powell Northwest Con       7000.00
    07         8166      14          0         811212    Payroll
Bruce R. Corey             1634.40
    08         8166      26          0         811212    Payroll
Monty G. Butler            4336.00
    09         8166      26          0         811212    Payroll
James C. Lynch             7010.90
    10         8166      26          1         811130    Gasoline, etc.
Chevron USA                 825.00
    11         8166      26          1         811130    NOVEMBER
Lumbermen's, Inc.          2740.10
    12         8166      37          1         811130    NOVEMBER
Olympic Glass Co., I       5584.20
    13         8166      40          1         811130    NOVEMBER
David Bryan Contract        554.40
    14         8166      62          1         811130    November Retainage
Nelson's Htg & Air C       5310.90
    15         8166      62          1         811130    November (90%)
```

FIGURE 6-10.
Job master list 80-column display

TITLES, assigns JOB COST SYSTEM—SAMPLE REPORT 1 to the top of each page. You can also print footings at the bottom of each page, as well as the date and page number. Titles can be centered, left-justified, or right-justified.

The second division, FIELD PRINTING, formats the actual data lines in the report. All fields except JOB NUMBER are printed out, along with the starting column number. You don't have to print fields in the same order in

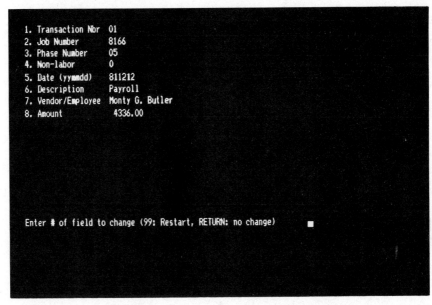

```
1. Transaction Nbr  01
2. Job Number       8166
3. Phase Number     05
4. Non-labor        0
5. Date (yymmdd)    811212
6. Description      Payroll
7. Vendor/Employee  Monty G. Butler
8. Amount           4336.00




Enter # of field to change (99: Restart, RETURN: no change)  ■
```

FIGURE 6-11.
Job file QUERY

which they appear in the FD. Figure 6-14 shows you the screen after defining all the report fields except AMOUNT. The edit screen is similar to the FD screen, allowing you to change lines and fields without using CONTROL key sequences. FMS-80 provides prompts as shown in Figure 6-14.

You produce a simple report with page headings and a cost record with one line per job. Job totals and grand totals require more work. Refer to Figure 6-12 again. The report's FIELD BREAK division (Page 3) has captions to the right of the seven lines. Another FD, previously hidden from you, defined a temporary file containing one record with the first field, Job Total Amount, and the second, Grand Total Amount. (The captions describe these hidden functions.) Line 1 adds the Job Record Amount to the Job Total Amount field, and line 5 adds the Job Total Amount to the Grand Total Amount.

The remaining lines control printing.

You can set up a PAGE BREAK division which prints totals for all the records on a page at the bottom of the page. The last division, END OF REPORT, prints a caption and Grand Total Amount on a separate page at the end of the report.

Now for a few words on the mechanics of defining and running reports. As usual, more files are involved, namely one .RD file for each Report Definition. To create this file select DEFINE REPORT from the File Definition Menu. To print the report, select REPORT from the File Reports Menu, specifying JOBR1 as the RD name and JOB/PHAS as the file (in this case index) name.

The report of Figure 6-12 doesn't break down job costs by phase. Also, each job should start on a new page, and the job number should come before the job's data instead of after it.

```
04/18/82               F M S - 8 0                    PAGE 1
               R E P O R T   D E F I N I T I O N
     LINES/PAGE: 66  COLS/LINE: 79  RD: JOBR1.    FD: JOB.  TEMP FD: A:JOBR1.


     TITLES:
     CH JOB COST SYSTEM - SAMPLE REPORT 1
     LH
     LH Trans    Phase      Date    Description    Vendor/Employee    Amount
     LH


04/18/82               F M S - 8 0                    PAGE 2
               R E P O R T   D E F I N I T I O N
     LINES/PAGE: 66  COLS/LINE: 79  RD: JOBR1.     FD: JOB.  TEMP FD: A:JOBR1.
                     FIELD PRINTING
               LINE  COL  FUNC  FIELD  LITERAL

               1.  1    1    F      1     Transaction Nbr
               2.  1   10    F      3     Phase Number
               3.  1   14    F      4     Non-labor
               4.  1   17    F      5     Date (yymmdd)
               5.  1   25    F      6     Description
               6.  1   46    F      7     Vendor/Employee
               7.  1   71    F      8     Amount


04/18/82               F M S - 8 0                    PAGE 3
               R E P O R T   D E F I N I T I O N
     LINES/PAGE: 66  COLS/LINE: 79  RD: JOBR1.     FD: JOB.  TEMP FD: A:JOBR1.
                        FIELD BREAK
        FUNC  BREAK  DEST  SOURCE  LINE  COL  LITERAL

     1.  +      0     1T     8P      0    0                  *add amount to job
     2.  L      2     0      0P      1   24   Total for      *caption
     3.  L      2     0      0P      1   40   Job Number
     4.  F      2     0      2P      1   50   Job Number     *print job number
     5.  +      2     2T     1T      0    0                  *add amount to grand
     6.  Z      2     0      1T      1   69   Job total      *zero & print amount
     7.  L      2     0      0P      2    1                  *blank line after


04/18/82               F M S - 8 0                    PAGE 4
               R E P O R T   D E F I N I T I O N
     LINES/PAGE: 66  COLS/LINE: 79  RD: JOBR1.     FD: JOB.   TEMP FD: A:JOBR1.
                        END OF REPORT
        FUNC  BREAK  DEST  SOURCE  LINE  COL  LITERAL

     1.  L      0     0      0P      2   24   Grand total    *caption
     2.  F      0     0      2T      2   69   Grand total    *amount
```

FIGURE 6-12.
Report Definition (RD) number 1

```
              JOB COST SYSTEM - SAMPLE REPORT 1
Trans    Phase   Date  Description           Vendor/Employee        Amount

01       05  0  811212  Payroll              Monty G. Butler        4336.00
02       05  1  811130  DEC PICKUP           George A. Pirrie, Jr    1550.00
03       07  1  811130  NOVEM                Evergreen Septic Tan     158.00
04       07  1  811130  NOVEMBER - JOBS      Pacific Northwest Be    1955.60
05       08  1  811130  NOVEMBER             ABC Rentals            1152.50
06       09  1  811130  NOV RETAINAGE        Powell Northwest Con    7000.00
07       14  0  811212  Payroll              Bruce R. Corey         1634.40
08       26  0  811212  Payroll              Monty G. Butler        4336.00
09       26  0  811212  Payroll              James C. Lynch         7010.90
10       26  1  811130  Gasoline, etc.       Chevron USA             825.00
11       26  1  811130  NOVEMBER             Lumbermen's, Inc.      2740.10
12       37  1  811130  NOVEMBER             Olympic Glass Co., I   5584.20
13       40  1  811130  NOVEMBER             David Bryan Contract    554.40
14       62  1  811130  November Retainage   Nelson's Htg & Air C   5310.90
15       62  1  811130  November (90%)       Nelson's Htg & Air C    987.40
                        Total for Job Number        8166          45135.40

17       05  0  811212  Payroll              Glen Sunderlin         6529.20
18       05  1  811130  NOVEMBER - JOBS      Texaco                  890.00
22       08  1  811130  NOVEMBER             Star Rentals, Inc.     1719.10
23       09  1  811130  NOVEMBER             ABC Rentals            3293.30
24       10  0  811205  Payroll              Robert L. Stewart      3810.00
25       10  1  811130  NOVEM                Bremerton Concrete P   7336.90
26       10  1  811130  NOVEMBER             Kitsap Mechanical Co   4412.50
27       15  0  811212  Payroll              James D. Young         4165.70
28       15  0  811212  Payroll              Douglas M. Seals       4165.70
29       15  0  811212  Payroll              Bruce R. Corey         1225.80
30       15  1  811130  NOVEMBER             Oxygen Sales & Servi    138.00
31       16  0  811205  Payroll              Glen Sunderlin         2292.70
32       16  0  811212  Payroll              Glen Sunderlin         2176.40
33       16  0  811212  Payroll              Floyd E. Amos          8518.00
34       16  0  811205  Payroll              Francis L. Tence       4971.70
35       16  0  811212  Payroll              Francis L. Tence       3314.40
38       16  1  811113? NOVEMBER             Addison Pacific Supp    930.00
39       16  1  811130  NOVEM                Fred Hill Materials,   8852.10
40       16  1  811130  NOVEMBER             Parker Lumber Co.      2505.50
41       16  1  811130  NOVEMBER             Mike Schmuck, Conc.P   1810.00
43       38  0  811212  Payroll              George P. Stromberg    4971.60
44       38  0  811212  Payroll              Francis L. Tence       4971.60
45       38  1  811130  NOVEMBER             Roblin Building Prod   7861.80
46       54  1  811130  NOVEMBER             Allied Bolt Co.        3334.20
47       58  1  811130  NOVEMBER             B & E Equipment Co.,    552.10
                        Total for Job Number        8169          94748.30


                Grand total                                      139883.70
```

FIGURE 6-13.

Sample report 1

```
A:JOBR1.RD                      FIELD PRINTING



*6        1  46  F  7    Vendor/Employee
1         1   1  F  1    Transaction Nbr
2         1  10  F  3    Phase Number
3         1  14  F       Non-labor
4         1  17  F  5    Date (yymmdd)
5         1  25  F  6    Description


1. LINE #:          01
2. COLUMN:          071
3. FUNCTION:        F
4. FIELD #:         008 Amount
5. LITERAL:         Amount


        COMMANDS: UP,DOWN,BEFORE,AFTER,CHANGE,KILL,WINDOW,SCREEN,QUIT
ENTER # OF ITEM TO CHANGE OR RETURN:
```

FIGURE 6-14.
Formatting the
report fields

Figure 6-15 shows one page of the improved report and Figure 6-16 shows the associated RD, called JOBR2. Notice the page number. It's starting to look just like it came from the data processing department.

While the examples have illustrated most of the Report Generator's features, there are a few you haven't seen. You are not limited to just one line per record, but you can define as many lines as you need, including blank lines. You can print one record per page or one per several pages. The program calculates (add, subtract, multiply, divide) within the report to create total lines and generates as many levels of subtotals as you need.

Your fundamental limitation is the restriction to one file. This can be overcome by writing an EFM program (FMS-82) to combine data from several files into one temporary file for reporting. Of course, with EFM you can always write programs, but you need the Report Generator for headings, page breaks, total breaks, and so on. EFM will be described later in this chapter.

There is one minor irritation. You can freely update the lines describing field printing and breaks, but you can only edit individual heading and footing lines. If you need new lines, you must erase the entire heading or footing and start over.

Selecting Records and Fields

Up to now you have been printing, querying, and reporting using all the data in the job cost file. Suppose you want to see only non-labor items, or only job 8166, or only non-labor items for jobs 8166 and 8169. You are selecting records for later processing. If you want to see only Job Number, Phase Number, and Amount,

```
                  JOB COST SYSTEM - SAMPLE REPORT 2

            LC   Date    Description        Vendor/Employee      Amount
Job number 8166

             0  811212  Payroll            Monty G. Butler      4336.00
             1  811130  DEC PICKUP          George A. Pirrie, Jr 1550.00
                                                Phase 05 total  5886.00

             1  811130  NOVEM              Evergreen Septic Tan   158.00
             1  811130  NOVEMBER - JOBS     Pacific Northwest Be 1955.60
                                                Phase 07 total  2113.60

             1  811130  NOVEMBER            ABC Rentals          1152.00
                                                Phase 08 total  1152.00

             1  811130  NOV RETAINAGE       Powell Northwest Con 7000.00
                                                Phase 09 total  7000.00

             0  811212  Payroll            Bruce R. Corey        1634.40
                                                Phase 14 total  1634.40

             0  811212  Payroll            Monty G. Butler      4336.00
             0  811212  Payroll            James C. Lynch       7010.90
             1  811130  Gasoline, etc.     Chevron USA           825.00
             1  811130  NOVEMBER            Lumbermen's Inc.     2740.10
                                                Phase 26 total 14912.00

             1  811130  NOVEMBER            Olympic Glass Co., I 5584.20
                                                Phase 37 total  5584.00

             1  811130  NOVEMBER            David Bryan Contract  554.40
                                                Phase 40 total   554.40

             1  811130  November Retainage  Nelson's Htg & Air C 5310.90
             1  811130  November (90%)      Nelson's Htg & Air C  987.40
                                                Phase 62 total  6298.30

                                                Job total      45135.40

Page 1
                  JOB COST SYSTEM - SAMPLE REPORT 2

            LC   Date    Description        Vendor/Employee      Amount

                                                Grand total   139883.70

Page 3
```

FIGURE 6-15.

Report number 2

```
04/18/82                 F M S - 8 0                    PAGE 1
                  R E P O R T   D E F I N I T I O N
LINES/PAGE: 66  COLS/LINE: 79  RD: JOBR2.   FD: JOB.   TEMP FD: A:JOBR2.

 TITLES:
CH JOB COST SYSTEM - SAMPLE REPORT 2
LH
LH   LC   Date      Description     Vendor/Employee   Amount
LH
LF
LF
LF Page #
LF
LF
LF
LF
```

```
04/18/82                 F M S - 8 0                    PAGE 2
                  R E P O R T   D E F I N I T I O N
LINES/PAGE: 66  COLS/LINE: 79  RD: JOBR2.   FD: JOB.   TEMP FD: A:JOBR2.
                        FIELD PRINTING
                  LINE  COL  FUNC  FIELD  LITERAL

            1.     1    14    F      4     Non-labor
            2.     1    17    F      5     Date (yymmdd)
            3.     1    25    F      6     Description
            4.     1    46    F      7     Vendor/Employee
            5.     1    71    F      8     Amount
```

```
04/18/82                 F M S - 8 0                    PAGE 3
                  R E P O R T   D E F I N I T I O N
LINES/PAGE: 66  COLS/LINE: 79  RD: JOBR2.   FD: JOB.   TEMP FD: A:JOBR2.
                         FIELD BREAK
      FUNC  BREAK  DEST  SOURCE  LINE  COL  LITERAL

1.  +     0     1T     8P      0    0               *add amount to
                                                     phase total
2.  L     3     0      0P      1    55   Phase       *caption
3.  F     3     0      3P      1    61   Phase Number *print phase
                                                     number
4.  L     3     0      0P      1    64   total       *caption
5.  +     3     2T     1T      0    0                *add amount to job
                                                     total
6.  Z     3     0      1T      1    69   Phase total  *zero & print phase
                                                     total
7.  L     3     0      0P      2    1                *blank line
8.  L     2     0      0P      1    55   Job total    *caption
```

(continued)

FIGURE 6-16.
RD for job report number 2

```
  9.  +       2     3T      2T      0     0               *add amount to
                                                           grand total
 10.  Z       2     0       2T      1    69   Job total   *zero & print job
                                                           total
 11.  P       2     0       0       0     0               *new page on new
                                                           job
 12.  L       2     0       OC      2     1   Job number  *caption
 13.  F       2     0       2C      2    12   Job Number  *print job number
 14.  L       2     0       OC      3     1               *blank line



 04/18/82                    F M S - 8 0                  PAGE 4
                     R E P O R T   D E F I N I T I O N
 LINES/PAGE: 66  COLS/LINE: 79  RD: JOBR2.   FD: JOB.   TEMP FD: A:JOBR2.
                            END OF REPORT
         FUNC  BREAK  DEST  SOURCE  LINE  COL  LITERAL

     1.  L      0     0      OP      2    55   Grand total  *caption
     2.  F      0     0      3T      2    69   Grand total  *amount
```

FIGURE 6-16.
RD for job report number 2 (continued)

you would select fields for later use. You create a file called a Selection Definition (not SD, that already stands for Screen Definition) identified in this example as JOBNON-L.SEL. This will select Job Number, Phase Number, and Amount fields for non-labor records only. Figure 6-17 shows the screen after this has been set up. Although the record selection "non-labor only" is rather simple, you can set up more complicated ones like

(Labor Code = 1)
(Job Number = 8166 or Job Number = 8169)

Divide the selection into two groups, defining each group as a series of connected expressions, then connect the groups—all via a menu. This allows selection definitions with up to "one level of parentheses," which should be good enough for most applications. See Figure 6-18 for a printout of the Selection Definition.

Now that you have a Selection Definition, what do you do with it? The most obvious thing is to print the qualifying records, and the PRINT function conveniently lets you specify the .SEL file to go with the data (.DAT) file. Figure 6-19 shows the printout of the selected records from the main data file.

You can also QUERY using the Selection Definition, but you cannot selectively REPORT unless you first build a special index which points only to selected records.

You can also use the Selection Definition to make a new data file containing selected records and selected (and possibly rearranged) fields. Choose SUBFILE & AUTO FD from the File Maintenance Menu, specifying the Selection Definition described above, to generate a new FD, as shown in Figure 6-20, plus a corresponding data file physically arranged like the "pseudo" data file printed in Figure 6-19.

The SUBFILE selection adds RDBMS features to FMS-80. It offers the only way, short

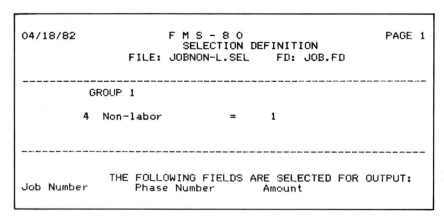

```
CREATING SELECT CRITERIA. FILE:A:JOB.FD  SELECT NAME: A:JOBNON-L.SEL
1. FIELD # : 004 Non-labor
2. MIN :
   MAX :
   EQUALS:  1
   NOT  = :
3. CONNECTOR (A OR O):        ■

   _____
ENTER THE CONNECTOR TO THE NEXT FIELD OR RETURN
```

FIGURE 6-17.
Select definition
screen

```
04/18/82                 F M S - 8 0                      PAGE 1
                      SELECTION DEFINITION
            FILE: JOBNON-L.SEL     FD: JOB.FD
-------------------------------------------------------------------
        GROUP 1

      4   Non-labor            =        1


-------------------------------------------------------------------
              THE FOLLOWING FIELDS ARE SELECTED FOR OUTPUT:
Job Number        Phase Number          Amount
```

FIGURE 6-18.
Selection definition
printout

of EFM programming, to physically rearrange data. You can eliminate fields and records, but you can't add new ones.

Defining Screens

Figure 6-7 showed the job transaction entry screen that FMS-80 generates automatically.

```
 04/18/82              F M S - 8 0                    PAGE 1
    FD: JOBNON-L.FD        SELECT: (NONE)      FILE: JOBNON-L.SFL
 -----------------------------------------------------------------
 Job        Phase      Amount
 Number     Number
 -----------------------------------------------------------------

    8166      05       1550.00
    8166      07        158.00
    8166      07       1955.60
    8166      08       1152.50
    8166      09       7000.00
    8166      26        825.00
    8166      26       2740.10
    8166      37       5584.20
    8166      40        554.40
    8166      62       5310.90
    8166      62        987.40
    8169      05        890.00
    8169      08       1719.10
    8169      09       3293.30
    8169      10       7336.90
    8169      10       4412.50
    8169      15        138.00
    8169      16        930.00
    8169      16       8852.10
    8169      16       2505.50
    8169      16       1810.00
    8169      38       7861.80
    8169      54       3334.20
    8169      58        552.10
```

FIGURE 6-19.
Printout of selected
records and fields

```
 04/18/82                 F M S - 8 0                  PAGE 1

                  FILE GLOSSARY FOR JOBNON-L.AFD

   --PROMPT/HEAD---    TYPE   LEN    -----------PICTURE------------

 1. Job Number         D      004
 2. Phase Number       D      002
 3. Amount             D      008        XXXXX.XX
```

FIGURE 6-20.
Auto-generated FD

This screen is sufficient unless you have more than 21 fields, need "invisible" fields, or just want a fancier screen. To define your own screen, select DEFINE SCREEN from the File Definition Menu. Through a process similar to File Definition, you lay out the screen, specifying line numbers, column numbers, and field numbers. The Screen Definition (SD) is listed in Figure 6-21. Compare the new screen in Figure 6-22 with that of Figure 6-7. Notice the same Add, Change, Delete, and Inquire choices at the bottom.

The Screen Definition is used with transaction entry and direct query in place of the default layout. While the custom screen makes this example "prettier," the examples in the next section require several Screen Definitions.

Defining Menus

Menu Definition (MD) is crucial if your system will be operated by office personnel. Without it, operators work from the FMS-80 menus (Figure 6-1) and must remember all the FD, SD, and control file names. A system developer also saves time with early menu definition.

Consider the completed job cost menu in Figure 6-23. Notice the improvement over the standard FMS-80 menus. What's behind the menu? The answer is the commands shown in Figure 6-24, which you set up through the DEFINE MENU step in the File Definition Menu. How do commands get into a menu-driven system? FMS-80 uses commands internally. Behind every menu, whether it is generated by

04/18/82			F M S - 8 0		PAGE 1
			SCREEN DEFINITION		
			FILE: JOBS1.SD		FD: JOB.FD
	SCREEN LINE	COL	FUNCTION	FIELD	LITERAL
1.	1	2	5	LITERAL	0	JOB COST TRANSAC
2.	1	2	20	LITERAL	0	TION ENTRY
3.	1	4	20	HEADER	1	Transaction Nbr
4.	1	4	36	COLLECT	1	Transaction Nbr
5.	1	6	5	HEADER	2	Job Number
6.	1	6	21	COLLECT	2	Job Number
7.	1	6	40	HEADER	3	Phase Number
8.	1	6	55	COLLECT	3	Phase Number
9.	1	7	5	LITERAL	0	Labor Code
10.	1	7	21	COLLECT	4	Non-labor
11.	1	7	40	HEADER	5	Date (yymmdd)
12.	1	7	55	COLLECT	5	Date (yymmdd)
13.	1	9	5	HEADER	6	Description
14.	1	9	21	COLLECT	6	Description
15.	1	10	5	HEADER	7	Vendor/Employee
16.	1	10	21	COLLECT	7	Vendor/Employee
17.	1	11	5	HEADER	8	Amount
18.	1	11	21	COLLECT	8	Amount

FIGURE 6-21. Job Screen Definition (SD) printed out

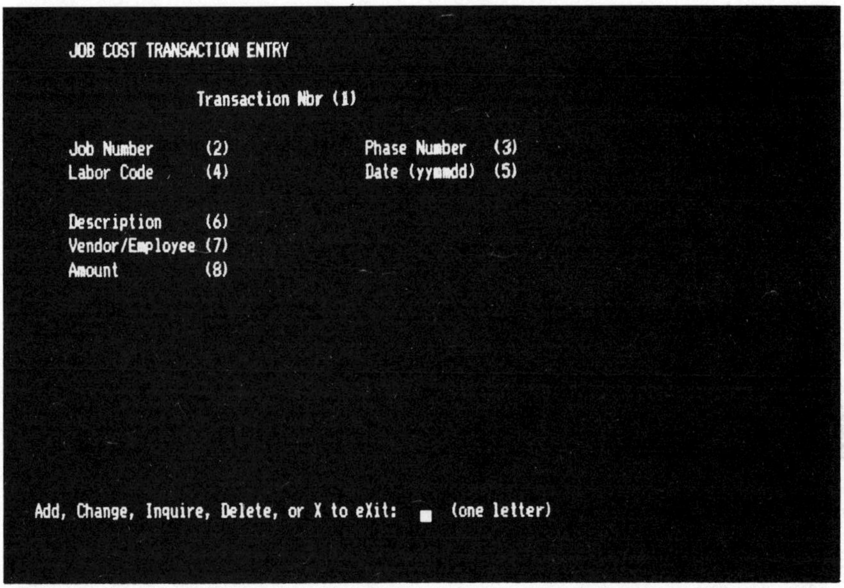

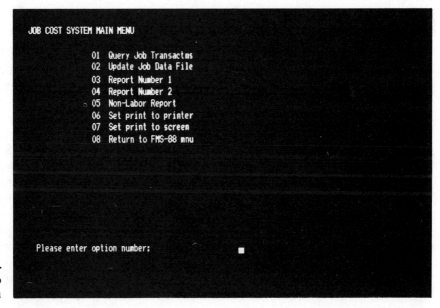

FIGURE 6-22.
New job
transaction screen

FIGURE 6-23.
Completed job
cost menu

```
 04/18/82                 F M S - 8 0                      PAGE 1
                         MENU DEFINITION
                         FILE: MASTER.MD
          FUNCTION     LINE   COL   OPTION   PROGRAM/BATCH FILE/MENU   JOB COST SYSTEM
                                                                      MAIN MENU
   1.     TEXT         01     05
   2.     TEXT         01     25
   3.     PROGRAM      03     20    01       QUERY JOB.IDX JOBS1.SD    Query Job
                                                                      Transactns
   4.     BATCH FILE   04     20    02       JOBUPDT Update Job Data File
   5.     PROGRAM      05     20    03       REPORT JOBR1.RD JOB/PHAS.IDX   Report
                                                                      Number 1
   6.     PROGRAM      06     20    04       REPORT JOBR2.RD JOB/PHAS.IDX   Report
                                                                      Number 2
   7.     PROGRAM      07     20    05       PRINT JOBNON-L.SEL JOB.DAT   Non-labor
                                                                      Report
   8.     PROGRAM      08     20    06       PIP LOCATE.SYS=LOCATE.PRN   Set print
                                                                      to
                                                                      printer
   9.     PROGRAM      09     20    07       PIP LOCATE.SYS=LOCATE.SCR   Set print
                                                                      to
                                                                      screen
  10.     PROGRAM      10     20    08       FMS80                     Return to
                                                                      FMS-80
                                                                      mnu
```

FIGURE 6-24.
Job cost Menu Definition (MD)

FMS-80 or you, is a table of these commands. If you choose REPORT from FMS-80's File Reports Menu, you are asked for the FD name and the RD name, whereupon the command REPORT JOBR1.RD JOB.FD brings up the report program and passes it the two file names. Your menu does the same thing, except the RD and FD names are "in the table" so you don't need to type them each time. Figure 6-24 shows the job menu listing with functions, line numbers, column numbers, option numbers, commands, and prompts. The menu program displays the options to the left of the prompts, accepts the operator's input, and then sends the command. FMS-80 always returns control to the same menu after the commands complete except after QUIT (which exits to CP/M) and FMS80 (which branches to the main menu).

There are two menu choices to switch listing output between the video screen and the line printer. These tie into FMS-80's LOCATE.SYS file which will be explained later in this chapter.

This menu is named MASTER.MD because FMS-80 looks for a menu of that name on startup. After data entry, control is passed directly to this menu, bypassing the FMS-80 menus completely. In addition, the FMS-80 Main Menu option USER MENU links into this menu if you key in the name MASTER when prompted.

CP/M File Summary

In the example, FMS-80 generated numerous new CP/M files for you to keep track of. These are summarized here.

JOB.FD
>   File Definition containing the data dictionary

JOB.CTL
>   Control file defining Transaction Number as the key

JOBNON-L.CTL
>   Control file for the non-labor selection

JOB.TRX
>   Transaction file (temporary, lasts through UPDATE)

JOB.REJ
>   Rejected transactions

JOB.DAT
>   Job data file

JOB.IDX
>   Job index on transaction number (linked to JOB.CTL)

JOB/PHAS.IDS
>   Job index on Job Number and Phase Number

JOBR1.RD
>   Report Definition for report 1

JOBR2.RD
>   Report Definition for report 2

JOBNON-L.SEL
>   Selection definition for non-labor transactions

JOBNON-L.AFD
>   Automatic File Definition for selected job fields

JOBNON-L.SEL
>   Data file from automatic select

JOBS1.SD
>   Screen Definition

JOBUPD.SUB
>   Batch file for update

MASTER.MD
>   User-defined menu

FMS-82

FMS-81 limits you to the functions described in the previous section. FMS-82 adds a programming language called Extended File Management (EFM) which lets you perform more tasks, including

· More complex reports
· Special, interactive, full-screen data entry
· Multifile access
· Posting
· File reorganization.

You write EFM programs using a text editor, then **PREPARE** them with the built-in compiler. The compiler doesn't generate machine-language instructions, but rather intermediate interpretive codes similar to those of CBASIC2. You can run these programs from CP/M, from the FMS-80 File Maintenance Menu, or from your own menu.

If you program in interpretive BASIC, you can probably learn EFM in a few days. An interpretive language lets you make program changes instantly, but, like other compiled languages, EFM forces you to recompile the program after every change. It would be difficult to learn if EFM were your first computer language; it doesn't have the level of support available for BASIC programmers.

Example:
Bicycle Track Racing

This is a sports statistics program for bicycle track racing sponsored by a federation of bicycle clubs. It could apply, with minor changes, to any multievent competition such as track and field meets, motorcycle races, steeplechases, or dog shows.

There are 250 regular track riders in four classes, each with a number. Evening races are weekly, and there are 14 events. Riders participate in several events, and 60 riders race each week. Points are given for each event, 5 points for first place, 3 for second, and so on. The track announcer needs quick access to the information, which must be current from the last race.

For each rider, grouped by class, the announcer must know

- Season point totals for each event
- Points for each event from the last race
- Date of the last race
- Total season points
- Total points from the last race.

For each class, the announcer must know

- The season's top ten riders with season totals
- The season's top three riders in each event with event season totals.

Data input includes

- Rider maintenance
  a. add new riders
  b. delete inactive riders
  c. modify season event totals
  d. modify last race evening event totals.
- Race event point entry.

Season event totals, rider totals, and last race date are automatically maintained, but there must be a way to recalculate after points are corrected. Also, all totals must be made zero at season's end.

Defining Files and Screens, Generating Reports

To understand this system, look at the parts constructed without EFM, starting with the

File Definition (data dictionary) shown in Figure 6-25. The rider file, RIDERS.DAT, has basic information such as name and class, plus space for season and evening points for all events. Because EFM programs are keyed to field numbers, the file was structured to accommodate new events without changing present numbers.

Since there are 40 fields, a Screen Definition is necessary. Even though all fields could fit on one screen, there is a logical separation between evening and season points. These go onto two screens, one for rider maintenance and the other for race data entry. Figures 6-26 and 6-27 show the Screen Definitions for the two screens, and Figures 6-28 and 6-29 show the resulting screens. FMS-80 displays numbers in parentheses next to fields that the user may update. Notice that the rider maintenance screen allows changes to last name, class, first name, date of last race, and season totals, but the evening data entry screen allows only event point entry. The fields are the same ones entered for the FD. If an event name changes, a new heading in the FD will be reflected on the screen.

FMS-80 performs this rider maintenance without programming help. Once the FD and the maintenance SD are built, transaction-based UPDATE takes over using Rider Number as the unique key. Now a test file can be entered to provide data for reports and future EFM programs. The race entry SD can be built and used through UPDATE/QUERY on the test file.

The rider detail report, shown in Figure 6-30, comes from the FMS-80 Report Generator. The RD is shown in Figure 6-31. The report is driven from an index sorted by Class, then Rider Number. The main menu in Figure 6-32 comes from the MD (Menu Definition) in Figure 6-33. The associated batch files RIDERUPD and RIDERMOD are listed in Figure 6-34.

To summarize, the FMS-81 system has

```
04/18/82              F M S - 8 0                    PAGE 1

                 FILE GLOSSARY FOR RIDERS.FD

  --PROMPT/HEAD---   TYPE   LEN    ------------PICTURE-------------

  1. Rider Number     D     003        XX^X
  2. Class            D     001
  3. Last Name        A     015
  4. First Name       A     010
  5. Place            D     003        XX^X
  6. Date last race   D     008        XX/XX/XX
  7. Evening Total    D     003        XX^X
  8. Season Total     D     003        XX^X
  9. spare            D     001
 10. spare            D     001
 11. Miss & Out  (E)  D     003        XXX^
 12. Miss & Out  (S)  D     003        XXX^
 13. 3 lap (E)        D     003        XXX^
 14. 3 lap (S)        D     003        XXX^
 15. 4 lap (E)        D     003        XXX^
 16. 4 lap (S)        D     003        XXX^
 17. 6 lap (E)        D     003        XXX^
 18. 6 lap (S)        D     003        XXX^
 19. 6 x 1 (E)        D     003        XXX^
 20. 6 x 1 (S)        D     003        XXX^
 21. 4 x 3 (E)        D     003        XXX^
 22. 4 x 3 (S)        D     003        XXX^
 23. 4 x 2 (E)        D     003        XXX^
 24. 4 x 2 (S)        D     003        XXX^
 25. 3 x 3 (E)        D     003        XXX^
 26. 3 x 3 (S)        D     003        XXX^
 27. 3 x 2 (E)        D     003        XXX^
 28. 3 x 2 (S)        D     003        XXX^
 29. 4000 meters (E)  D     003        XXX^
 30. 4000 meters (S)  D     003        XXX^
 31. 8000 meters (E)  D     003        XXX^
 32. 8000 meters (S)  D     003        XXX^
 33. Final (E)        D     003        XXX^
 34. Final (S)        D     003        XXX^
 35. Madison (E)      D     003        XXX^
 36. Madison (S)      D     003        XXX^
 37. Sports loop (E)  D     003        XXX^
 38. Sports loop (S)  D     003        XXX^
 39. Other (E)        D     003        XXX^
 40. Other (S)        D     003        XXX^
```

FIGURE 6-25.
Rider FD (data dictionary)

```
04/18/82                    F M S - 8 0                        PAGE 1
                               SCREEN DEFINITION
                         FILE: RIDER-RE.SD          FD: RIDERS.FD
            SCREEN   LINE   COL   FUNCTION   FIELD        LITERAL

     1.       1       1     20    LITERAL      0     EVENING DATA ENT
     2.       1       1     36    LITERAL      0     RY
     3.       1       3      1    HEADER       1     Rider Number
     4.       1       3     20    COLLECT      1     Rider Number
     5.       1       3     40    HEADER       2     Class
     6.       1       3     60    DISPLAY      2     Class
     7.       1       4      1    HEADER       3     Last Name
     8.       1       4     20    DISPLAY      3     Last Name
     9.       1       4     40    HEADER       4     First Name
    10.       1       4     60    DISPLAY      4     First Name
    11.       1       5      1    HEADER       5     Place
    12.       1       5     20    DISPLAY      5     Place
    13.       1       5     40    HEADER       6     Date last race
    14.       1       5     60    DISPLAY      6     Date last race
    15.       1       6      1    HEADER       7     Race total
    16.       1       6     20    DISPLAY      7     Race total
    17.       1       6     40    HEADER       8     Season Total
    18.       1       6     60    DISPLAY      8     Season Total
    19.       1       8     20    LITERAL      0     ** EVENING TOTAL
    20.       1       8     36    LITERAL      0     S **
    21.       1      10      1    HEADER      11     Miss & Out (R)
    22.       1      10     20    COLLECT     11     Miss & Out (R)
    23.       1      11      1    HEADER      13     3 lap (R)
    24.       1      11     20    COLLECT     13     3 lap (R)
    25.       1      12      1    HEADER      15     4 lap (R)
    26.       1      12     20    COLLECT     15     4 lap (R)
    27.       1      13      1    HEADER      17     6 lap (R)
    28.       1      13     20    COLLECT     17     6 lap (R)
    29.       1      14      1    HEADER      19     6 x 1 (R)
    30.       1      14     20    COLLECT     19     6 x 1 (R)
    31.       1      15      1    HEADER      21     4 x 3 (R)
    32.       1      15     20    COLLECT     21     4 x 3 (R)
    33.       1      16      1    HEADER      23     4 x 2 (R)
    34.       1      16     20    COLLECT     23     4 x 2 (R)
    35.       1      10     40    HEADER      25     3 x 3 (R)
    36.       1      10     60    COLLECT     25     3 x 3 (R)
    37.       1      11     40    HEADER      27     3 x 2 (R)
    38.       1      11     60    COLLECT     27     3 x 2 (R)
    39.       1      12     40    HEADER      29     4000 meters (R)
    40.       1      12     60    COLLECT     29     4000 meters (R)
    41.       1      13     40    HEADER      31     8000 meters (R)
    42.       1      13     60    COLLECT     31     8000 meters (R)
    43.       1      14     40    HEADER      33     Final (R)
    44.       1      14     60    COLLECT     33     Final (R)
    45.       1      15     40    HEADER      35     Madison (R)
    46.       1      15     60    COLLECT     35     Madison (R)
    47.       1      16     40    HEADER      37     Sports loop (R)
    48.       1      16     60    COLLECT     37     Sports loop (R)
    49.       1      17     40    HEADER      39     Other (R)
    50.       1      17     60    COLLECT     39     Other (R)
```

FIGURE 6-26.
SD for rider maintenance

```
04/18/82              F M S - 8 0                      PAGE 1
                            SCREEN DEFINITION
                      FILE: RIDER-MN.SD       FD: RIDERS.FD
         SCREEN   LINE   COL    FUNCTION   FIELD      LITERAL

  1.        1      1      20    LITERAL      0     RIDER FILE MAINT
  2.        1      1      36    LITERAL      0     ENANCE
  3.        1      3       1    HEADER       1     Rider Number
  4.        1      3      20    COLLECT      1     Rider Number
  5.        1      3      40    HEADER       2     Class
  6.        1      3      60    COLLECT      2     Class
  7.        1      4       1    HEADER       3     Last Name
  8.        1      4      20    COLLECT      3     Last Name
  9.        1      4      40    HEADER       4     First Name
 10.        1      4      60    COLLECT      4     First Name
 11.        1      5       1    HEADER       5     Place
 12.        1      5      20    DISPLAY      5     Place
 13.        1      5      40    HEADER       6     Date last race
 14.        1      5      60    COLLECT      6     Date last race
 15.        1      6       1    HEADER       7     Race total
 16.        1      6      20    DISPLAY      7     Race total
 17.        1      6      40    HEADER       8     Season Total
 18.        1      6      60    DISPLAY      8     Season Total
 19.        1      8      20    LITERAL      0     ** SEASON TOTALS
 20.        1      8      36    LITERAL      0     **
 21.        1     10       1    HEADER      12     Miss & Out (S)
 22.        1     10      20    COLLECT     12     Miss & Out (S)
 23,        1     11       1    HEADER      14     3 lap (S)
 24.        1     11      20    COLLECT     14     3 lap (S)
 25.        1     12       1    HEADER      16     4 lap (S)
 26.        1     12      20    COLLECT     16     4 lap (S)
 27.        1     13       1    HEADER      18     6 lap (S)
 28.        1     13      20    COLLECT     18     6 lap (S)
 29.        1     14       1    HEADER      20     6 x 1 (S)
 30.        1     14      20    COLLECT     20     6 x 1 (S)
 31.        1     15       1    HEADER      22     4 x 3 (S)
 32.        1     15      20    COLLECT     22     4 x 3 (S)
 33.        1     16       1    HEADER      24     4 x 2 (S)
 34.        1     16      20    COLLECT     24     4 x 2 (S)
 35.        1     10      40    HEADER      26     3 x 3 (S)
 36.        1     10      60    COLLECT     26     3 x 3 (S)
 37.        1     11      40    HEADER      28     3 x 2 (S)
 38.        1     11      60    COLLECT     28     3 x 2 (S)
 39.        1     12      40    HEADER      30     4000 meters (S)
 40.        1     12      60    COLLECT     30     4000 meters (S)
 41.        1     13      40    HEADER      32     8000 meters (S)
 42.        1     13      60    COLLECT     32     8000 meters (S)
 43.        1     14      40    HEADER      34     Final (S)
 44.        1     14      60    COLLECT     34     Final (S)
 45.        1     15      40    HEADER      36     Madison (S)
 46.        1     15      60    COLLECT     36     Madison (S)
 47.        1     16      40    HEADER      38     Sports loop (S)
 48.        1     16      60    COLLECT     38     Sports loop (S)
 49.        1     17      40    HEADER      40     Other (S)
 50.        1     17      60    COLLECT     40     Other (S)
```

FIGURE 6-27.

SD for race data entry

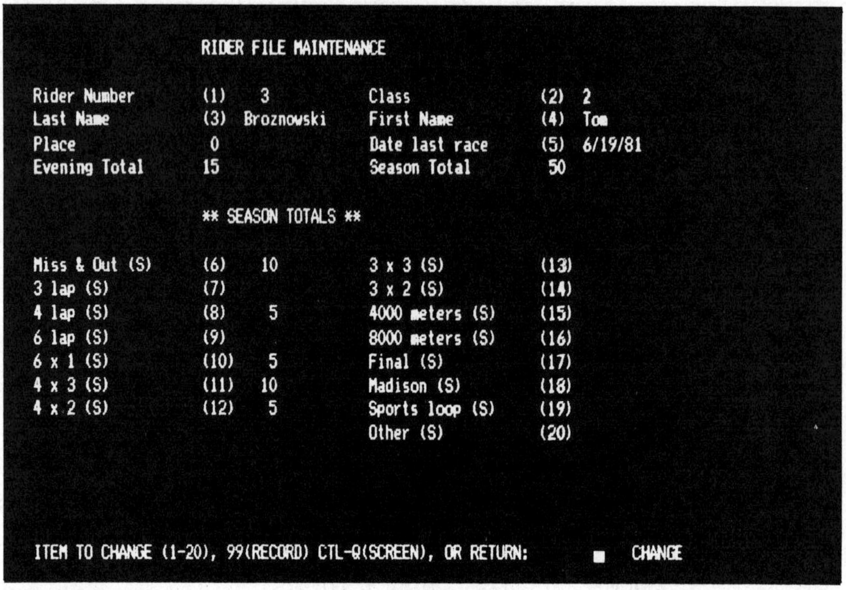

```
                RIDER FILE MAINTENANCE

Rider Number      (1)   3        Class            (2) 2
Last Name         (3)  Broznowski First Name       (4) Tom
Place              0              Date last race   (5) 6/19/81
Evening Total     15             Season Total      50

                ** SEASON TOTALS **

Miss & Out (S)    (6)   10       3 x 3 (S)        (13)
3 lap (S)         (7)            3 x 2 (S)        (14)
4 lap (S)         (8)    5       4000 meters (S)  (15)
6 lap (S)         (9)            8000 meters (S)  (16)
6 x 1 (S)         (10)   5       Final (S)        (17)
4 x 3 (S)         (11)  10       Madison (S)      (18)
4 x 2 (S)         (12)   5       Sports loop (S)  (19)
                                 Other (S)        (20)




ITEM TO CHANGE (1-20), 99(RECORD) CTL-Q(SCREEN), OR RETURN:    ■   CHANGE
```

FIGURE 6-28.
Rider maintenance
screen

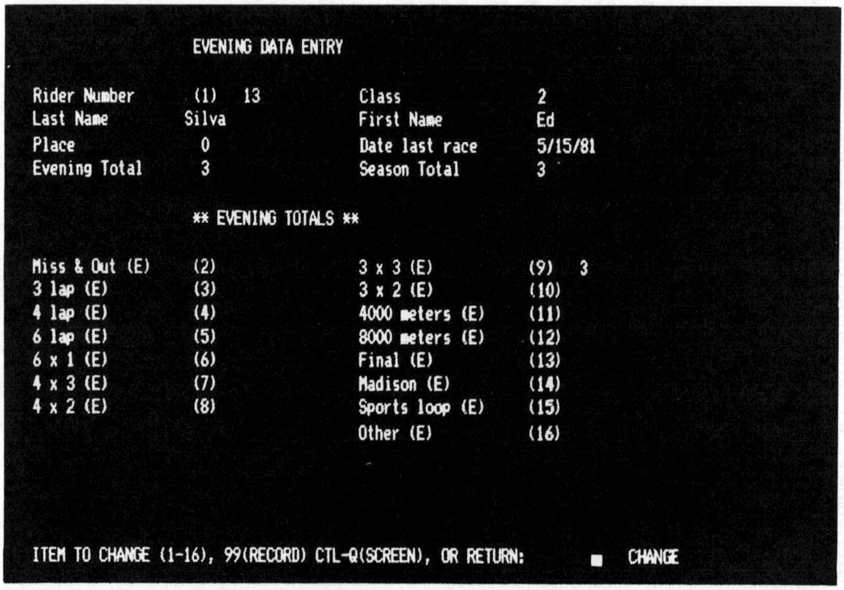

```
                EVENING DATA ENTRY

Rider Number      (1)   13       Class             2
Last Name         Silva          First Name        Ed
Place              0             Date last race    5/15/81
Evening Total      3             Season Total       3

                ** EVENING TOTALS **

Miss & Out (E)    (2)            3 x 3 (E)         (9)   3
3 lap (E)         (3)            3 x 2 (E)         (10)
4 lap (E)         (4)            4000 meters (E)   (11)
6 lap (E)         (5)            8000 meters (E)   (12)
6 x 1 (E)         (6)            Final (E)         (13)
4 x 3 (E)         (7)            Madison (E)       (14)
4 x 2 (E)         (8)            Sports loop (E)   (15)
                                 Other (E)         (16)



ITEM TO CHANGE (1-16), 99(RECORD) CTL-Q(SCREEN), OR RETURN:    ■   CHANGE
```

FIGURE 6-29.
Race data entry
screen

```
FIRST LINE: Evening Totals          R+E CYCLES TRACK STATISTICS          Date: 06/19/81
SECOND LINE: Season Totals          5627 UNIVERSITY WAY NE                      PAGE 1

num name         place last race  M/O 3lap 4lap 6lap 6x1 4x3 4x2 3x3 3x2 4K 8K Final Mad Spt L Other Total.

Class 2

  3 Tom Broznowski    0  6/19/81    5         5         5  10   5                  5               15
                                   10                           5                 15               50

  6 Lionel Space      0  6/19/81    1                                                                1
                                    2                                                  3            5

 12 Ken Meyer         0  6/19/81    7         1               3                               3      3
                                                             3                                      11

 13 Ed Silva          0  5/15/81                                     3                               3
                                                                     3                               3

 23 Bill Turina       0  6/19/81    3              3                              4                   3
                                    6                                                               13

 36 Ron Mahugh        0  5/15/81    3                                1                               4
                                    3                                1                               4

 40 Bob Stezelecki    0  5/22/81         3       2                                              2     5
                                         3       2                                                    7

 48 John Roper        0  5/22/81         2                               2                      2     2
                                         2                                                            6

 75 Steve Curry       0  6/19/81    2         1        1                       2               5      3
                                                       1                       3                     12

123 Jason Leach       0  6/19/81    1    1                                    9                 2     2
                                    6    4                                                           21
```

FIGURE 6-30.
Rider detail report.

```
04/18/82              F M S - 8 0                    PAGE 1
              R E P O R T   D E F I N I T I O N
LINES/PAGE: 66  COLS/LINE: 132  RD: RIDER.  FD: RIDERS.  TEMP FD: D:RIDERS.


  TITLES:
L+ FIRST LINE: Evening Totals
C+ R+E CYCLES TRACK STATISTICS
RH DATE %
L+ SECOND LINE: Season Totals
C+ 5627 UNIVERSITY WAY NE
RH PAGE #
LH
L+ num    name    place last race  M/O    3lap  4lap  6lap   6x1  4x3  4x2
RH 3x3  3x2  4K   8K   Final Mad Spt L  Other     Total..
LH
LF
LF
LF
LF



04/18/82              F M S - 8 0                    PAGE 2
              R E P O R T   D E F I N I T I O N
LINES/PAGE: 66  COLS/LINE: 132  RD: RIDER.  FD: RIDERS.  TEMP FD: D:RIDERS.
                              FIELD PRINTING
        LINE  COL  FUNC  FIELD  LITERAL

  1.      1    1    F      1    Rider Number      *first line
  2.      1    5    F      4    First Name
  3.      1   12    F      3    Last Name
  4.      1   26    F      5    Place
  5.      1   31    F      6    Date last race
  6.      1   41    F     11    Miss & Out (R)
  7.      1   47    F     13    3 lap (R)
  8.      1   53    F     15    4 lap (R)
  9.      1   59    F     17    6 lap (R)
 10.      1   65    F     19    6 x 1 (R)
 11.      1   70    F     21    4 x 3 (R)
 12.      1   75    F     23    4 x 2 (R)
 13.      1   80    F     25    3 x 3 (R)
 14.      1   85    F     27    3 x 2 (R)
 15.      1   90    F     29    4000 meters (R)
 16.      1   95    F     31    8000 meters (R)
 17.      1  100    F     33    Final (R)
 18.      1  105    F     35    Madison (R)
 19.      1  110    F     37    Sports loop (R)
 20.      1  116    F     39    Other (R)
 21.      1  127    F      7    Race total
 22.      2   41    F     12    Miss & Out (S)    *second line
 23.      2   47    F     14    3 lap (S)
                                              (continued)
```

FIGURE 6-31.
RD for rider detail report

```
24.      2    53   F       16   4 lap (S)
25.      2    59   F       18   6 lap (S)
26.      2    65   F       20   6 x 1 (S)
27.      2    70   F       22   4 x 3 (S)
28.      2    75   F       24   4 x 2 (S)
29.      2    80   F       26   3 x 3 (S)
30.      2    85   F       28   3 x 2 (S)
31.      2    90   F       30   4000 meters (S)
32.      2    95   F       32   8000 meters (S)
33.      2   100   F       34   Final (S)
34.      2   105   F       36   Madison (S)
35.      2   110   F       38   Sports loop (S)
36.      2   116   F       40   Other (S)
37,      2   127   F        8   Season Total
38.      3     1   L        0                    *skip a line


04/18/82              F M S - 8 0                    PAGE 3
                 R E P O R T   D E F I N I T I O N
LINES/PAGE: 66  COLS/LINE: 132  RD: RIDER.  FD: RIDERS.  TEMP FD: D:RIDERS.
                            FIELD BREAK
     FUNC  BREAK  DEST  SOURCE  LINE  COL  LITERAL

1.    P      2     0      2      0    0            *new page on new class
2.    H      2     0      2C     1    1   Class    *print caption
3.    F      2     0      2C     1    7   Class    *print class number
4.    L      2     0      0C     2    1            *blank line
```

FIGURE 6-31.
RD for rider detail report (continued)

produced the following:

File Definition
Rider number control file
Two Screen Definitions
Standard update procedure
Class/rider control file
Detail report
Custom menu

This minimum working system will accept data and print reports, all controlled by the custom menu. There are a few missing pieces however. Remember that the evening race totals must be added to the season totals. This is called *posting* in data processing terminology and is used in updating general ledger accounts from transactions. Unlike some file management systems, this package has no automatic posting feature; you must use EFM. The Report Generator for FMS-80 won't handle the rider summary report shown in Figure 6-35, and the end-of-season cleanup and the rider total recompute reports are both difficult.

The following four EFM programs are necessary for the bicycle track system (the figure references are to figures in Appendix B):

End-of-season cleanup	Figure B-1
Rider total recompute	Figure B-2
Rider update	Figure B-3
Summary report	Figure B-4

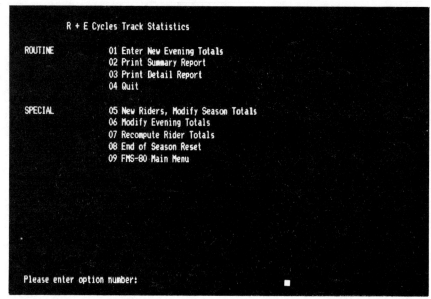

FIGURE 6-32.

Track system
main menu

Look ahead to these figures in the Appendixes to see the complexity of these programs. The next section explains how they work. If you aren't a programmer, you may not be interested; however, you should understand how posting works. For example, when Brosnowski races, his event points are added to his season points. If he didn't participate, the event points remain from his last race. Because the points are only posted for riders who actually race, the "update totals" program must be transaction-driven. A file of transactions containing event points is created, one record for each participating rider. The EFM program sequentially processes this transaction file and does the following for each record:

· Looks up the rider record in the rider data file by matching the rider number in the index

· Adds each event point count from the transaction record to the corresponding rider season

total in the rider record (this is posting)

· Adds all the event points in the rider record, storing the sum in the rider evening total

· Adds all the season totals in the rider record, storing the sum in the rider season total.

File Restructure Program

You have seen *what* EFM does; now you will find out *how* it does it. The simplest, most useful EFM program adds a new field to an existing data file by creating a new file with an extra slot. Go back to the job cost system for a minute. If you need a new field, HOURS, in the job transaction file and if you want it between Vendor/Employee and Amount, you write and run the EFM program shown on the following page. This program copies the JOB.DAT file into the JOBHOURS.DAT file, adding the new field. It also creates a new FD, JOBHOURS.FD, from information you supply in the "output" statement.

```
/* RESTRUCT.EFM adds a new field to JOB.DAT */
''Hours'',d,4,'XX.X'/* Define the new
   field */
input(JOB, JOB) /* old file */
output(JOBHOURS: 1,1 1,2 1,3 1,4 1,5 1,6 1,
   7 0,
1 1,8) /* new file /*
2,(1-7) = 1,(1-7);/* Copy fields 1
   through 7 */
2,8 = 0;/* Set new Hours field (8) to 0 */
2,9 = 1,8;/* Copy the Amount field*/
write 2;
end;
```

It is not like languages you've seen before. The semicolons and "/ ∗∗ /" comment delimiters are from C and PL/I, but that's where the similarity ends. Two important features shown here are concise field references and automatic record looping. There is no READ statement or end-of-file test because that's done automatically; the program processes each record in the file and stops when it's done. The fields are referenced by number: "2,9" is field 9, Amount, in file 2, the output file; "1,(1-7)" means fields 1 through 7 in file 1, the input file. Field "0,1" is a working variable defined earlier as a decimal number four digits long.

	FUNCTION	LINE	COL	OPTION	PROGRAM/BATCH FILE/MENU	
04/18/82		F M S - 8 0				PAGE 1
			MENU DEFINITION			
			FILE: MASTER.MD			
1.	TEXT	01	20		R + E	Cycles Track Statistics
2.	TEXT	01	40			
3.	TEXT	03	10		ROUTINE	
4.	BATCH FILE	03	30	01	RIDERUPD	Enter New Evening Totals
5.	TEXT	03	54			
6.	PROGRAM	04	30	02	DO RIDERSUM	Print Summary Report
7.	PROGRAM	05	30	03	REPORT RIDER.RD RIDERCLN.IDX	Print Detail Report
8.	PROGRAM	06	30	04	QUIT	Quit
9.	TEXT	08	10		SPECIAL	
10.	BATCH FILE	08	30	05	RIDERMOD	New Riders, Modify Season Totals
11.	TEXT	08	54			
12.	PROGRAM	09	30	06	QUERY RIDERS.IDX RIDER-RE.IDX	Modify Evening Totals
13.	TEXT	09	54			
14.	PROGRAM	10	30	07	DO RIDERCMP	Recompute Rider Totals
15.	TEXT	10	54			
16.	PROGRAM	11	30	08	DO RIDERZER	End of Season Reset
17.	PROGRAM	12	30	09	FMS80	FMS-80 Main Menu

FIGURE 6-33.
MD for the main menu

```
/* RIDERUPD.SUB
 *    batch file to update race transactions to rider master
 */
TRANSACT RIDERS.FD RIDER-RE.SD    /* enter transactions */
DO RIDERUPD                       /* EFM update program (Fig B-4) */
ERA D:RIDERS.TRX                  /* delete used transaction file */
INDEX RIDERCLR RIDERS             /* rebuild class/rank index */
SORT RIDERCLR.IDX


/* RIDERMOD.SUB
 *    batch file to add/change/delete rider master records
 */
TRANSACT RIDERS.FD RIDER-MN.SD    /* enter transactions */
APPLY RIDERS.FD                   /* standard FMS-80 update */
DO RIDERCMP                       /* EFM program to recompute totals (Fig B-3)
                                     */INDEX RIDERCLN RIDERS/* rebuild
                                     class/rider# index */
SORT RIDERCLN.IDX
INDEX RIDERCLR RIDERS             /* rebuild class/rank index */
SORT RIDERCLR.IDX
```

FIGURE 6-34.
Batch files referenced
from main menu

End-of-Season Total Zero Program

Figure B-1 in Appendix B shows a more complicated program used in the bicycle track system to return a rider's points to zero at season's end. Here the automatic record looping is turned off because EFM can't be used to update in place, rewriting the record it just read sequentially. Instead a classical loop is programmed around the "nread" and "rewrite" statements. The statement "nread" gets the next record from the rider data file, and fields 7 through 40 are set to zero. Next, the "rewrite" statement writes it back to disk. The rest of the program makes sure that the operator really wants to make all the totals zero.

Two features you will notice in this program are the "if, endif" construct and cursor-addressed data entry. The "if" statements allow the relational tests = (equal), ! = (not equal), > (greater than), and < (less than), but they don't allow >= (greater than or equal to) or < = (less than or equal to). Any number of statements can be grouped together for conditional execution, but nested "if's" are not allowed. An "else" clause is allowed, however. The cursor is positioned with the "curse" command, specifying row and column numbers. The "enter" command ("enteru" for upper-case conversion) gets data from the keyboard. The one-character, alphanumeric field "0,1" is entered here. Working variables are these file-zero fields which must be set up at the start of the program. In addition, the letters "A" through "Z" may be used as numeric variables.

Update Program

Figure B-2 in Appendix B shows the update program for posting race points to season totals.

Here there are two files: File 1 is the transaction file with race points, and file 2 is a data file with season totals. The program automatically reads each transaction record, then looks up the rider record with the "kread" statement. Next there's a loop which steps through all 14 events, adding the race points to the season total and totaling evening and season points by rider. Afterward, the rider record is written back to disk with the "rewrite" statement. "W" and "V" are numeric variables used as "subscripts" to identify fields. Notice that EFM has no "do while" or "for-next" constructions; all

```
                              R+E CYCLE TRACK STATISTICS                    DATE 06/19/81
                                5627 UNIVERSITY WAY NE                            PAGE 1

  TOP TEN IN THE II CLASS

  rider number    name          season points

  NO. 1     3  Tom    Broznowski    50
  NO. 2   123  Jason  Leach         21
  NO. 3    23  Bill   Turina        13
  NO. 4    75  Steve  Curry         12
  NO. 5    12  Ken    Meyer         11
  NO. 6    40  Bob    Stezelecki     7
  NO. 7    48  John   Roper          6
  NO. 8     6  Lionel Space          5
  NO. 9    36  Ron    Mahugh         4
  NO. 10   13  Ed     Silva          3

  EVENT                    FIRST                  SECOND                 THIRD

  Miss & Out (S)   Tom    Broznowski  10   Ken   Meyer       7   Jason  Leach       6

  3 lap (S)

  4 lap (S)        Tom    Broznowski   5   Jason Leach       4   Steve  Curry       2

  6 lap (S)

  6 x 1 (S)        Tom    Broznowski   5   Bob   Stezelecki  3   John   Roper       2

  4 x 3 (S)        Tom    Broznowski  10   Bill  Turina      3   Bob    Stezelecki  2

  4 x 2 (S)        Tom    Broznowski   5   Ken   Meyer       3   Steve  Curry       1

  3 x 3 (S)        Ed     Silva        3   John  Roper       2   Ron    Mahugh      1

  3 x 2 (S)        Jason  Leach        9

  4000 meters (S)
```

FIGURE 6-35.
Rider summary report

repetitive execution must be done with loops. There is only one arithmetic operation allowed per statement, so "X = (A+B)/C" becomes "X = A+B; X = X/C."

Report Program

This last sample program, shown in Figure B-4 in Appendix B, prints the rider summary report shown in Figure 6-35. It is structured into a main module and four submodules accessed by "call" statements. Each record of the rider file is sorted by class and season totals and read in the nonautomatic mode. Auto mode doesn't work here because there is no way to gain control for the last summary at the end of the job. The top ten riders in each class are routed to "printline" and all are sent to "tablestore" for accumulation. "Tableprint" is called from "heading," and at end-of-file it prints the first-, second-, and third-place summary for each class.

There is a 90-entry table defined at the top of the program for storage of the first-, second-, and third-place totals. This is equivalent to the BASIC statement

```
DIM RIDER(3,15),STOTAL(3,15)
```

The table is a one-dimensional array of three-digit numbers, with Rider Number and season Event Total stored by rank. Just before "tableprint" prints the table, it uses Rider Number to look up Rider Name from the file. The rider file is really one file, but the program looks at it through two indexes—the class/total index (file 1) and the rider number index (file 2).

In the "heading" module, notice the "print" statements which allow tabbing to print positions with the "at" clause. A new line results from a "print" with no "at." The statement "print at(1) h(1,W)" prints the field heading from the FD starting in column 1. This means the event titles (Miss & Out, and so on) aren't "hard coded" into the report. If the event name changes, changing the FD will ensure an accurate summary but not a detailed report.

Look at the "case" statement which selects the proper title for each class. This will often make up for the lack of a nested "if."

Additional EFM Features

It is possible to use EFM for data entry programs which outperform the FMS-81 transaction entry and query functions. In the bicycle track system, a single EFM program could have handled race data entry and added the event points directly to the rider season totals. This would have meant extra programming and increased the risk of duplicate entries. If you need to validate data on entry, EFM would allow a quick file lookup. In an invoice entry application, for example, you could program a lookup to the Customer file, bringing information about names and addresses into the invoice.

EFM allows access to the shell (see Chapter 4). You can redirect the program's input, allowing a disk file to supply the equivalent of keystrokes. You can even execute another program with control returning to the point of call. This is a slow process because the calling program is "swapped" out to disk and restored after the called program exits.

A recently released version of the EFM Compiler allows nested "ifs," named file and field references, and more.

CP/M File Summary

The following are the CP/M files for the bicycle track example. The list includes the EFM source and object files.

RIDERS.FD
  File Definition

RIDERS.CTL
  Control file—rider number is key

RIDERCLN.CTL
  Control file—class/rider is key

RIDERCLR.CTL
  Control file—class/rank is key

RIDERS.TRX
  Transaction file—temporary during updates

RIDERS.REJ
  Reject file—unmatched rider numbers, duplicates

RIDERS.DAT
  Rider data file

RIDERS.IDX
  Index on rider number

RIDERCLN.IDX
  Index on class/rider

RIDERCLR.IDX
  Index on class/rank

RIDER.RD
  Report Definition

RIDER-RE.SD
  Screen Definition—race data entry

RIDER-MN.SD
  Screen Definition—maintenance

RIDERZER.EFM
  Source code—end-of-season zero

RIDERCMP.EFM
  Source code—total recompute

RIDERUPD.EFM
  Source code—update

RIDERSUM.EFM
  Source code—summary report

RIDERZER.E
  Object code—end-of-season zero

RIDERCMP.E
  Object code—total recompute

RIDERUPD.E
  Object code—update

RIDERSUM.E
  Object code—summary report

RIDERMOD.SUB
  Batch file—add/change/delete

RIDERUPD.SUB
  Batch file—update race transactions

MASTER.MD
  Main menu

SYSTEM NOTES

Transfer to or from Non-FMS-80 Files

There is no explicit way to read or write non-FMS-80 files. However, FMS-80 files are simply structured and can be read from and written to by other programs with some restrictions. The FMS-80 records are fixed-length ASCII records without delimiters or CARRIAGE RETURN or LINE FEED. COBOL and PL/I programs should have no trouble with them, and Microsoft BASIC fielded records are permissible if they don't contain binary numbers. Other BASIC files (including CBASIC2) with commas and quotes that delimit the fields are incompatible. CBASIC2 can communicate with FMS-80 if you define a CARRIAGE RETURN/ LINE FEED at the end of the FMS-80 record. Your CBASIC program must output one string per record using the "&" format, and it must read with a READ LINE statement. The program has to "field" the input/output string itself, using string concatenations and the "$MID" function.

Because FMS-80 files can be read directly by other programs, there is no time delay for file conversion. Non-FMS-80 programs can be called directly from FMS-80 menus and batch files, and this gives you some flexiblity. You could, for instance, link in a BASIC program to compute means and standard deviations on some data accumulated in update function or FMS-80.

Documentation

DJR Associates provides a 325-page FMS-80 manual that documents both FMS-81 and FMS-82. The manual is organized in three parts of almost equal length—tutorial, reference, and appendixes. The tutorial section was recently rewritten and appears in a neatly typeset 64-page handbook called the *FMS-80 Primer*. The manual's tutorial and only use the primer, are essentially the same.

Tutorial

Like all DBMS manuals, this one presents an "Introduction to CP/M," but this section isn't strong enough to substitute for a thorough study of CP/M. After this introduction, the manual introduces you to configuration (more on that later) and alteration of LOCATE.SYS. If you are not a CP/M expert, you will need your dealer's help. Save this part of the manual as a reference.

The tutorial assumes you have a computer and uses a sales analysis problem with the following defined fields:

Transaction Number
Department
Salesman
Item code
Quantity
Price

With the tutorial you practice FD entry, control definition, update, and selection definition. You use the report generator to make two reports—one a simple listing and the other a single, subtotal problem similar to the report shown in Figure 6-13. The tutorial that comes with the system (especially in the report genera-

tor section) really does take you by the hand, capitalizing on the "learn by doing" principle.

The manual concludes with an introduction to EFM, starting with a "Hello, world" example—a program written solely to print those words on the screen. The EFM section concludes with an interactive selection example—a program allowing the operator to write out selected fields from a file, display the first three fields, and permit modification of the last field.

Absent from the tutorial are lessons on Screen Definition and Menu Definition. Because these are similar to File Definition, there really isn't a need for further explanation.

Reference

The reference section starts with a five-page "road map" that associates functions like "Create Screen Definition" with commands (EDITSD, SDPRINT). You find the command names in a road map and then look them up in a reference section. Also included with the road map are listings of the FMS-80 menus, similar to that found in Figure 6-1 of this book. These menu listings associate the command names with the option numbers.

Each of the 36 commands is explained in the main reference section. Command titles are written in boldface at the top of the page, making lookups easy. You soon learn the functions of each and wean yourself from the road map.

An EFM reference section continues where the EFM tutorial left off. Each feature of EFM is described, including input/output, data types, execution sequence, and individual statements. The following is an example of the EFM reference section:

CURSE STATEMENT
Form: curse <line>,<column>;
   (both are rvalues)

<line> and <column> are converted to numbers, and the cursor is positioned to that line and column.

Excerpted from FMS-80 File Management System User's Manual, copyright © 1978 DJR Associates.

Next some EFM program examples are given, including a multi-index inquiry/direct update application. The reference concludes with a "SHELL-80 Interface Guide for EFM Programmers," a listing of EFM error messages, and an EFM summary.

A complete index covers both the tutorial and the reference.

The manual concludes with the following appendixes:

A. FMS-80 error messages
B. Extension Summary
C. Application Note #1 — Indexes
   Application Note #2 — Updates
   Application Note #3 — Spaces
D. The FMS-80 Report Generator with examples included.

Some final pages show notes for users of previous FMS-80 versions.

Support

Support is just a long-distance telephone call away (a local call if you live in Palo Alto). Expect your call to be returned within 24 hours by a courteous and knowledgeable person who will answer your questions.

Configuration

FMS-80 is shipped with a number of terminal-specific disk files supporting the following terminals:

ADDS 200
Micro-Term ACT IV,V
Lear Seigler ADM-3A
Beehive B150
Datapoint 3000
Hazeltine 1420,1500
Soroc IQ-120
Imsai VIO-C
Intertec Intertube
Televideo
DIRECT
Vector Memory-mapped

If you have an ADM-3A terminal, for example, you type REN PARM.SYS = ADM3A.PRM and you're ready to go. You do this once and FMS-80 always remembers which terminal you have. All terminal modules are set up for a two-drive system, preventing you from referencing drive C:, D:, and so on. This is a handy feature that eliminates CP/M errors from miskeyed entries. If you have more than two drives, you run a program called DISPARM which reconfigures FMS-80 for three, four, or more drives.

The DISPARM module allows you to configure for a terminal other than those listed above. You are prompted to enter cursor addressing sequences, screen clear codes, and so on, but this is a job better suited for your dealer.

Using LOCATE.SYS

If you have a two-drive diskette computer, you probably want all your data files on the B: drive. With a hard disk, you may want them on the C:, D:, or E: drives. Because it's a waste of time to qualify each file with the drive name, FMS-80 stores drive configuration data on a special file called LOCATE.SYS with each file type (.FD, .CTL, and so on) linked to a drive name. In addition, LOCATE.SYS maintains the specifications on the following items:

Date format (mm/dd/yy or dd/mm/yy)
Print spacing (single or double)

Page width (80 to 132 columns)

Page length (33 to 112 lines)

Transaction print option

Diskette mount messages

Index sort option

Sort output naming

Print output to video screen or printer

Duplicate key option

There is a special interactive utility program, written in EFM, which lets you maintain the LOCATE.SYS file. It is difficult, however, to invoke this program while operating FMS-80. If you need to switch print output between the printer and the video screen, make two files, LOCATE.PRN and LOCATE.SCR, and copy these into LOCATE.SYS as needed. The job cost user menu (Figure 6-24) does exactly that.

Error Handling

An extremely stable system, FMS-80 is difficult to crash. The only error you may encounter is a DISK FULL condition which terminates the job. The ^C or BREAK key is trapped, causing an ABORT? prompt on the screen's lower right. If you answer "N," program execution continues; if you answer "Y," the job in process is terminated with control returned to the appropriate FMS-80 menu.

One problem was observed when the record size was pushed above 10,000 characters—the sort died without warning.

EFM has its own set of fully documented error messages. Compiling (PREPARE) produces one set of messages and execution (DO) produces another. Occasionally something slips through the the compiler such as "1,(1,7)" instead of "1,(1-7)" and causes an execution crash, but this is rare. Of course you can program an infinite loop in EFM, just as in any other language.

Technical Information

FMS-80 uses a shell, as described in Chapter 4. You can run non-FMS-80 programs in the FMS-80 environment, but these programs have about 5K less available memory than under straight CP/M. Each FMS-80 module, such as the REPORT program or the MAIN MENU, gets loaded into low memory by the shell, which is located in high memory. Each program module is totally self-contained and must open its files on startup. Consequently there is a 10-second time delay as each program, menus included, is loaded.

Because FMS-80 modules are self-contained, you can run them directly from CP/M without the shell, saving yourself all the menu overhead during system development. Thus you have a command-driven system similar to Condor and dBASE II. However, this system isn't recommended for beginners.

Data is stored in files in the simplest way possible. Fixed-length records are ASCII-coded without delimiters. There is no way to tell how many records a file contains. Variable-length records are allowed, with one variable-length field last in the record. These records are delimited, and no indexing is permitted.

As mentioned before, the "indexes" of FMS-80 are really pointer files with a header linking them to the FD. On transaction entry and QUERY/UPDATE, the program does a binary search through this pointer file. This works well until the pointer file no longer fits into memory, then the process slows down. See the following performance section for details.

FMS-80 tries to make you keep data files in primary key order by leading you through the update procedure similar to a merge. Since you must have a separate index for querying, it seems unnecessary to add the merge time to the already long indexing time. It is better to

APPEND the transactions to the file's end, regardless of key order, since the index always reorganizes in proper sequence.

When you sort a file or index, FMS-80 selects either an internal, in-memory sort or a disk sort/merge, depending on the file size. It is unclear what algorithm is used, but the execution times are reasonable.

Performance

Benchmark

1635 records, 151 characters each, 5-digit key

Floppy Disk:

Index build (5:45)
Sort Index(3:20)
Index setup (0:20 10-second program load, 10-second setup)
Indexed access (1 to 2 seconds)
Sequential Pass (4:50)

Hard Disk:

Index build (3:45)
Sort Index(3:00)
Index setup (0:05)
Indexed access (½ second)
Sequential Pass (3:30)

Benchmark

20,216 records, 22 characters each, 18-character key

Hard Disk:

Index build (19:00)
Sort Index (Index was already sorted)
Index setup (4:30)
Indexed access (20 seconds)
Sequential Pass (8:00)

Carefully review the index build and sort times and remember you need to recreate all indexes after each addition to a file. With the 1635-record, floppy-based system you must wait nine minutes for each index—an acceptable time if these updates are infrequent.

FMS-80 is not acceptable for the 20,216-record file. The 4 1/2-minute index setup time prior to each query session is a problem as is the 20-second access time. It appears that the slowdown starts when the index becomes larger than available memory.

Restrictions

The limits of 255 characters per field and 255 fields per record are generous, but don't forget that one record of 255 255-character fields would use up your entire 64K of memory. The practical limit for record size in a 64K system is about 10,000 characters, a size large enough for most applications.

If you wish to modify data using the key "Smith," there may be a problem if there are several Smiths in the file. Transaction processing requires a unique key in each record in order to use FMS-80. If your application doesn't have natural, unique identifiers like part number, customer number, and so on, you must invent them. You can avoid this restriction by writing an interactive file update program using EFM or by changing records only through query.

If you were using FMS-80 to enter a payables entry with vendor verification and you encountered an invoice for a new vendor, you would have to either put that one aside, or do the entire vendor update procedure, a task which could take 15 minutes. FMS-80 is clearly not good for files that need a quick update.

For data entry, you can use a screen formatted through the Screen Definition procedure, or you can write an EFM program. If you need to look up the vendor number as it is keyed into an invoice form, you must do it all in EFM.

Security

FMS-80 has no security features *per se*, but you can easily build a very secure system if you eliminate paths to the FMS-80 menus from your own custom menus. To be safe, you can even eliminate modules like REPORT from working disks. If you access files through Screen Definitions, you can make certain fields invisible. You can create a special password file and have EFM check it against an operator's entered password.

FMS-80 MENU SUMMARY

File Definition

· Enter and print data dictionary
· Define and print sort/access keys
· Define and print record or field selection criteria
· Define and print report definitions
· Compile an EFM program
· Define and print custom menu

File Maintenance

· Update a file by merging or appending transactions
· Generate a new data dictionary and file with a subset of the original fields
· Sort a file or index
· Run an EFM program

· Build a multikey index on a whole file or on selected records

File Reports

· Print a file using optional selection criteria within an automatic format
· Count occurrences of selected records
· Print an already defined report
· Direct query or update by key

Utilities

· File directory
· Delete file
· Rename file

7

MDBS III from
Micro Data Base Systems

ake a moment to stir up the alphabet
soup, and see what floats to the top.

- *DBMS (Data Base Management System)*. A software package.
- *MDBS (Micro Data Base Systems, Inc.)*. The name of a software development company.
- *ISE (International Software Enterprises, Inc.)*. A software distributor and corporate relation of MDBS.
- *MDBS III*. The principle product of MDBS—a particular data base management system.
- *NDBMS (Network/Hierarchical Data Base Management System)*. The generic term used in this book. MDBS III is the leading NDBMS for microcomputers.
- *RDBMS (Relational Data Base Management System)*. Not the same system as NDBMS.

If you're a programmer fearing that data base management systems will eliminate your job, worry no more. MDBS III is a *programmer's DBMS* that demands every bit of your skill. If you aren't a programmer, prospective programmer, or manager of programmers, this

chapter may be too technical for you. While MDBS III may meet your needs, you will require the services of a programmer to evaluate and implement it. For this reason programs for this chapter are included in the text, rather than in a separate appendix. This DBMS is entirely different from the FMS and RDBMS because it doesn't claim to be "user friendly." It's a tool for experienced applications program developers—classified as a Network/Hierarchical Data Base Management System (NDBMS), but technically an *extended network* system.

Micro Data Base Systems' advertising claims it has the only real microcomputer DBMS, and that's true according to the strict definition for large systems. That definition excludes the microcomputer RDBMS because its databases are too much like files. However, it doesn't stop those packages from being useful, and indeed they do meet *most* of the DBMS criteria summarized in Chapter 1. Both the NDBMS and the RDBMS can be used to set up complex applications, and each has its own distinct advantages. MDBS III is ideal for difficult business and scientific problems with intricate relationships between data items. As illustrated by the simple NDBMS wine example in Chap-

167

SYSTEM OVERVIEW

DBMS Checklist

☒ Data Dictionary
  Specified with Data Definition Language (DDL)

☒ Query Facility
  With add-on Query Retrieval System (QRS)

☒ Report Generator
  QRS performs this function, but only minimally

☒ File Compatibility
  Reads and writes to or from any file

☐ Restructure Capability
  To be released later

☒ Effective Error Handling
  Programmer responsibility

☒ Documentation and Support
  Excellent

☒ Multiple Files
  Data base is one physical file with multifile function

☐ Full-Screen Editing
  Must be user programmed; screen handler to be released

☐ On-Screen Display Format

☒ Password Security
  Very comprehensive

☒ Multiuser Capability
  With multiuser operating systems

☐ Menu-driven

☒ Program-driven
  Host language communicates through CALLs or function invocations

☒ Command-driven
  Only with add-on Interactive Data Manipulation Language (IDML)

☐ Built-in Language

☒ Established Language
  BASIC, COBOL, FORTRAN, PL/I, Pascal, C, and Assembler used as host language

☒ Access Time
  One-half second, 1 of 1685 records, hard disk

☒ Processing Speed
  Runs 280 records per minute, hard disk very dependent on available memory, disk hardware, and data base design

☐ Data Access Method
  Virtual memory, with data items grouped into records connected invisibly using the *set* construct with modified B^+-*trees* and *hashing* for quick access

Price (10/82)

	8-Bit CP/M Version (Single User)	16-Bit Unix/ Xenix Versions (Multiuser)
DDL/DMS (minimum system)	$2250	$6675
QRS (Query/Retrieval)	1125	2500
RTL/RCV (Transaction Logging, Recovery)	2225	3350
IDML (Interactive Data Manipulation)	900	2000
DMU (password update, space statistics)	1150	1700
Three-day training seminar	850	850
Total (includes 15% 6-module discount)	7225	14,513
Total (minimum useful system, excluding RTL/RCV and training — 10% discount)	4,882	11,588
Each added language interface	450	725
Annual service and maintenance: free for first year, 15% of current price thereafter		

NOTE: Multiuser prices vary depending on operating systems and number of users.

SYSTEM OVERVIEW (Continued)

Developer

Micro Data Base Systems, Inc.
Box 248
Lafayette, IN 47902
(317) 448-1616

Distributor

ISE-USA
85 West Algonquin Road
Arlington Heights, IL 60005
(312) 577-6800
(800)323-3629

System Requirements

The MDBS III as described in this chapter runs on a Z-80 microcomputer under CP/M. There is an 8080/8085 CP/M version plus other 8-bit versions for MP/M and Radio Shack TRSDOS. Versions with 16 bits run on 8086/8088 and PDP-11 processors, and a version for the 68000 chip is forthcoming. Multiuser versions are available for multiuser operating systems. The following are requirements for 8-bit CP/M versions:

· Z-80 or 8080/8085 microprocessor system

· The CP/M or MP/M operating system

· 64K bytes of memory

· Two or more disk drives, each with a capacity of 500K bytes or more

· A 24 × 80-character video display

Specifications for 8-Bit CP/M Systems

The following are MDBS III specifications for 8-bit CP/M systems. CP/M and the usual 64K of available memory impose additional constraints.

Data record size	65,524 bytes
Data item size	
Character	65,535 bytes
String (variable length, compressed)	250 bytes
Binary (variable length)	65,535 bytes
Real	16 bytes
Internal decimal	130 bytes
Time (compressed)	3 bytes
Date (compressed)	2 bytes
Unsigned integer	16 bytes
Integer	16 bytes
Data items per record type	65,535
Record types per data base	255
Sets per data base	no limit
Sort fields per set	no limit
Disk files per data base	16
Record occurrences per data base	limited by disk storage
Disk storage per data base	4.2 billion bytes
Simultaneous users	1

ter 2, extensive advance planning is necessary before programming begins. Once you've designed the schema and written the programs, changing the system is difficult.

The cost alone of an MDBS III requires that it be used for more meaningful tasks than Christmas lists or simple sorting. Indeed, the $4882 initial cost for a minimum system is more expensive than that of most microcomputers. Perhaps this is a sneak preview of the brave new world where software costs more than hardware. An *applications developer* planning to sell several hundred copies of a system would pay the $4882 plus a royalty depending on quantity and include MDBS III components. If the royalty were $400 per unit and 100 systems were sold at $4000, the total MDBS III costs would be $44,882, more than most programmers' annual salaries, but only 11 percent of the total gross. If the application is complex enough, MDBS III might actually save some-one a year of labor, bring the product to market earlier, and impress prospective clients by being state-of-the-art software.

The economics are different if MDBS III is being used to develop a single, in house system. If a compiler plus programming cost $7000, the total software cost is about $12,000. Only a diligent systems analysis will determine whether the cost is worth the benefits. You must always ask whether a $500 or a $1000 FMS or RDBMS will be sufficient for the job.

MDBS III is usually worth its price because it lets you create applications not possible with conventional programming techniques. It actually expands the potential of the micro-computer, but not without a certain amount of pain. It will take up to a month just to learn the basics—to get a simple system up and running—and it will take much longer to unlock the package's real power. Micro Data Base Systems points out that its product is easier to learn than many large-computer data base management systems and that their three-day training course gives participants a sub-stantial head start.

If you're used to interpretive BASIC, you have some more learning to do. There isn't room in an 8-bit single-user system for MDBS III to coexist with an interpreter. You will need a *compiler* such as Microsoft BASCOM, FORTRAN, COBOL, PL/I, CB-80, C, or any widely used Pascal.

A great attraction of MDBS III is its *trans-portability* among various machines. If you develop programs on a Z-80 you can run them on a 68000, assuming the host language also transports. The 16-bit processors allow for true multiuser operations, and MDBS provides the necessary record locking and reentrancy, as described in Chapter 3. In addition, the extra memory space available with the new 16-bit

chips should make programs run 10 or more times faster. You could almost say MDBS III was made for 16 bits; using it on an 8-bit machine should be a temporary measure, giving you a head start in developing your new, multiuser software. Eight-bit, multiple CPU networks offer some possibilities with a version of MDBS III scheduled for the Turbodos oper-ating system.

The bulk of this chapter is devoted to two examples. The first is a parts catalog and order history system, not really complex enough to deserve MDBS III. It's in the book because it's easy to understand and lets you compare the MDBS III approach with the conventional approach. The second example is a fragment from a real commercial software package built around a data base. Hundreds of people are pounding away on that system while you read this.

PARTS CATALOG

This is almost an inventory problem, which details a shop that sells about two thousand different parts and needs an up-to-date mail-order catalog plus reports listing previous orders by part and by vendor. Quantity on hand is entered only during physical inventory and is not updated daily. This MDBS III sys-tem was derived from a real working system written in dBASE II which, in turn, was origi-nally written using Pearl Level 2 (see Chapter 8). The shop is a bicycle shop, but the parts system analysis could equally apply to auto parts, electronic components, and so on.

Similar systems running with both an RDBMS and an NDBMS provide a unique opportunity to make comparisons. While the parts system analysis is too simple to justify the use of MDBS III, it serves well as a beginning example.

The parts system currently running under dBASE II performs the following steps:

1. Prints a well formatted mail-order catalog for selected parts.

2. Prints reports for other selection criteria, such as out-of-stock parts or tools.

3. Prints the order report for all parts, showing the last three orders with date, vendor, and cost.

4. Allows entry of new parts and updating of existing ones.

5. Supports a function called carding. When new orders are entered, the operator updates the selling price, entering the new information based on order cost and percentage of markup.

The dBASE II system was built using one major database, PARTS, with the data dictionary shown in Figure 7-1. Another small database holds vendor names. Figure 7-1 shows three occurrences each of DATE, VENDOR, QUANTITY, and COST, implying that there is room for only three orders. If three orders have

FLD	NAME	TYPE	WIDTH	DEC
001	NUM1	C	002	
002	NUM2	C	003	
003	FLAG1	L	001	
004	MAJORPRT	L	001	
005	CATALOGE	L	001	
006	TANDEM	L	001	
007	TOOL	L	001	
008	OUT	L	001	
009	EMERG	L	001	
010	FLAG8	L	001	
011	MANU	C	010	
012	DESCRI	C	030	
013	PRICE	N	007	002
014	MARKUP	N	002	
015	DATE1	N	006	
016	VENDOR1	N	002	
017	QUANT1	N	004	
018	COST1	N	007	002
019	DATE2	N	006	
020	VENDOR2	N	002	
021	QUANT2	N	004	
022	COST2	N	007	002
023	DATE3	N	006	
024	VENDOR3	N	002	
025	QUANT3	N	004	
026	COST3	N	007	002
027	MAN:NUM	C	010	
028	YTD:PARTS	N	004	
029	YTD:DOL	N	007	002
030	INVENT	N	004	
031	SPARE	N	005	
** TOTAL **			00150	

FIGURE 7-1. Original dBASE II parts data dictionary

been recorded, a fourth order causes the stack to be "pushed," thereby dropping the oldest order. There are eight select flags, which may be used individually or in combination to print the catalog, the out-of-stock list, or other reports. Parts are indexed by the two-field part number, NUM1 and NUM2. All in all, it is a straightforward application, ideal for a relational data base.

There are a few things the parts system can't do in this relational form. Because the database is not in *normal form* (it has multiple order "subrecords"), it can't provide a list of all orders *by vendor*. Also, to select every report, the RDBMS must make a sequential pass of all the part records. The new MDBS III system plugs the holes, allowing orders-by-vendor reports and quick access to selected records.

Schema Design

MDBS III is based on records and sets as described in a data base *schema*. There are no files except for one big file containing the data base itself; although records are used, fields become data items. Chapter 2 explains what sets and schemas are all about, so this may be a good time to review the section on Network/ Hierarchical Data Base Systems.

Figure 7-2 shows the starting schema, which is nearly equivalent to the relational system. There are two record types, PART and ORDR, and two sets: SYSPART is the set of all parts, and PARTORD is the set of all orders for each part. Figure 7-3 shows some sample data. There is still no orders-by-vendor information, nor is there quick access to selected records. However, more than three orders per part can now be listed, since the PARTORD set can contain an unlimited number of members. If there are fewer than three orders, space will be saved.

Adding a new record type, VENDOR, as shown in Figure 7-4, along with two more sets, SYSVEND and VENDORD, allows listing orders by vendors. Just follow the right-hand path down from SYSTEM to VENDOR to ORDR. To get the part description, go up one to the left from ORDR to PART.

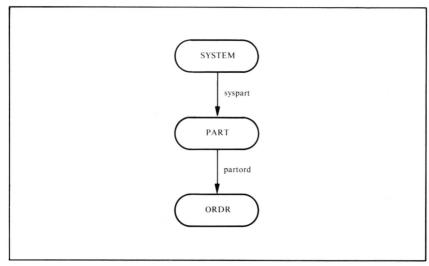

FIGURE 7-2.
Starting schema for parts system

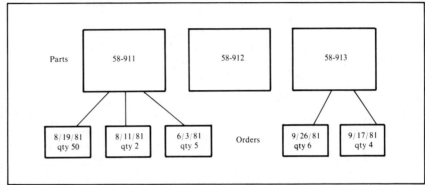

FIGURE 7-3.
Sample part and
order data

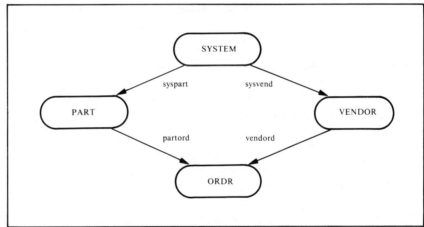

FIGURE 7-4.
Parts schema with
VENDOR added

Up to now, all sets have had a *one-to-many* relationship. This works because there is just one part for a particular order and one vendor for that order. One-to-many won't work when the SELECT record is introduced as illustrated in Figure 7-5. As previously mentioned, there are eight occurrences of the SELECT record, each corresponding to a select flag. The catalog SELECT record occurrence, for instance, is connected to all PART records to be included in the mail-order catalog; the tool occurrence is connected to all parts classified as tools. Note that a particular part can be *both* a catalog item and a tool. This makes the SYSPART set a *many-to-many* relationship as indicated by the double arrow in Figure 7-5.

MDBS III Procedure Summary

After thorough analysis and schema design, you are ready to build the system. The process is long and complicated and is explained in some detail using the parts inventory example.

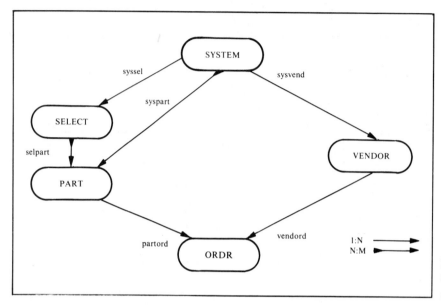

FIGURE 7-5.
Complete parts scheme

Here is a summary of that system-building process:

1. Specify the data base using the Data Description Language (DDL). You may use a text editor, word processor, or the line editor MDBS supplies.

2. Feed the specification to DDL, a stand-alone MDBS III program that analyzes your DDL statements and, if everything is perfect, generates an empty database file on disk.

3. Repeat steps 1 and 2 until DDL indicates no errors.

4. Prepare some test data in an ordinary CP/ M file or group of files.

5. Write a data base load program in BASIC or another host language. Use the MDBS Data Manipulation Language (DML), which amounts to CALL statements in-line with the BASIC statements. These statements permit the program to interact directly with the DBMS in order to store and load data.

6. Compile the program.

7. Link the compiled program with the MDBS access routines contained in a library called the Data Manipulation System (DMS).

8. Run the compiled and linked program to initialize the data base.

9. Repeat steps 5 through 8 until there are no errors.

10. Use QRS, the MDBS III Query/Retrieval System, to "explore" the new data base.

11. Write, compile, link, and test some of your own report, query, and data entry programs.

MDBS III Data Description Language (DDL)

Return to the parts schema system shown in Figure 7-5. That diagram shows the names of each record (SELECT, PART, ORDR, VENDOR) and the name, type, owner record, and member record of each set. The *partord* set has owner PART and member ORDR and is of type *one-to-many* (1:N), as indicated by the single arrow. The *selpart* relationship is *many-to-many* (N:M), as indicated by the double arrow.

Missing from the diagram are the field descriptions, security levels, and some important set information. This next level of detail is found in the DDL *source specification*, or data dictionary, as shown in Figure 7-6. This specification is written in a nonprocedural "language" described in the MDBS III documentation. The language is free-form, using about 90 reserved words such as "ascending," "highest," and "sorted." Field names, record names, and set names are alphanumeric and must be distinct from the reserved words. Comments are bracketed by "/*" and "*/" as they are in the PL/I and C languages.

You have a choice when preparing your DDL source specification. You can use your full-screen text editor or the built-in line editor. The text editor is a fine way to write the first draft, but the DDL analysis is terminated on the *first error*. Then you must return to the text editor, then back to DDL, and so forth. If you use the DDL internal line editor (similar to the ED text editor of CP/M), you are operating interactively and are able to correct errors immediately.

So much for the mechanics of DDL. How does a DDL specification relate to the schema? Look again at Figure 7-6. It is divided into four sections.

Identification Section

Here you specify the data base disk file name. Large data bases may be split into several *areas*, each of which is assigned to a physical file and drive. You also may specify the page size and number of pages. This is largely guesswork, but

you can start by computing the space required for a non-data base file system. MDBS III should require less space, but there are some unpredictable effects which depend on record length and page size. A page size of 1024 bytes is realistic. For the PARTS data base with DDL shown in Figure 7-6, the data base size is 300×1024, or 307,200 bytes, not all of which are used.

User Section

User names, passwords, and corresponding security codes are defined here. The codes relate to the codes in the record and set sections.

Record Section

Each record type corresponding to the oval shape in Figures 7-2 through 7-5 is defined in this section. Read and write access is defined for the record as a whole, but this may be overridden for individual fields (COST and MARKUP). Notice the *calc key* clause which sets up a *hashing* algorithm with part number as the key. The PART records are spread evenly over all 300 pages in the data base, permitting MDBS III to quickly access any part.

After general information for each record, each *data item* is described with data type, length, optional value range, repeating items, encryption, synonyms, and so on. Observe that MARKUP is readable only by "b" users, overriding the record read permission. The types of data allowed are summarized in the MDBS III Specifications section at the start of this chapter.

Set Section

Each set, represented by an arrow in the schema, is described individually. Owner record, member record, and order are the necessary parameters, and the order may be

```
/***************************************************
 *                  PARTS.DDL                      *
 *           A sample schema for MDBS III          *
 ***************************************************

 /****   I D E N T I F I C A T I O N   S E C T I O N  ****/

 db PARTS
         file "C:PARTS.DB"
         size 300 pages, page size 1024
         title "PARTS schema"

 /***************   U S E R   S E C T I O N   *********/

 user "ANYONE" with "PASS"
         read access is (a)
         write access is (a)
 user "OWNER" with "IMPORTANT"
         read access is (b)
         write access is (b)


 /************   R E C O R D   S E C T I O N   **********/

 record PART in any area calc key (NUM1,NUM2) nodup
         read access is (a,b)
         write access is (b)
         item NUM1        int  1     range 0 to 99
         item NUM2        int  2     range 0 to 999
         item MANU        str 10
         item DESCRI      str 30
         item PRICE       real 4     range 0 to 99999.99
         item MARKUP      int 1      range 0 to 99
                 read access is (b)
         item MANNUM      str 10
         item YTDPARTS    int 2      range 0 to 9999
         item YTDDOL      real 4     range 0 to 99999.99
         item INVENT      int 2      range 0 to 9999
         item SPARE       real 4

 record VENDOR
         read access is (a,b)
         write access is (b)
         item VENDORID    int 1
         item VENDOR      str 10

 record SELECT
         read access is (a,b)
         write access is (b)
         item SELECTID    int 1
         item SELECT      str 10

 record ORDR in area of owner of PARTORD
         read access is (a,b)
         write access is (b)
         item ORDATE      date
```

(continued)

FIGURE 7-6.
Parts DDL
specification

```
            item QUANTITY    int 2
            item COST        real 4
                    read access is (b)

/**************  S E T   S E C T I O N  **************/

set SYSPART, type 1:n
        read access is (a,b)
        write access is (a,b)
        owner SYSTEM
        member PART, order sorted ascending (NUM1,NUM2)
                        duplicates not allowed
                        insertion auto

set SYSVEND, type 1:n
        read access is (a,b)
        write access is (a,b)
        owner SYSTEM
        member VENDOR, order sorted ascending VENDORID
                        duplicates not allowed
                        insertion auto

set SYSSEL, type 1:n
        read access is (a,b)
        write access is (a,b)
        owner SYSTEM
        member SELECT, order sorted ascending SELECTID
                        duplicates not allowed
                        insertion auto

set SELPART, type n:m
        read access is (a,b)
        write access is (a,b)
        owner SELECT, order immat
        member PART, order sorted ascending (NUM1,NUM2)
                        duplicates not allowed

set PARTORD, type 1:n
        read access is (a,b)
        write access is (a,b)
        owner PART
        member ORDR, order sorted descending ORDATE
                        insertion auto

set VENDORD, type 1:n
        read access is (a,b)
        write access is (a,b)
        owner VENDOR
        member ORDR, order sorted ascending ORDATE
                        insertion auto

end
```

FIGURE 7-6.
Parts DDL
specification
(continued)

sorted, first-in first-out (FIFO), last-in first-out (LIFO), next-after-current, or prior-to-current. Access codes are necessary for some sets to avoid unauthorized requests like "list all employees in order by pay rate." *Insertion auto* means that all new records are automatically connected into the set, saving the programmer some effort. This works with one-to-many sets but not with many-to-many sets; in the SEL-PART set, a new PART record might have several owners in the SELECT set. The program must find the owners and connect the PART record to each.

Data base *security* needs some explanation. There are two *access codes* in the PARTS data base. If you sign on with user name ANYONE and enter the password PASS, you are allowed to see everything except Markup and Cost—but you don't have write permission and you can't change any data. If you sign on as OWNER with the password IMPORTANT, you can access and change everything. The letters "a" and "b" are like keys (as found on keyrings); ANYONE carries the "a" key, and OWNER carries the "b" key. The records, data items, and sets have locks; some locks are opened by both "a" and "b" keys while others are opened by the "b" key only.

Data Manipulation Language

Even though a finished system built around MDBS III might appear to be menu-driven or command-driven, MDBS III is really driven by *programs* written in a host language, such as BASIC, that communicate with the data base through CALL statements as described in Chapter 2. There are 111 data manipulation *commands* listed at the end of this chapter, and all are accessible through the CALL statements. If

you need to store a record in the data base, for instance, you insert a variation of the statement

```
CALL CRS( ''RECNAME,BLOCKNAME'' )
```

into your program. CRS is the command mnemonic for Create Record and Store, REC-NAME is the name of the MDBS III record as defined in the DDL specification, and BLOCK-NAME is the name of a group of program variables corresponding to the data items in the record.

The exact form of the CALL statement depends on which host language is used, with the above example specific to the Microsoft BASIC compiler. The program variables are grouped together by the MDBS III command DEFINE. The variable BLOCKNAME is really a "supervariable" consisting of several individual BASIC variables.

You will probably use only a dozen or so of the 111 commands in a given application. Those commands fall into four broad classes.

- *Navigation Commands.* These allow movement among sets within the schema, finding specific owners and members and stepping through sequences of owners and members.

- *Create, Delete, and Modify Commands.* Record occurrences may be added and deleted, and both records and individual data items may be stored and retrieved. The already described CRS command is included in this class.

- *Connect and Disconnect Commands.* Members and Owners may be connected and disconnected when the DDL specification does not call for automatic insertion.

- *Boolean Commands.* These permit creation of new sets from logical operations on existing sets. The command AMM (And of Members with Members) applies to the wine schema shown in Chapter 2. This command allows you to create a new set of all-Vigeant wines from California. Your program must be sure to connect any new bottles into this special set.

Miscellaneous Commands. These include data base open and close, multiuser locking, recovery control, and utility operations.

The concept of *currency* is central to MDBS III data manipulation theory. For each set in the data base, MDBS III maintains a *current owner* and a *current member*. These are used to mark the place as you would use a bookmark or a finger to keep your place in a book while looking up an appendix. Inserting a new record into an auto-insertion set, as with the CRS command, demands that there be a current owner. If your program hasn't established this current owner, MDBS III returns an error code. Many commands make certain well-documented assumptions about currency.

In addition to current members and owners, MDBS III maintains a *current of the run unit* (CRU). There is only one CRU for a single-user system, and this is the record last accessed by a data manipulation command. The CRS command, for example, leaves its newly created record as the CRU, and this would be a necessary input for a subsequent insertion command such as IMS (Insert Member into Set). If another command were executed between CRS and IMS, the program would have to "save and restore" the CRU via commands available for that purpose.

Data Manipulation System (DMS)

After a successful DDL run you have a new, empty data base of fixed size; the next step is to put something into it. The MDBS III Interactive Data Manipulation Tool (IDML) lets you input data directly from the keyboard, but this is not useful for initial loading; if you reinitialize the data base, you would have to rekey all the data. A better approach is to create some ordinary disk files containing test data. The source can be an existing system or simply a text editor. Once you capture the data on disk, you can feed it into the data base over and over until you are satisfied that the data base works.

This loading of a data base from files does not imply that your finished product will be a batch system. On the contrary, MDBS III is ideal for interactive systems, but you must have a minimum amount of data in the data base to start. After that IDML is ideal for "prototyping" on-line update and inquiry programs, thus saving compiling time.

In the parts example, the test files are BASIC-compatible versions of the main dBASE II PARTS database (Figure 7-1) and a short VENDOR database containing only vendor names. The files are loaded by the BASIC program PARTLOAD.BAS, written for the Microsoft BASCOM compiler and shown in Figure 7-7. The code is similar to BASIC-80, with which you may be familiar, but with two exceptions: Line numbers are necessary only when the line is referenced by a GOTO or GOSUB, and the %INCLUDE statement copies in blocks of code at compile time.

The following points don't attempt to explain the PARTLOAD program, but rather they help you understand what MDBS III programming involves.

1. The included module PARTSTUP.BAS (Figure 7-8) is the "boilerplate" included in all programs which use the PARTS data base.

2. The main purpose of PARTSTUP is to set up the data base by opening it, specifying the user and the password.

3. The PARTSTUP module also defines data blocks, an activity unique to BASIC and other languages that don't allow grouping of variables. Look at the DDL specification in

```
'     ********************************
'     *    PARTLOAD.BAS              *
'     * loads PARTS database         *
'     ********************************

      PRINT "** MDBS 3 PARTS load program **"
%INCLUDE PARTSTUP.BAS
'                ** Main Program **
'                set up vendor records
      OPEN "I",#1,"C:VENDOR.ASC"
      VENDOR.ID%=1
      WHILE EOF(1) <> -1
          INPUT#1,VENDOR$
          CO$="VENDOR,VENDOR"
          CALL CRS(CO$)                     'create VENDOR record
          IF EO% THEN 6000
          VENDOR.ID%=VENDOR.ID%+1
      WEND
      CLOSE #1


             set up select records
      SEL$(1)="FLAG1":SEL$(2)="MAJORRPT":SEL$(3)="CATALOG":SEL$(4)="TANDEM"
      SEL$(5)="TOOL":SEL$(6)="OUT":SEL$(7)="EMERG":SEL$(8)="FLAG8"
      FOR SELECT.ID%=1 TO 8
          SELECT$=SEL$(SELECT.ID%)
          CO$="SELECT,SELECT"
          CALL CRS(CO$)                     'create SELECT record
          IF EO% THEN 6000
      NEXT SELECT.ID%


             set up parts and orders records
      OPEN "I",#1,"C:PARTS.ASC"
      WHILE EOF(1) <> -1                    'read a sequential record
          INPUT#1,NUM1$,NUM2$,SEL$(1),SEL$(2),SEL$(3),SEL$(4),SEL$(5),_
              SEL$(6),SEL$(7),SEL$(8),MANU$,DESCRI$,PRICE,MARKUP%,_
              ORDATE(1),VENDOR.ID%(1),QUANTITY%(1),COST(1),_
              ORDATE(2),VENDOR.ID%(2),QUANTITY%(2),COST(2),_
              ORDATE(3),VENDOR.ID%(3),QUANTITY%(3),COST(3),_
              MAN.NUM$,YTD.PARTS%,YTD.DOL,INVENT%,SPARE
          NUM1%=VAL(NUM1$): NUM2%=VAL(NUM2$)
          PRINT "part ";NUM1%;NUM2%

          CO$="PART,PART"
          CALL CRS(CO$)                     'create PART record
          IF EO%=19 OR EO%=30 OR EO%=33 THEN_
              PRINT "***ERROR***";EO%: GOTO 2000
          IF EO% THEN 6000
          CO$="USER"
          CALL SUC(CO$)                     'save CRU for inserts
          IF EO% THEN 6000
```

(continued)

FIGURE 7-7.
PARTLOAD.BAS program listing

```
                     insert part into select set for all true flags
             FOR SELECT.ID%=1 TO 8
                 IF SEL$(SELECT.ID%)<>"Y" AND SEL$(SELECT.ID%)<>"T" THEN 500
                 CO$="SYSSEL,SELKEY"
                 CALL FMSK(CO$)              'find SELECT record
                 IF EO% THEN 6000
                 PRINT SELECT.ID%;
                 CO$="SELPART,SYSSEL"
                 CALL SOM(CO$)               'make SELECT owner of PART
                 IF EO%>0 THEN 6000
                 CO$="USER"
                 CALL SCU(CO$)               'restore CRU from part create
                 IF EO% THEN 6000
                 CO$="SELPART"
                 CALL IMS(CO$)               'insert PART into select set
                 IF EO% THEN 6000
500          NEXT SELECT.ID%
             PRINT

             FOR I%=1 TO 3                   'create up to three order records
                 IF ORDATE(I%) = 0 THEN 1000
                 YY=INT(ORDATE(I%)/10000)    'convert yymmdd date to string
                 MM=INT((ORDATE(I%)-10000*YY)/100)
                 DD=ORDATE(I%)-10000*YY-100*MM
                 ORDATE$=RIGHT$(STR$(MM),2)+"/"+RIGHT$(STR$(DD),2)+_
                         "/19"+RIGHT$(STR$(YY),2)
                 PRINT ORDATE$
                 QUANTITY%=QUANTITY%(I%)
                 COST=COST(I%)

                 VENDOR.ID%=VENDOR.ID%(I%)
                 CO$="SYSVEND,VENDKEY"
                 CALL FMSK(CO$)              'find VENDOR record
                 IF EO%=-1 THEN_
                     PRINT "**VENDOR ERROR**";VENDOR.ID%: GOTO 1000
                 IF EO% THEN 6000

                 CO$="VENDORD,SYSVEND"
                 CALL SOM(CO$)               'set VENDOR owner of ORDR
                 IF EO%>0 THEN 6000

                 CO$="PARTORD,SYSPART"
                 CALL SOM(CO$)               'set PART owner of ORDR
                 IF EO%>0 THEN 6000

                 CO$="ORDR,ORDR"
                 CALL CRS(CO$)               'create ORDR record
                 IF EO%=30 OR EO%=33 THEN_
                     PRINT "***ERROR***";EO%: GOTO 1000
                 IF EO% THEN 6000
```

(continued)

FIGURE 7-7.
Partload.bas program listing
(continued)

```
1000            NEXT I%
2000      WEND
          CLOSE #1
          GOTO 6500

  ,             Error trap
5900      PRINT "** Basic error";ERR;"in line";ERL;"**"
          RESUME 6500

  ,             DMS error routine
6000      PRINT "** DMS error";E0%;"during ";CO$;" **"

  ,             Quit
6500      CALL DBCLS
          IF E0%<>0 AND E0%<>38
          THEN PRINT "** DMS error";E0%;"during DBCLS **"
END
```

FIGURE 7-7.
PARTLOAD.BAS program listing
(continued)

Figure 7-6. The PART record consists of eleven fields, NUM1, NUM2, MANU, and so on. The CALL DEFINE and CALL EXTEND statements in PART LOAD create a new pseudo-variable, PART, which is really a block of pointers to the eleven BASIC variables, NUM1%, NUM2%, MANU$, and so on.

4. The first job for PARTLOAD is to read in the vendor records. The DMS call *CRS* (Create Record and Store) is the only necessary MDBS III interaction. It is used once for each input record to create a data base VENDOR record with vendor number and vendor name. The input variable "VENDOR,VENDOR" tells MDBS III that the record name is VENDOR and the BASIC data block name is VENDOR.

5. When PART records are being loaded, it is necessary to *find* which SELECT records the part is associated with. The program steps through all eight select flags in the input data record, and uses the DMS call *FMSK* (Find Member based on Sort Key) to locate the future owner for the SELPART set. Here the key is a number, 1 through 8. After the PART record is found, it may be connected to the select flag with *IMS* (Insert Member into Set).

6. When ORDR records are being created, the "insertion is auto" feature comes into play. Two *SOM* (Set Owner based on Member) calls establish the PART and VENDOR which are owners of the new ORDR record. When the *CRS* is executed, the record is inserted into both PARTORD and VENDORD sets without the need for an *IMS* call.

7. After every call to MDBS III, a command status is returned in the variable E0%. The program must check this variable *every* time to decide whether this is an acceptable condition or a disaster such as media failure or a full data base. Exception processing is a significant part of an MDBS III program because the status of *every* DBMS call must be examined.

If you're overwhelmed, don't worry too much. It's harder to program *input* to the data base than it is to program *output* from it, but input always comes before output. The much simpler CATALOG program in Figure 7-9 may

```
             ****************************
             *   PARTSTUP.BAS           *
             *  setup module for PARTS  *
             ****************************

                  Dimension dms buffer array
             The dms buffer should be as large as possible.

             DIM DMSBUF%(6143)          ' 12K bytes
             DIM ORDATE(3),VENDOR.ID%(3),QUANTITY%(3),COST(3),SEL$(8)
                  Set error trap
             This is a safety precaution to protect your data base while
             it is open for modify in the event of a BASIC error.

             ON ERROR GOTO 5900

                  Open DB, define data blocks
             DBU$="OWNER": DBP$="IMPORTANT"
             DBO$="M": DBF$="C:PARTS.DB"

                  set E0% to be the command status return variable
             CALL VARCS(E0%)

                  set DMS buffer
             I%=12288
             CALL SETPBF(DMSBUF%(0),I%)
             IF E0% THEN 6000

                  open block
             I%=4: C0$="OPEN"
             CALL DEFINE(C0$,I%,DBU$,DBP$,DBO$,DBF$)
             IF E0% THEN 6000

                  open db
             C0$="OPEN"
             CALL DBOPN(C0$)
             IF E0% THEN 6000

                  VENDOR data block
             I%=2: C0$="VENDOR"
             CALL DEFINE(C0$,I%,VENDOR.ID%,VENDOR$)
             IF E0% THEN 6000

                  SELECT data block
             I%=2: C0$="SELECT"
             CALL DEFINE(C0$,I%,SELECT.ID%,SELECT$)
             IF E0% THEN 6000
```

(continued)

FIGURE 7-8.
Listing of PARTSUP,
setup module for the
Parts system programs

```
                 vendor key data block
        I%=1: CO$="VENDKEY"
        CALL DEFINE(CO$,I%,VENDOR.ID%)
        IF EO% THEN 6000


                 select key data block
        I%=1: CO$="SELKEY"
        CALL DEFINE(CO$,I%,SELECT.ID%)
        IF EO% THEN 6000


                 part key data block
        I%=2: CO$="PARTKEY"
        CALL DEFINE(CO$,I%,NUM1%,NUM2%)
        IF EO% THEN 6000


                 PART data block
        I%=4: CO$="PART"
        CALL DEFINE(CO$,I%,NUM1%,NUM2%,MANU$,DESCRI$)
        CALL EXTEND(CO$,I%,PRICE,MARKUP%,MAN.NUM$,YTD.PARTS%)
        I%=3
        CALL EXTEND(CO$,I%,YTD.DOL,INVENT%,SPARE)
        IF EO% THEN 6000


                 ORDR data block
        I%=3: CO$="ORDR"
        CALL DEFINE(CO$,I%,ORDATE$,QUANTITY%,COST)
        IF EO% THEN 6000


                 user indicator user block
        I%=1: CO$="USER": U%=1
        CALL DEFINE(CO$,I%,U%)
        IF EO% THEN 6000


                 Alter end of set
        We recommend using ALTEOS as it simplifies error
        checking on commands that could return end of set.


        CALL ALTEOS
        IF EO% THEN 6000
```

FIGURE 7-8.
Listing of PARTSUP,
setup module for the
Parts system programs (continued)

be easier to understand.

After you finish the program, you *compile* it using the BASCOM compiler. This is a quick procedure that requires only a few seconds. *Linkage* is the step which connects the MDBS code to your code. That procedure takes about two minutes and requires the command

```
L80 PARTLOAD/N,PARTLOAD,BASCOM80,CPMDMS/S/E
```

L80 is the Microsoft link program, and BASCOM80 and CPMDMS are *libraries* consisting of individual MDBS routines, especially

```
'       *******************************
'       *    CATALOG.BAS              *
'       * print mail-order catalog    *
'       *******************************

        PRINT "*** MDBS 3 PARTS mail-order catalog"
%INCLUDE PARTSTUP.BAS
'               ** Main Program **
        DESCRI$=SPACE$(30)              'initialize strings
        MANU$=SPACE$(10)                ' very important
        MAN.NUM$=SPACE$(10)
        ENDFILE%=0
        PAGE%=0
        LINE.COUNT%=99
        DATE$="05/10/82"
        SELECT.ID%=3                    'select records with CATALOG flag
        CO$="SYSSEL,SELKEY"
        CALL FMSK(CO$)                  'find SELECT record #3
        IF EO% THEN 6000
        CO$="SELPART,SYSSEL"
        CALL SOM(CO$)                   'SELECT is owner of parts
        IF EO% THEN 6000
        WHILE ENDFILE%<>-1
            CO$="SELPART,PART"
            CALL GETM(CO$)              'get PART from SELECT set
            IF EO% THEN 6000
            LINE.COUNT%=LINE.COUNT%+1
            IF LINE.COUNT% > 50 THEN_
                GOSUB 1000              'new page if necessary
            LPRINT USING "##_-###";NUM1%;NUM2%;   'print detail line
            LPRINT TAB(10);MANU$;" ";DESCRI$;
            LPRINT USING "   $####.##";PRICE
            CO$="SELPART"
            CALL FNM(CO$)               'find next PART
            IF EO%>0 THEN 6000
            ENDFILE%=EO%                'ENDFILE% is -1 at end of set
            IF INKEY$ <> "" THEN_
                PRINT "operator job abort":_
                ENDFILE%=-1
        WEND
        GOTO 6500

'               Page heading subroutine
1000    PAGE%=PAGE%+1
        LPRINT CHR$(12);DATE$;TAB(22);"PARTS CATALOG";
        LPRINT TAB(54);"PAGE ";PAGE%
        LPRINT
        LPRINT "Part Nbr    Manu            Description";
        LPRINT TAB(55) "Price"
        LPRINT
        LINE.COUNT%=5
        RETURN                                      (continued)
```

FIGURE 7-9.
CATALOG.BAS program listing

```
        ⁄            Error trap
     5900     PRINT "** Basic error";ERR;"in line";ERL;"**"


              RESUME 6500
        ⁄            DMS error routine
     6000     PRINT "** DMS error";EO%;"during ";CO$;" **"

        ⁄            Quit
     6500     CALL DBCLS
              IF EO%<>0 AND EO%<>38_
               THEN PRINT "** DMS error";EO%;"during DBCLS **"
     END
```

FIGURE 7-9.
Catalog.bas program listing
(continued)

adapted to CP/M and the Microsoft compiler. If your program uses only the MDBS calls GETM and FNM, for instance, only the routines necessary to support those functions are linked in. Code for CRS and other unused calls is not brought in.

After linking, you have an executable program, PARTLOAD.COM. Just type PARTLOAD and the data base gets loaded. It's a good idea to start off with a small subset of the data because it takes three hours to load in the full 1685 parts, and that's using a hard disk. Like all MDBS III activities, load times are very dependent on schema design, hardware configuration, and disk operating system. Most data base loads would occur after hours because operator interaction is not required.

Query Retrieval System (QRS)

Now that the data is there, it's time to experiment with it. You had no choice but to write a load program for data *input*. For data *output* you can start off with MDBS-QRS, neatly

avoiding tedious programming and increasing your understanding of MDBS III concepts. QRS is unusually simple to use, with the main command, **list**, having the syntax

list fields [*by* break fields] [*for* condition] *thru* path

The best way to understand QRS is to see it in action. After typing QRS, you are asked for the data base name PARTS, then the user ANYONE and the password PASS. Here the PARTS data base is a small grouping of just 57 parts with 47 total orders. The QRS prompt is →, and upper and lower cases are equivalent.

Suppose you want a list of *all* parts in numerical order, showing part number and description. After the prompt, you type in the following:

→list NUM1 NUM2 DESCRI thru SYSPART

and you receive the list of parts as shown in Figure 7-10.

You didn't really need seven decimal places for the part number, nor did you need to know the standard deviation and variance. These little "extras" can be tuned out by adjusting defaults as follows: "set" changes the query environment in various ways, "of" is output format, and "53" means five digits to the left and three to the right of the decimal. For example, by typing in the following:

```
→set of 53
→list NUM1 NUM2 MANU DESCRI PRICE thru SYSPART
```

you will see the amended parts list shown in Figure 7-11.

Now all numbers have two decimal places in the PRICE column. The minimum, maximum, and average actually have some meaning. The clause "thru SYSPART" in the command line is the very important *path* clause, telling QRS how to navigate through the data base, in this case, telling it to step through all members of the SYSPART set.

Suppose you don't need to see *all* the parts, but only those with NUM1 between 50 and 58. The QRS LIST command has the syntax

list fields [*by* break fields] [*for* condition] *thru* path

The *condition* clause with the "for" takes care of the selection, but QRS still has to process *all* part records. A full data base with over 1600 parts requires about seven minutes' processing time with QRS and only a little less with your own program. For example, by entering the following command:

```
→set of 50
→list NUM1 NUM2 MANU DESCRI for
    NUM1 > 50 and NUM1 < 58 thru SYSPART
```

you call up on the screen a partial parts list as shown in Figure 7-12.

```
        NUM1                NUM2    DESCRI

    13.0000000          910.0000000   STANDARD REPLACEMENT FORK
    13.0000000          940.0000000   PRO FORK
    22.0000000          912.0000000   EXPANDER+CONE
    23.0000000          911.0000000   STREAMERS (PAIR)
    ..................
    58.0000000          996.0000000   FRONT FRAME WASHER-SQU #1056
    58.0000000          997.0000000   AS ABOVE.BUT ROUND
    58.0000000          998.0000000   REAR FRAME WASHER WEIN #451W
    74.0000000          910.0000000   BIKE WALLET

        NUM1                NUM2    DESCRI

  no. of observations:    57
    2681.0000000        53921.0000000            sum
      99.0000000          998.0000000            max
      13.0000000          910.0000000            min
      47.0350877          945.9824561            ave
     299.3558897         1035.3389724            var
      17.3019042           32.1766837            std
```

FIGURE 7-10.
Parts listed in numerical order

```
   NUM1      NUM2   MANU        DESCRI                               PRICE

   13.00    910.00  JAPAN       STANDARD REPLACEMENT FORK            17.00
   13.00    940.00  TANGE       PRO FORK                             42.00
   22.00    912.00  PIVO        EXPANDER+CONE                         1.50
   23.00    911.00  MISC.       STREAMERS (PAIR)                      0.75
            . . . . . . . . . . . . .

   58.00    996.00  MISC.       FRONT FRAME WASHER-SQU #1056          0.15
   58.00    997.00  MISC.       AS ABOVE.BUT ROUND                    0.35
   58.00    998.00  MISC.       REAR FRAME WASHER WEIN #451W          0.35
   74.00    910.00  ECLIPSE     BIKE WALLET                           2.50

   NUM1      NUM2   MANU        DESCRI           PRICE

   no. of observations:    57
 2681.00  53921.00                           246.07 sum
   99.00    998.00                            42.00 max
   13.00    910.00                             0.00 min
   47.04    945.98                             4.32 ave
  299.36   1035.34                            42.97 var
   17.30     32.18                             6.55 std
```

FIGURE 7-11.
Parts list without decimals

If you're curious about how much money the shop owner makes from the sale of each part, you could look at the Markup.

```
→list NUM1 NUM2 MARKUP thru SYSPART

NUM1    NUM2      MARKU

DMS command status    44
user may not read this item
```

Read access to Markup is not permitted for user ANYONE. QRS doesn't let you see any of the part fields as long as Markup is in the field list.

It's time to look at some orders. Here the path clause is critical. Referring to the schema in Figure 7-5, you start at the SYSTEM record, then go down the SYSPART set to PART, then on down the PARTORD set to ORDR. This gets you all orders grouped by part, but you're missing the vendor name. Just go *up* the VENDORD set from the ORDR record to pick up vendor. SYSPART PARTORD >VENDORD defines the path, with the ">" symbol indicating "upstream" movement.

```
→list NUM1 NUM2 ORDATE QUANTITY VENDOR
   for NUM1 = 58 thru SYSPART PARTORD
   >VENDORD
```

The resulting list (Figure 7-13) shows the vendor for each part number you specify.

Notice that this list shows three entries for part 58-911 because there are three orders. If a part has no orders it isn't shown because there is no complete path. If you need to know the total quantity ordered for each part, use the *break* clause with "by." You'll get subtotals by part as well as grand totals.

```
NUM1        NUM2        MANU            DESCRI

  52          980       WEINMANN        RIM WASHERS(72)
  56          910       BARGE           CEMENT 3/4 OZ TUBE OR CAN
  56          915       BR/ALLEZ        TIRE SAVERS (EA)
  56          920       KINGBRIDGE      TIRE SAVERS
  56          925       RAL/VITTOR      TIRE HOLDER
  56          930       HOLDSWORTH      WHEEL COVERS
  56          946       JOVELOT         TIRE LIFE (LATEX)

no. of observations:      7
```

FIGURE 7-12.
Partial parts list

```
NUM1        NUM2        ORDATE          QUANT       VENDOR

  58          911       08/19/1981        50        WEST COAST
  58          911       08/11/1981         2        SPECIALIZD
  58          911       06/03/1981         5        R.H. BROWN
  58          912       09/26/1981         6        MISC.
  58          912       09/17/1981         0        MISC.
  58          913       09/26/1981         6        MISC.
  58          913       09/17/1981         0        MISC.
  58          920       10/15/1980         5        WEST COAST
```

FIGURE 7-13.
List of vendors

→list NUM1 NUM2 ORDATE QUANTITY VENDOR by NUM1
  NUM2 for NUM = 58 thru SYSPART PARTORD
  >VENDORD

See Figure 7-14 for an example of what you would see on the screen.

So much for queries by part number. Suppose you want to see orders listed by vendor. Just take a different path, starting at the SYSTEM record, going down the SYSVEND set through VENDOR, on down the VENDORD set to ORDR and back up to PART via PARTORD to pick up the part number and description.

By keying in

→list VENDOR NUM1 NUM2 DESCRI
  ORDATE thru SYSVEND VENDORD
  > PARTORD

you can see a list of orders by vendor, as shown in Figure 7-15.

Now for some explorations via the select flags. First, just list the flag names.

→list SELECTID SELECT thru SYSSEL

Then view the resulting screen shown in Figure 7-16.

Now list all parts with the CATALOG flag set. QRS cycles through *all eight* members of the SYSSEL set, but it only processes those 14 parts in SELPART with owner CATALOG. (Be sure to look back at the schema in Figure 7-5.) This select method can save time in processing large data bases because it saves having to process *all* the PART records.

The command

→list NUM1 NUM2 MANU DESCRI for SELECT
  ='CATALOG' thru SYSSEL SELPART

```
NUM1    NUM2   ORDATE         QUANT   VENDOR

  58     911   08/19/1981        50   WEST COAST
  58     911   08/11/1981         2   SPECIALIZD
  58     911   06/03/1981         5   R.H. BROWN

   no. of observations:     3
 174    2733                     57              sum
        ...................

  58     938   10/22/1981         2   SPECIALIZD
  58     938   08/31/1981         3   SPECIALIZD
  58     938   03/13/1981         4   SPECIALIZD

   no. of observations:     3
 174    2814                      9              sum
        ...................

   no. of observations:    20
1160   18613                   1261              sum
  58     994                   1000              max
  58     911                      0              min
  58     931                     63              ave
   0     602                  49011              var
   0      25                    221              std
```

FIGURE 7-14.
Parts list with totals

```
VENDOR         NUM1    NUM2   DESCRI                          ORDATE

MEL PINTO        25     910   STEEL POST-1IN STANDARD LENGTH  11/14/1980
MEL PINTO        81     965   14-17                           11/14/1980
SPECIALIZD       28     950   END BUTTON FOR TOE STRAP        10/22/1981
SPECIALIZD       58     938   CARDED (SET OF 4)               10/22/1981
        ...........

WEST COAST       13     910   STANDARD REPLACEMENT FORK       09/20/1980
TEN SPEED        58     931   FINNED PAD SET                  06/05/1981
BP PACIFIC       56     946   TIRE LIFE (LATEX)               06/25/1981
BP PACIFIC       56     946   TIRE LIFE (LATEX)               05/15/1981

   no. of observations:    47
```

FIGURE 7-15.
Orders listed by vendor

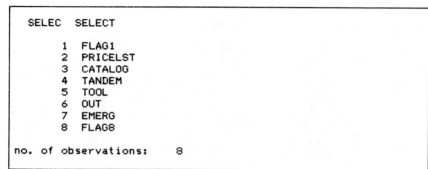

```
SELEC  SELECT

    1  FLAG1
    2  PRICELST
    3  CATALOG
    4  TANDEM
    5  TOOL
    6  OUT
    7  EMERG
    8  FLAG8

no. of observations:      8
```

FIGURE 7-16.
Select flags

produces the CATALOG flag set shown in Figure 7-17.

Another try, this time for out-of-stock parts, yields the following:

→ list NUM1 NUM2 MANU DESCRI for SELECTID = 6
  thru SYSSEL SELPART

The resulting screen is shown in Figure 7-18.

If you would like to see which select flags are set for each product, go into the data base via the SYSPART set, then go up via the SELPART set to pick up the flag name.

→ list NUM1 NUM2 SELECT thru SYSPART > SELPART

The resulting screen is shown in Figure 7-19.

The preceding examples make a good introduction to QRS. If you dig deeper you will discover some more capabilities.

1. A DISPLAY command shows pieces of the DDL specification. This is superfluous if you keep a printed copy handy.

2. It is easy, by means of the SET command (don't confuse this with MDBS III sets) to change the operating environment. You can suppress printing of variances and standard deviations, echo input and output to the printer, spool printer output to disk, suppress column headings, and so on.

3. You can build sequences of commands called *macros*, saving yourself some keystrokes.

4. Relational expressions in the LIST command are very flexible. Wild cards are permitted for character matching so that "*spoke*" finds any occurrence of the word "spoke" in a part description, and "ti$e" matches "tire," "time," "tile," and so on, in a four-character field. "Sm[i,y]th" matches on "Smith" and "Smyth" only. Any combination of AND, OR, XOR, and NOT, with parentheses, is permitted in a relational expression.

5. A SPEW command sends a file to the Super-Calc spread sheet program in a form similar to the LIST output. The required version of SuperCalc, 1.07, was not available for testing.

6. Value labels permit substitution of phrases for numeric values. "Butcher" could appear in place of occupation code 357.

QRS is a useful learning and experimentation tool, but it stops just short of being a report generator. What is most irritating is the limitation that all numeric columns must have the same number of decimal places; if Price has two places, then Part Number must also. A little more control over page headings, column widths, and field breaks would make a world of difference.

```
NUM1    NUM2   MANU          DESCRI

  13     910   JAPAN         STANDARD REPLACEMENT FORK
  13     940   TANGE         PRO FORK
  23     912   BIKIT         WATCH-HOLDER
  25     930   OMAS          ALUM SEATPOST BOLT FOR CAMPY
         ..................

  56     910   BARGE         CEMENT 3/4 OZ TUBE OR CAN
  56     925   RAL/VITTOR    TIRE HOLDER
  56     930   HOLDSWORTH    WHEEL COVERS
  58     931   MATHAUSER     FINNED PAD SET

  no. of observations:    14
```

FIGURE 7-17.
CATALOG flag set

```
NUM1    NUM2   MANU          DESCRI

  25     910   MISC.         STEEL POST-1IN STANDARD LENGTH
  25     920   MISC.         STEEL POST-1IN LONG
  56     946   JOVELOT       TIRE LIFE (LATEX)
  58     911   MISC.         CASING-ALL COLORS (PER FOOT)

  no. of observations:    4
```

FIGURE 7-18.
Out-of-stock
parts list

```
NUM1    NUM2   SELECT

  13     910   CATALOG
  13     940   EMERG
  13     940   CATALOG
  23     912   CATALOG
  25     910   OUT
         ............

  58     931   TOOL
  58     931   CATALOG
  58     931   PRICELST
  81     965   TANDEM

  no. of observations:    33
```

FIGURE 7-19.
Select flags for
each product

Interactive Data Manipulation Language (IDML)

Consider all the DMS commands (FMSK, SOM, CRS, and so on) in the PARTLOAD program. Most of these can be used in an *interactive mode* with the MDBS-IDML module. Suppose you have the PARTS data base running, and you want a quick way to add new orders. You could write another BASIC program, but IDML will save you some time and effort. You won't have to wait around for compiles and links.

First you sign on as you did with QRS, but you must use the OWNER/IMPORTANT user/ password combination because you are now "writing" to the data base. The dialog for entering one order follows, with "I:" as the IDML prompt.

```
I: FMSK?
   syntax of FMSK is: FMSK set [data]

I: FMSK SYSPART
   enter NUM1: 58
   enter NUM2: 911

I: FMSK SYSVEND
   enter VENDORD: 4

I: SOM?
   syntax of SOM is: SOM set set

I: SOM VENDORD SYSVEND
I: SOM PARTORD SYSPART

   DMS command status 255
   record not found

I: CRS?
   syntax of CRS is: CRS record [data]

I: CRS ORDR
   enter ORDATE: 05/22/1982
   enter QUANTITY: 50
   enter COST: .25

I:
```

A few words of explanation might help. Each command has a *syntax* corresponding to its use in the host language. Commands need some combination of record names and set names. Where the host language requires block names, IDML accepts data interactively from the keyboard and displays data on the screen. If you don't know the syntax, you type a "?" following the command, and IDML helps you.

The following is a reminder of what the commands do:

- *FMSK* finds the member of a set, here a part first and a vendor second.
- *SOM* sets the owner of one set to be the same as the member of another set. The part and vendor are defined as owners of the soon-to-be added order record.
- *CRS* actually creates the record occurrence and fills it with data. Because the schema (Figure 7-5) specified *automatic insertion*, the new order is connected to part and vendor.

Notice the "record not found" command status message. This is normal because there were no preexisting orders for part 58-911, but you must be able to distinguish this message from real error messages. The error number is the clue; 255 indicates that no members of PARTORD were found.

If you need to enter more than one order, the IDML *macro* facility will make things easier. Macros are simply named sequences of commands stored on disk (in the data base itself, as a matter of fact). To create a new one, type DEFINE, which will result in the following menu:

```
Macro Definition Utility

Macro/Synonym Functions:

(A)Add a Macro
(C)Change a Macro
(D)Delete a Macro
```

```
(I)Index of Macro/Synonym Names
(L)List Macros and Synonyms
(?)Print This Command List
(Q)Quit Define Mode
```

Entering "A" for a new macro, you type in the following commands:

```
FMSK SYSPART
FMSK SYSVEND
SOM VENDORD SYSVEND
SOM PARTORD SYSPART
CRS ORDR
```

You can *execute* the macro, named NEW-ORDR, by typing its name. IDML then prompts you for the data.

```
I: NEWORDR
    enter NUM1: 58
    enter NUM2: 911
    enter VENDORD: 4
    enter ORDATE: 05/22/1982
    enter QUANTITY: 50
    enter COST: .25


I:
```

In addition to data input, IDML may be used for data output, one record or data item at a time. Often, however, QRS is a better tool for that job.

Programmed Data Access

To sidestep QRS's inability to produce nicely formatted reports, you must either use QRS to produce a sequential disk file to feed to a separate report generator program, or you must resort to the host language. Take the mail-order catalog as an example. It is sent out to about a thousand mail-order customers, and it includes the subset of parts with the CATALOG select flag set. The path through the schema is the same as in the preceding QRS example, but the program has to step through all parts in the

SELPART set for CATALOG. "Pseudo code" for the necessary program is

· Open the data base
· Define data blocks
· Find the CATALOG record in the SYSSEL set
· Set owner of SELPART based on member of SYSSEL
· While not end-of-file
    a. Get member record (PART) from SELPART
    b. Print a page heading if necessary
    c. Print a report detail line
    d. Find next member of SELPART
    e. Give operator a chance to break out of report
· End of while loop
· Close the data base.

Figure 7-9 shows the Microsoft BASIC program, CATALOG.BAS. After the setup code in PARTSTUP is removed, the program is just over a page long—not too unreasonable. A fragment of the resulting price list is shown here.

05/10/82		PARTS CATALOG	PAGE2
Part Nbr	Manu	Description	Price
21-420	SR	WORLD CUSTOM	$14.25
21-520	SR	RANDONEAUR	$14.95
21-610	PHILLIPE	FLAT OR ANGLED	$11.00
21-640	SR	ALL-ROUNDER	$ 9.76
21-652	TTT	UPRIGHT BARS	$10.00
22-110	CINELLI	ROAD STEM	$34.25

Another program, DISPLAY.BAS, gives a screen display of everything you want to know about a part. It finds a part through SYSPART, goes up through SYSSEL to list all the select flags, then goes down through SYSORD and up through VENDORD to print order information. Figure 7-20 shows the program, and Figure 7-21 shows a photo of the resulting display. The operator can choose an individual part or step through parts sequentially by keying <CR>.

```
'          ****************************
'          *    DISPLAY.BAS           *
'          * display PART info on screen*
'          ****************************
           PRINT "** MDBS 3 display PARTS program"
%INCLUDE PARTSTUP.BAS
'              ** Main Program **
           DESCRI$=SPACE$(30)              'initialize strings
           MANU$=SPACE$(10)                'very important
           MAN.NUM$=SPACE$(10)
           VENDOR$=SPACE$(10)
           SELECT$=SPACE$(10)
           ORDATE$=SPACE$(10)
           ENDFILE%=0
           CO$="SYSPART"
           CALL FFM(CO$)                   'find first PART in system set
           IF EO% THEN 6000
           WHILE ENDFILE%<>-1
               INPUT "ENTER PART NUMBER (nn-nnn)";PART.NBR$
               IF PART.NBR$="99-999" THEN_
                   ENDFILE%=-1: GOTO 100   'exit on all 9's
               IF PART.NBR$="" THEN_
                   GOSUB 2000:_            'next part on null entry
               ELSE_
                   GOSUB 1000             'specific part
               IF EO%=-1 THEN_
                   PRINT "Part not found": GOTO 100
               GOSUB 3100                  'print PART information
               CO$="SELPART,SYSPART"
               CALL SMM(CO$)               'PART is member of select set
               IF EO%>0 THEN 6000
               ENDSEL%=EO%                 'ENDSEL% is -1 if no owners
               WHILE ENDSEL%<>-1
                   GOSUB 3200              'print select flag names
               WEND
               PRINT:PRINT
               PRINT "Order date  Quantity    Cost       Vendor"
               PRINT
               CO$="PARTORD,SYSPART"
               CALL SOM(CO$)               'PART is owner of orders
               IF EO%>0 THEN 6000
               ENDORD%=EO%
               WHILE ENDORD%<>-1
                   GOSUB 3300              'print ORDER/VENDOR information
               WEND
               PRINT
100        WEND
           GOTO 6500

               find specified part
1000       NUM1%=VAL(LEFT$(PART.NBR$,2)):_
           NUM2%=VAL(RIGHT$(PART.NBR$,3)):_
```

(continued)

FIGURE 7-20.

DISPLAY.BAS program listing

```
              CO$="SYSPART,PARTKEY"
              CALL FMSK(CO$)                      'find PART by key
              IF E0%>0 THEN 6000
              RETURN


    '              get next part
2000          CO$="SYSPART"
              CALL FNM(CO$)                       'find next PART
              IF E0%>0 THEN 6000
              RETURN


    '              get and print PART information
3100          CO$="SYSPART,PART"
              CALL GETM(CO$)                       'get PART record
              IF E0% THEN 6000
              PRINT CHR$(12);                      'clear screen
              PRINT TAB(20);"** PART DISPLAY **
              PRINT
              PRINT USING "##_-###";NUM1%;NUM2%;
              PRINT "   ";MANU$;" ";DESCRI$
              PRINT                                'print PART data items
              PRINT "Price: ";
              PRINT USING "$####.##";PRICE;
              PRINT TAB(40);"Markup: ";MARKUP%
              PRINT "Manufacturer number: ";MAN.NUM$;
              PRINT TAB(40);"YTD quantity sold: ";YTD.PARTS%
              PRINT "YTD sales dollars: ";
              PRINT USING "$######.##";YTD.DOL;
              PRINT TAB(40);"Inventory level: ";INVENT%
              PRINT
              PRINT "Select Flags: ";
              RETURN


    '              get and print select flags
3200          CO$="SELPART,SELECT"
              CALL GETO(CO$)   'get the owner record
              IF E0% THEN 6000
              PRINT SELECT$;"   ";                 'print SELECT flag names
              CO$="SELPART"
              CALL FNO(CO$)     'try for the next owner
              IF E0%>0 THEN 6000
              ENDSEL%=E0%                          'ENDSEL% is -1 when done
              RETURN


    '              get and print this part's orders
3300          CO$="PARTORD,ORDR"
              CALL GETM(CO$)                       'get the ORDR record
              IF E0% THEN 6000
              PRINT ORDATE$,QUANTITY%;TAB(20);
              PRINT USING "$####.##";COST;          'print the ORDR data
              CO$="VENDORD,PARTORD"
```

(continued)

FIGURE 7-20.
DISPLAY.BAS program listing
(continued)

```
            CALL SMM(CO$)                   'make ORDR member of VENDOR
            IF EO% THEN 6000
            CO$="VENDORD,VENDOR"
            CALL GETO(CO$)                  'get the VENDOR record
            IF EO% THEN 6000
            PRINT "   ";VENDOR$             'print VENDOR name
            CO$="PARTORD"
            CALL FNM(CO$)                   'try for the next ORDR
            IF EO%>0 THEN 6000
            ENDORD%=EO%                     'ENDORD% is -1 when done
            RETURN

'                   Error trap

5900        PRINT "** Basic error";ERR;"in line";ERL;"**"
            RESUME 6500

'                   DMS error routine
6000        PRINT "** DMS error";EO%;"during ";CO$;" **"

'                   Quit
6500        CALL DBCLS
            IF EO%<>0 AND EO%<>38_
              THEN PRINT "** DMS error";EO%;"during DBCLS **"
END
```

FIGURE 7-20.
DISPLAY.BAS program listing
(continued)

Design Modification Unit (DMU)

MDBS-DMU does three useful things.

1. It allows you to change the user names and passwords.
2. It shows you how much free space is left in the data base.
3. It lets you "expand" an *empty* data base which was shipped to you in a compact form.

If you buy MDBS III you really need DMU and should include the extra cost in the budget. Keep in mind that DMU does *not* allow you to change the size of an active (not empty) data base, nor does it perform data base restructuring. Figure 7-22 shows a photo of the free space display, indicating the quantity and size of free blocks. These numbers will be meaningful after you've worked with MDBS III for a while.

COMMERCIAL SOFTWARE PRODUCTS

Micro Data Base Systems promotes MDBS III as "the premier system for serious applications developers." Among the first commercial products built around MDBS III is *Solomon Series Software* from TLB, Inc., of Findlay, Ohio. TLB got a head start working with an earlier MDBS version, MDBS I, and has since converted to MDBS III.

There are presently two packages: Solomon I—

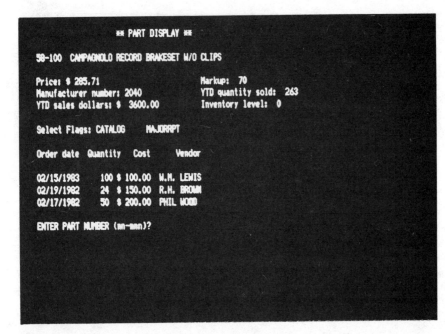

```
        ** PART DISPLAY **

58-100  CAMPAGNOLO RECORD BRAKESET W/O CLIPS

Price: $ 285.71               Markup:  70
Manufacturer number: 2040     YTD quantity sold:  263
YTD sales dollars: $  3600.00 Inventory level:  0

Select Flags: CATALOG    MAJORRPT

Order date  Quantity  Cost     Vendor

02/15/1983     100 $ 100.00  W.M. LEWIS
02/19/1982      24 $ 150.00  R.H. BROWN
02/17/1982      50 $ 200.00  PHIL WOOD

ENTER PART NUMBER (nn-nnn)?
```

FIGURE 7-21.
DISPLAY screen output

```
        Option:  A

For area PARTS  :


              Data Base Statistics
             (all values in hexadecimal)
Range:    0-21   33-100  101-200 201- 300 301- 400   totals

Bytes:  01D4E   043C7   06612   00000   00000   0C727
Freq.:  0021A   0006F   0004B   00000   00000   002D4

        Calculation Overflows:    0004C


        Statistics Menu:
All areas:             A
Individual area:       I
Exit to main DMU menu: E


        Option:
```

FIGURE 7-22.
DMU status display

General Accounting and Solomon II—General Accounting with Job Cost. Each of these packages is a *totally integrated* system. Solomon II, for example, includes general ledger, accounts payable, accounts receivable, payroll, fixed assets, job costing, and address maintenance, all part of *one* software package and all running from one master menu. The data for all subsystems resides in *one disk file*.

Accounts Payable—Data Base Versus Conventional Methods

In order to appreciate the Solomon series, consider how a *conventional* microcomputer accounting system handles accounts payable. (The system under scrutiny is described in the book *Accounts Payable & Accounts Receivable CBASIC* (Berkeley: Osborne/McGraw-Hill, 1979) and uses a common file-oriented approach to business programming.)

Consider the problem of *posting an invoice*. You have just received a bill from a vendor who sells to you on credit. The computer system must allow entry of this invoice into your accounts payable ledger under the proper vendor, recording how much is to be paid and when it must be paid. A ledger report should show all invoices by vendor, and a check-writer program should let you pay selected invoices, combining all payments for the same vendor on one check. In addition, the system must post to the general ledger; often an invoice must be *distributed* over several expense accounts, and there must be an offsetting credit to the accounts payable account.

This all sounds so simple; it can be completely described in one paragraph. Figure 7-23 illustrates how the system flows in the Osborne book. The disk files involved are the following:

· *Invoice Transaction File*. Holds an image of a

new invoice before it's added to the Invoice File.

· *Invoice File*. Holds the actual invoice records until you delete them. The *original* invoice file and the new transactions are merged, forming the *new* invoice file, whereupon the original is deleted.

· *Vendor File*. Contains the name and address of each vendor plus the year-to-date and prior year sales amounts.

· *General Ledger External Posting File*. Holds individual general ledger posting transactions: debits and credits to specific general ledger accounts.

· *General Ledger Account File*. Contains the account numbers, descriptions, and amounts for all general ledger accounts. For balance sheet accounts, the amount is the account balance; for income statement accounts, the amount is the period-to-date total.

As the invoice posting process is summarized below, refer to Figure 7-23.

1. A batch of invoice transactions is entered from the terminal. For each transaction, the vendor number is verified against the Vendor File and the newly entered invoice number is checked against the Invoice File to see if it already exists. The binary search technique is used for both lookups. The Transaction File is created, one record per transaction entered. There is a maximum of eleven general ledger account distributions allowed per invoice, and those accounts and amounts are stored as individual fields in the transaction record.

2. The transactions are *sorted* by vendor number and invoice number, the same order as the Invoice File, then printed to form an audit trail.

3. The sorted Transaction File is *merged* (see Chapter 3) with the Invoice File, creating a new Invoice File which replaces the original one (A/P Update Program). If any invoices

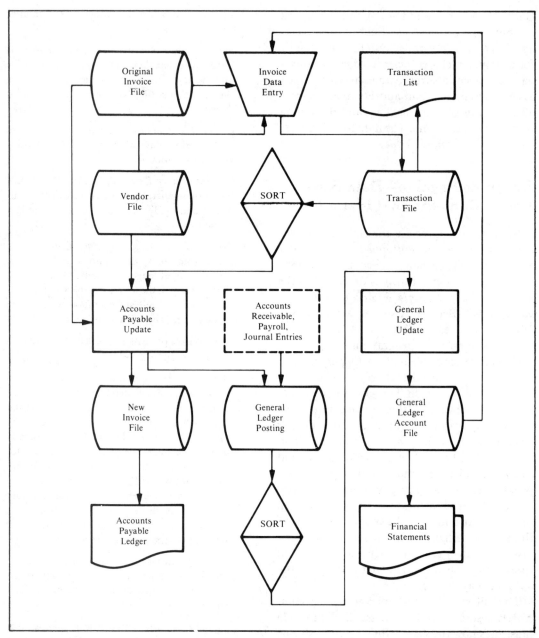

FIGURE 7-23.
Osborne accounts payable/general ledger
posting an invoice

were paid before being entered, the appropriate vendor's year-to-date sales amount is updated, requiring access to the Vendor File.

4. General ledger external postings are generated and are stored temporarily in the General Ledger External Posting File.

5. The Invoice Transaction File is deleted.

6. The general ledger postings are sorted, then *posted* to the General Ledger Account File (G/L Update Program). Debit postings increase the amounts; credit postings decrease them.

7. The General Ledger External Posting File is deleted.

8. The Accounts Payable Ledger, Financial Statements, and other reports may be printed.

Figure 7-24 shows the contrasting Solomon approach. The two SORTs and the two UPDATE

programs have been eliminated, and five physical files have been reduced to one—the data base. The simplified Solomon I schema shown in Figure 7-25 tells the story. When an invoice (called a voucher in Solomon) is entered, a VOUCHER HEADER record is created, along with a series of G/L POSTING records, corresponding to the expense distributions. Now the VOUCHER HEADER is connected to the VENDOR record, and the G/L POSTINGS are connected to *both* the VOUCHER HEADER and the proper G/L ACCOUNT record. Also, the VOUCHER HEADER is connected to a SESSION record, allowing a later listing of all vouchers entered during the current session.

In the Solomon system, when a voucher is entered, both the accounts payable ledger and the general ledger are automatically and instantly updated. There is no waiting around for SORTs and UPDATEs which take as much as

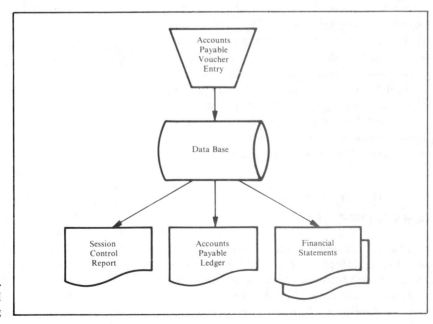

FIGURE 7-24.
Solomon Series I
voucher posting

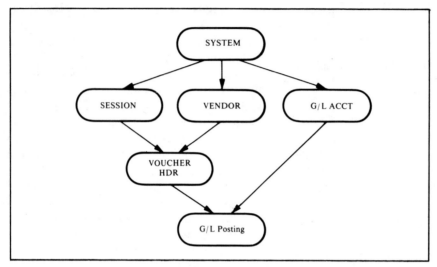

FIGURE 7-25.
Solomon simplified accounts payable schema

an hour with the Osborne system. The Accounts Payable Ledger report program moves down the path from SYSTEM to VENDOR to VOUCHER HEADER to G/L POSTINGS; financial statement report programs grab the opening balance from each G/L ACCOUNT record, then add up all the associated G/L POSTING values.

Solomon II takes the integration a step beyond Solomon I, allowing postings to Job Cost. The voucher is distributed to a number of Job/Phase/Service-codes, as well as to general ledger accounts, requiring a more complex schema than the one shown in Figure 7-25.

Payroll—PL/I-80 And MDBS III

The parts example in the preceding section was written using the Microsoft BASIC compiler because the source code is most familiar to microcomputer users. For the Solomon system, its developer, TLB, Inc., chose PL/I-80 from Digital Research, a language more sophisticated than BASIC and better suited to business applications. PL/I offers the following advantages over BASIC for use with MDBS III:

1. *Data structures* match MDBS records. The PL/I programmer codes

   ```
   1 employee
   2 name
   2 address
   2 Social Security number
   2 pay rate
   ```

   and then uses "name," "address," and so on, as program variables and uses "employee" in MDBS-DMS calls. This eliminates the CALL DEFINE as used in the BASIC parts example. The PL/I variable "name" corresponds to a field in the MDBS EMPLOYEE record.

2. Dollar amounts are stored in *decimal format*, eliminating roundoff errors. Try the double-precision BASIC program

   ```
   10 X# = 333.01
   20 PRINT USING ''#######.##'';X#*1000
   ```

which results in 333010.01. PL/I would round off to 333010.00.

3. *Overlays* are permitted. A complex accounting system has over a hundred program modules which won't all fit into memory at once. A lot of code is common to all modules, namely, the data base access routines. PL/I permits the common code to remain untouched in low memory, and only the unique code must be loaded from disk. The BASCOM compiler has only the %CHAIN command which loads an entire BASIC program.

4. Nested IF-THEN-ELSE structures are supported, all but eliminating GOTOs—a victory for *structured programming*.

The Solomon *payroll subsystem* is a good place to see PL/I-80 at work. First there is another schema to study, this one shown in Figure 7-26. This is not a simplification but the actual system. The DDL specification is given in Figure 7-27. The SYSTEM-COMPANY-DIVISION-EMPLOYEE hierarchy is straightforward. TIMESHEET entries (hours worked) are connected to both EMPLOYEE and DIVISION. Each EMPLOYEE can be connected, via *two* sets, to two STATE/LOCALITY records, allowing state and city income tax computations.

One feature of the Solomon system is a *common name and address list* for employees, vendors, customers, and other business contacts. If the same firm is both a vendor and a customer, there is only one address listed. There is a direct path to an ADDRESS record from the EMPLOYEE record, but there is another path through the ADSELCT record which works exactly the same as the SELECT path in the parts store example. You can request a listing or mailing label printout for any of 25 address subsets, and the "E" flag specifies employees. Thus, the same program that prints employee

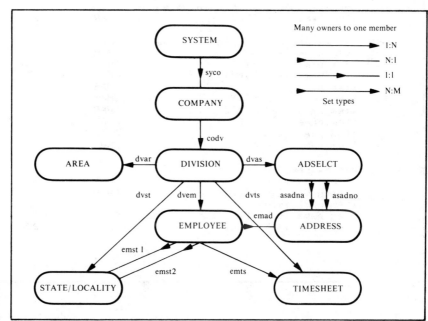

FIGURE 7-26. Solomon payroll schema

```
/********************************************
                FILES SECTION
********************************************/

database name is SOLIII
        file name is  "DATABASE.NO1"
        page size is 768 bytes


/********************************************
              PASSWORDS SECTION
********************************************/

user  is  ANYONE  with  XYZ

/********************************************
               RECORDS SECTION
********************************************/

record name is COMPANY within any area
        item name is COFILL                CHAR        81

record name is DIVISION within any area
        item name is DVNUM                 CHAR        2
        item name is DVFILL                CHAR        172

record name is AREA within any area
        item name is AREANO                CHAR        2
        item name is ARFILL                CHAR        81

record name is ADSELCT within any area
        item name is ASELCD                CHAR        1

record name is ADDRESS within any area
        item name is ADNO                  CHAR        6
        item name is ADNAME                CHAR        25
        item name is ADLINE1               CHAR        25
        item name is ADSTRT                CHAR        25
        item name is ADCITY                CHAR        12
        item name is ADSTATE               CHAR        6
        item name is ADZIP                 CHAR        9
        item name is ADPHONE               CHAR        10
        item name is ADFMT                 CHAR        1

record name is EMPLOYEE within any area
        item name is ENO                   CHAR        6
        item name is EMFILL1               CHAR        13
        item name is FRQENO                CHAR        7
        item name is EEXPACCT              CHAR        7
        item name is EMFILL2               CHAR        338
```

(continued)

FIGURE 7-27.
Solomon payroll DDL specification

```
record name is STAT within any area
        item name is STID                    CHAR         2
        item name is STFILL                  CHAR         121

record name is TIMESHEET within any area
        item name is TSFILL                  CHAR         100

/*****************************************
                SETS SECTION
*****************************************/

set name is DVAS
        type is 1:N
        owner is DIVISION
        member is ADSELCT
        order is sorted by ascending ASELCD
        insertion is AUTO

set name is ASADNA
        type is N:M
        owner is ADSELCT
        order is sorted by ascending ASELCD
        member is ADDRESS
        order is sorted by ascending ADNAME
        insertion is AUTO

set name is ASADNO
        type is N:M
        owner is ADSELCT
        order is sorted by ascending ASELCD
        member is ADDRESS
        order is sorted by ascending ADNO
        insertion is AUTO

set name is DVEM
        type is 1:N .
        owner is DIVISION
        member is EMPLOYEE
        order is sorted by ascending ENO
        insertion is AUTO

set name is EMST2
        type is N:1
        owner is EMPLOYEE
        member is STAT
        insertion is MANUAL

set name is EMST1
        type is N:1
        owner is EMPLOYEE
        member is STAT
        insertion is MANUAL
```

(continued)

FIGURE 7-27.
Solomon payroll DDL specification
(continued)

```
set name is DVST
        type is 1:N
        owner is DIVISION
        member is STAT
        order is sorted by ascending STID
        insertion is AUTO

set name is SYCO
        type is 1:1
        owner is SYSTEM
        member is COMPANY
        insertion is AUTO

set name is CODV
        type is 1:N
        owner is COMPANY
        member is DIVISION
        order is sorted by ascending DVNUM
        insertion is AUTO

set name is DVAR
        type is 1:N
        owner is DIVISION
        member is AREA
        order is sorted by ascending AREANO
        insertion is AUTO

set name is EMAD
        type is N:1
        owner is EMPLOYEE
        member is ADDRESS
        insertion is MANUAL

set name is DTS          /* temporary set for duration of payroll */
        type is N:1
        owner is DIVISION
        member is TIMESHEET
        insertion is AUTO

set name is EMTS         /* temporary set for duration of payroll */
        type is N:1
        owner is EMPLOYEE
        member is TIMESHEET
        insertion is AUTO

end.
```

FIGURE 7-27.
Solomon payroll DDL specification
(continued)

mailing labels prints vendor and customer labels. Another data base triumph.

Figure 7-28 shows some fragments of the Solomon PL/I program which allows adding, changing, and deleting employees. Don't attempt to understand the program, but just try to get a feeling for the PL/I-MDBS interaction. Here are a few points of interest.

- Solomon overlays call MDBS III *indirectly* through the CDB routine located in the memory-resident root module. The "get data from member" statement ERR = CDB('GETM, DVEM',ADDR(EMPLOYEE)) translates to ERR = GETM('DVEM,ADDR(EMPLOYEE)).

- Solomon uses its own built-in screen manager, accessed by statements like CALL SCRNED (9,21,EEXMPFD,3,0). This outputs data in decimal format (three digits, zero decimal digits, right-justified) at row 9, column 21 into the 3-character variable EEXMPFD. The end result is full cursor addressing with the ability to move backward and forward among fields.

- The %INCLUDE statements at the beginning of the program bring in the data declarations. One of these declaration files, EMPLOYEE.PLI, is partially shown in Figure 7-29. Many programs use this record layout, so if it must be changed, only one source file must be updated. When the programs are recompiled, they will access the record in its new form. As a matter of fact, MDBS III is unaware of the employee record's detailed layout. If you look at the DDL specification in Figure 7-27, you will notice that most of the employee data is hidden in EMFILL2, a 338-character "megavariable." This means, of course, that you can't use QRS because there is no way to separate the individual data items.

Figure 7-30 shows an "empty" employee maintenance screen, and Figure 7-31 shows a "full" one. Mr. Blake is assigned an employee ID of 000001, and also an address ID, in this case the same number. A separate screen, shown in Figure 7-32, permits entry of address information, doing triple duty as the vendor and customer address entry screen.

Recovery and Transaction Logging Module (RTL)

In the examples so far, no mention has been made of *error recovery*. If the power fails while you are calculating a payroll, you restore the most recent backup copy of the data base file and rekey the timecards. This method works when all inputs are paper documents, but it requires extra clerical labor.

MDBS-RTL makes error recovery possible on two levels. *Page-image processing*, called the first line of defense against data base failure, prevents a complex transaction sequence from going to disk until it is completed. Remember that MDBS III uses virtual memory and that newly added data for a transaction could be spread out over many pages, both in memory and on disk. If a system failure occurred before all necessary pages were written to disk, the data base on disk would be *inconsistent*, and therefore unusable. Special DMS commands, available only with the RTL option, enable the programmer to "bracket" a series of transactions, and send intermediate results to a temporary page-image file. Only when the transaction sequence is completed are the new pages written to the data base on disk. Unless the failure occurs during the short time when this batch of pages is being written, it will be possible to reopen the data base and continue processing.

Transaction logging, the second line of defense, creates a sequential disk file record on a *log file* for each transaction which changes the data base. If a system failure doesn't cause a disk directory crash, this file can be played back through the *recovery* utility program called

```
P02010:
  PROC;

/*****************************************************************/
/*                                                             */
/*      EMPLOYEE INFORMATION MAINTENANCE                       */
/*      E. FLUM   12/21/81                                     */
/*                                                             */
/*      COPYRIGHT 1981, TLB ASSOCIATES, INC.                  */
/*                                                             */
/*****************************************************************/

%INCLUDE 'B:EMPLOYEE.PLI';
%INCLUDE 'B:DECLARE.PLI';
  ..............

DECLARE          ASELCD  CHAR(1);
DECLARE
  LAB    LABEL VARIABLE,
  (FLAG,IFLAG,JFLAG)    BIT(1),
  (ERR,DAERR,DBERR,DCERR) FIXED BINARY,
  LCID          CHAR(2),
  B      CHAR(40) VARYING,
  ANS    CHAR(10) VARYING,
  L    FIXED,
  SELECT          CHAR(1),
  HOLD CHAR(10) VARYING,
  HOLDA CHAR(10) VARYING;

ON ERROR(250) GOTO LAB;
  ...............

CONTA:
      ADNO = '';
      DAERR = CDB('FMSK,DVEM',ADDR(ENO)); /* check to see if employee exists *
DBERR = 255;
      IF DAERR = 0 THEN
      DO;
        ERR = CDB('GETM,DVEM',ADDR(EMPLOYEE));  /* get the employee record */
        CALL CHLST;
        IF SELECT = 'A' THEN CALL MESS(ER(10),1);        /* add */

        IF SELECT = 'C' THEN DO;                          /* change */
          ANS = '';
          JFLAG = '1'B;
          IF ITFLG1 = '' THEN DO WHILE(JFLAG);
            CALL MESS(ER(11),1);
            IF ANS > '' THEN CALL MESS(ER(1),2);
            ANS = INPUT(22,42,1,1,0,'A','010'B);
            IF INDEX('YN',ANS) > 0 THEN JFLAG = '0'B;
            IF ANS = 'Y' THEN CALL ADPROC;
          END;
```

(continued)

FIGURE 7-28.
Fragments of Solomon employee
maintenance PL/I program

```
            ELSE ANS = 'Y';
            IF ANS = 'Y' THEN DO;
              ERR = CDB('SOM,EMAD,DVEM',NULL);    /* find address record if
                         connected to the employee record. If an address
                         record is not attached, then it has already been
                         created in the address maintenance screen. If this
                         is the case, attach the current address record to
                         the employee.   */
              IF ERR = 255 THEN ERR = CDB('AMS,ADDRESS,EMAD',NULL);
              ITFLG4 = STID !! LCID !! ' C';
              PROGRAM = 'P0201A';ITFLG1 = '';GOTO EXIT;
            END;
        END;

        ANS = '';
        JFLAG = '1'B;
        IF SELECT = 'D' THEN DO WHILE(JFLAG);    /* delete*/
          JFLAG = '0'B;
          CALL MESS(ER(12),1);
          IF ANS > '' THEN CALL MESS(ER(1),2);
          ANS = INPUT(22,42,1,1,0,'A','010'B);
          IF ANS = 'Y' THEN DO;
            FLAG = '1'B;
            DO L = 1 TO 12 WHILE(FLAG);
                IF ARR2(L) = 0 THEN FLAG = '0'B;
            END;
            IF FLAG THEN
                ERR = CDB('DRM,DVEM',NULL);   /* delete employee if no earnings *
            ELSE CALL MESS('Employee may not be deleted',1);
          END;
          ELSE IF ANS = 'N' THEN JFLAG = '1'B;
        END;
      END;
      ELSE DO;
        IF SELECT = 'A' THEN DO;
          IF ITFLG1 = '' THEN CALL ADPROC;
          ITFLG1 = '';
          ITFLG3 = ENO;
          ITFLG4 = '      A';
          PROGRAM = 'P0201A';
          GOTO EXIT;
        END;
        CALL MESS(ER(9),1);
      END;
      END;

CHLST:              /*  PRINT EMPLOYEE DATA  */
PROC;
      DBERR = CDB('SOM,EMAD,DVEM',NULL);
      IF DBERR = 0 THEN DO;
        ERR = CDB('GETM,EMAD',ADDR(ADDRESS));
        CALL ADLST();
      END;
```

(continued)

FIGURE 7-28.
Fragments of Solomon employee
maintenance PL/I program (continued)

```
        ERR=CDB('GETM,DVEM',ADDR(EMPLOYEE));
        BUFFER = EMSTAT;
        CALL SCREEN(8,23,BUFFER);           /* display employee data on screen *
        CALL SCRNED(9,21,EEXMPFD,3,0);      /* using screen handler routines   *
        CALL SCRNED(10,21,EEXMPST,3,0);
        CALL SCRNED(11,21,EEXMPCT,3,0);
    .....................

PEXIT:
        PROGRAM='P02000';
EXIT:
        RETURN;
END P02010;
```

FIGURE 7-28.
Fragments of Solomon employee
maintenance PL/I program (continued)

RCV, a part of the RTL package. If the data base is reloaded from the most recent backup, applying all the logged transactions will restore it to the point just before failure.

If page-image processing were in effect at the time of failure, any transactions in an incomplete sequence would not appear in the log file. Those log file records are only written at the end of the sequence.

Transaction logging permits recovery from operator error as well as from system failure. If one data base user had entered a bad batch of data, the data base could be reloaded from backup and *selective* recovery could apply to all transactions except the bad ones.

If you buy the RTL option, you can use transaction logging with *IDML*, as well as with your own programs. As a test, the NEWORDR macro (see the IDML material in the parts store example) was executed several times with RTL active. Two new orders were entered and the resulting log file saved. The data base was restored to its condition just before the addition of the new orders. The RCV utility used to list the logged transactions is illustrated in Figure 7-33.

The *Update* option was then used to apply the transactions to the data base, thus restoring the new orders.

RTL may be used with programs such as PARTLOAD by linking in the DMS-RTL routines instead of the plain DMS routines. A technical problem made testing impossible, but you can be sure RTL would have meant slower programs and fewer virtual memory pages.

Because the listed log transactions are somewhat cryptic (hexadecimal index numbers, for example) the non-technical user would have problems with RCV. Any system relying on RTL and RCV to log and restore transactions should have support staff on hand for recoveries.

Multiuser Operation

MDBS III is the first microcomputer DBMS to offer true multiuser operation. This operation isn't supported in the CP/M version because CP/M is a single-user operating system; however, there are MDBS III versions for MP/M, UNIX, Xenix, and other multi-user operating systems, and more are on the way.

```
DECLARE
  1 EMPLOYEE,
    2 ENO              CHAR(6),
    2 EMARSTA          CHAR(1),
    2 EEXMPST          FIXED BINARY(7),
    2 EEXMPFD          FIXED BINARY(7),
    2 EEXMPCT          FIXED BINARY(7),
    2 ESSN             CHAR(9),
    2 EPYFREQ          CHAR(1),
    2 ENOSORT          CHAR(6),
    2 EEXPACCT         CHAR(7),
    2 EPYTYP           CHAR(1),
    2 EFEDTAX          CHAR(1),
    2 EFICATAX         CHAR(1),
    2 EFUTATAX         CHAR(1),
    2 ESTATTAX         CHAR(1),
    2 ESUITAX          CHAR(1),
    2 EADDSTEX         FIXED DECIMAL(9,2),
    2 EADDSTCR         FIXED DECIMAL(9,2),
    2 ESALARY          FIXED DECIMAL(9,2),
    2 EPYRATE          FIXED DECIMAL(9,2),
    2 EMMSC(5),
      3 EMTYP          CHAR(1),
      3 EMPCT          FIXED DECIMAL(5,2),
      3 EMMIN          FIXED DECIMAL(9,2),
      3 EMMAX          FIXED DECIMAL(9,2),
..............
```

FIGURE 7-29.
%INCLUDE module for
employee record

While 8-bit MP/M is supported, its response time may not be acceptable. None of the multi-user features were tested, but according to the documentation, all the active and passive locking features are supported, as described in Chapter 3. If one user tries to access a record locked out by another user, MDBS makes periodic retries, based on some multiple of the system clock. There is a mechanism to prevent "deadly embrace" where user A waits for user B to release a record, while user B is waiting for user A to release it.

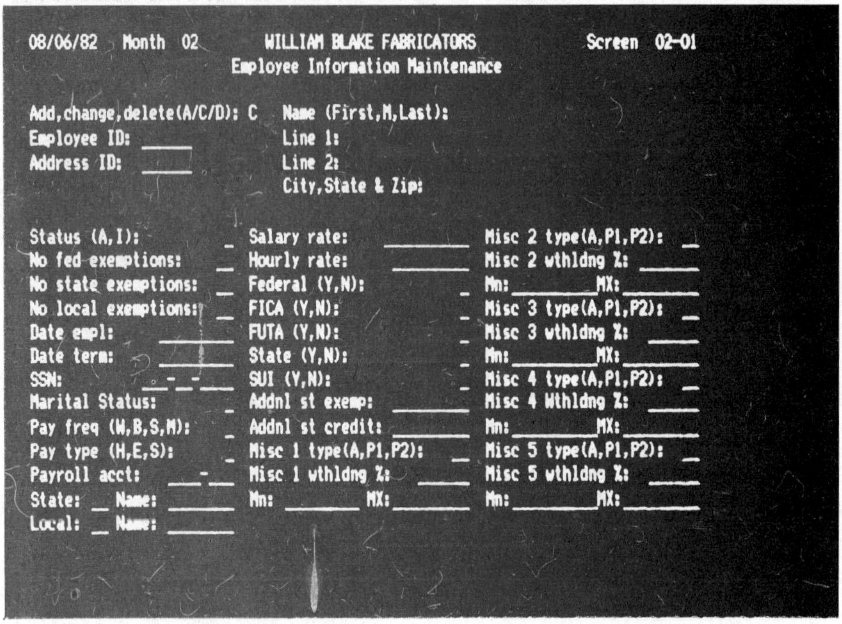

FIGURE 7-30.
Empty Solomon
employee
maintenance screen

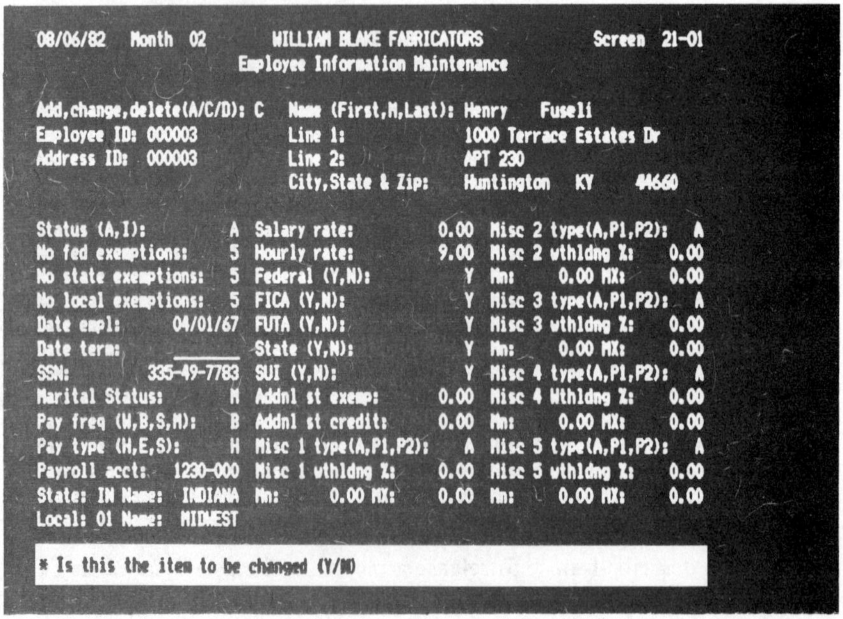

FIGURE 7-31.
Employee screen
with data added

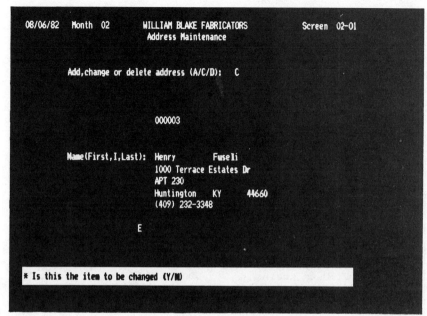

FIGURE 7-32.
Solomon address
screen

Data Transfer to or from Other Systems

Total flexibility is allowed for reading from and writing to conventional disk files, because MDBS III uses a host language. The PART-LOAD program in Figure 7-7 is an example of a program which reads BASIC files. Remember that a data base load program is seldom trivial.

Documentation

The large stack of manuals that confronts you after opening the MDBS box is nothing short of overwhelming. You must insert all the addenda sheets and the manuals in a loose-leaf binder. Plastic divider tabs separate the sections and subsections, making a very easy to use reference book. The text is particularly clear

and well organized, with a consistent format. All in all, the MDBS III documentation is a thoroughly professional effort.

The *User's Manual* is the principal reference document, with major sections for MDBS-DDL and MDBS-DMS. Additional sections for the add-ons, IDML, QRS, DMU, and RTL, fit into the same loose-leaf notebook, using the same color-coded index tab system. Each section forms a single document, complete with a table of contents, error message listings, appendixes, and an index.

The MBDS-DDL section contains the most general theory: defining the physical and logical structure of the data base and explaining the four kinds of sets. The section presents a complete specification of the DDL language, and data security and integrity information. The MDBS-DMS section describes all the DMS commands by function, as listed at the start of

```
 MDBS.RCV Ver 3.01a Transaction Recovery System
 (C) COPYRIGHT 1981, Micro Data Base Systems, Inc.
 Lafayette, IN 47092

 Serial Number:      99999999

      User Name: OWNER
      Password: (password is not echoed)

 Data Base Name: B:PARTS
 Transaction File? B:PARTS.LOG
 OPTIONS:  (List, Quit, Reset, Scan, Update)?L

 First transaction # [1] ?  (defaults are in brackets)
 Last transaction # [highest] ?
 User name [all]


 ID Tran No. Description
 --- --------- -----------

 0 00000001..Data Base Opened
 1 00000002..User Login          000000 OWNER
 1 00000003..Create Record          ORDR 06000382
 1 00000004..Insert Rec in Set    PARTORD 06000382 05003900
 1 00000005..Insert Rec in Set    VENDORD 06000382 0400B003
 1 00000006..Create Record Set       ORDR 0600ED02
 1 00000007..Insert Rec in Set    PARTORD 0600ED02 0800DD03
 1 00000008..Insert Rec in Set    VENDORD 0600ED02 0400C503
 1 00000009..User Logout
 0 0000000A..Data Base Closed

 OPTIONS:  (List, Quit, Reset, Scan, Update)?
```

FIGURE 7-33.
RCV utility

this chapter. This is an example of the *MDBS III User's Manual.*

SOM *Set Owner based on Member* **SOM**

Command and Arguments
SOM,set-1,set-2

Currency Indicators
Used: CM(set-2)
Changed: CO(set-1)
  <——CM(set-2)
  CM(set-1)
  <——first member
  CRU<——
  first member

Description

Set the current owner of **set-1** to be the same as the current member of **set-2**. This command is valid only if the owner record type(s) for **set-1** is the same as the member record type(s) for **set-2**. The first member of the new current owner of **set-1** becomes the new current member of **set-1** and the current of run unit. If the new current owner of **set-1** has no members via **set-1**, then the current member of **set-1** becomes null, the current of run unit becomes null and the command status is 255. If a user does not have read access to **set-1** and **set-2**, then a command status error is returned and no currency indicators change.

Examples of Command Usage

block/direct... E0 = SOM ("set-1, set-2")

block/indirect... E0 = DMS ("SOM, set-1, set-2")

record/direct... E0 = SOM ("set-1, set-2")

record/indirect... E0 = DMS ("SOM, set-1, set-2")

Excerpted with permission from MDBS Data Base Design Reference Manual, © 1982 Micro Data Base Systems, Inc.

A convenient feature of the *User's Manual* is the separation of fundamental information from advanced information. A thick vertical bar in the left column delineates the advanced material, focusing the reader's attention on the basics.

In addition to the *User's Manual*, there are *system-specific installation manuals*, one for each operating system and language combination. If you were using MDBS III with CP/M and the two languages BASCOM and PL/I, you would have two system-specific manuals, each giving installation instructions, calling conventions, and correspondence between MDBS data items and host language variables. Remember that if you use MDBS III with more than one host language, you must pay more for the additional interface programs and documentation.

To make the installation go smoothly, the system-specific manuals tie to a sample application, a book/keyword system similar to that described in Chapter 5. You are given the DDL schema specification and the source language program. After initializing the data base with MDBS-DDL, you compile the program, link it with the DMS routines, and test it. It's actually a good introduction to DDL and DMS coding.

Finally, there are two *tutorial* booklets by Dr. Clyde Holsapple, an MDBS consultant, titled *A Guide to Data Base Management* and *A Primer on Data Base Management Systems*.

Both develop MDBS III concepts with examples, notably a complex school problem with students, teachers, courses, sections, activities, and advisors. The *Guide* describes the first Micro Data Base Systems product, HDBS, a *hierarchical* data base management system and a subset of MDBS I, the predecessor of MDBS III. It shows DDL examples in an earlier format very different from that of MDBS III. The 54-page *Primer* explores the MDBS III *extended-network* approach with the school problem, then retreats to the hierarchical model, showing the network's superiority. Many illustrations, together with program fragments and narrative, make this booklet useful as an introduction to MDBS III.

Support

Service and maintenance for the first year is free and is provided by the customer support divisions of the various ISE companies. Service in subsequent years is available from ISE for 15 percent of the price then current. This buys you free updates as they are released, plus a maximum of four hours telephone consulting. A call to MDBS (now ISE) technical support yielded immediate answers to some problems, plus confirmation that a few bugs existed. The bugs, relating to range checks and duplicate key prevention, were supposed to be fixed in the next version. Without the support contract, you can get updates for a fee.

Error Handling

A great deal of your MDBS III programming effort will be devoted to error processing. Each call to MDBS III yields a command status code which, if non-zero, must be dealt with individually in the program. The MDBS-DMS manual section covers the command status codes in detail. A sample of the 100-odd numbered codes is listed here.

** 4**	Invalid data item for this record type
** 7**	Invalid data block name
14	Data base area already open
19	No duplicate record allowed
47	User may not write this area
51	Disk read or write error
255	Record not found

Standard procedure, as shown in the sample BASIC programs, dictates that your program process "expected" errors caused by operators and print out diagnostic messages for "unexpected" ones. If an on-line program is to run continuously, only media failure errors and program logic errors are really fatal.

Most unexpected errors appear during debugging, and the causes are easily identified. If you are writing an entire record to the data base, and one data item is bad, you have a problem because MDBS III's "invalid data item" message doesn't specify which item is invalid. Your alternative is to write each item individually.

Technical Information

MDBS III uses a *virtual* memory system as described in Chapter 3. You set the page size and number of pages on disk when you write the DDL specification, and you set the number of pages in memory when you write the programs. All programs should allow as much page space as possible for fast execution. In a typical 64K system, the maximum possible buffer size for the PARTLOAD program (Figure 7-7) is 12K, or twelve 1024-byte buffers.

Any increase in memory speeds up MDBS III processing considerably, and there are two ways to use extra memory banks. One method uses MP/M, together with a special single-user

MP/M version of MDBS III that permits all the MDBS code to reside in a separate 64K memory bank. This allows more page buffer space in the user bank. Another approach uses a special CP/M which buffers the disk through the extra memory bank, reading and writing whole tracks at a time. This creates a "three-level" virtual memory scheme with a large part of the data base in the disk buffer. MDBS thinks it's reading and writing pages from disk, but in reality it is moving data from one memory bank to another.

Those MDBS III sets that are *sorted* are accessed through an invisible multilevel balanced *index*. This proprietary method is very similar to a B$^+$-tree scheme, but is claimed to be marginally superior. FIFO and LIFO sets use a multilevel balanced *pointer* array, also invisible to the programmer. The indexes and pointer arrays still take up disk space. There is a formula for computing needed disk space based on numbers of records and sets. Trial and error methods are usually faster, though.

Random access will work through the indexing scheme, but you can make it faster by employing a hashing method using *calc keys*. You define random access records in the DDL specification, choosing one or more fields as the calc key (not necessarily the same as the set's sort key). MDBS III spreads the records over all the pages, determining a hashing algorithm based on the length of the keys and the number of allocated pages. Bear in mind that you can't change the data base size once you've initialized it. That requires unloading the old data base back to conventional disk files, then loading those files back into a newly initialized, larger data base.

MDBS III allows *variable-length records*, or rather variable-length data items within records. It is possible, with the use of calc keys, to randomly access these variable-length records, a feat quite impossible with most file-oriented systems.

Performance

It's unfair to compare the performance of MDBS III directly with that of RDBMS. Because the RDBMS physical data organization fits closely with CP/M, sequential passes of large databases are faster than the MDBS III equivalent. Also, it's important to remember that the performance of MDBS III depends on the amount of page buffer space available, the data base's physical location on disk, and so on. The following are the specifications for the parts store system.

Benchmark

1685 records, maximum length 70 bytes, organized as a one-to-many set, owner SYSTEM.

Floppy Disk:
    Sequential pass with QRS (14 minutes)
    Direct part access (1 second)

Hard Disk:
    Sequential pass with QRS (7 minutes)
    Sequential pass with BASIC program,
        12K buffer (6 minutes)
    Direct part access (1/2 second)

Remember that there are no sorts required with MDBS III except for an optional sort of QRS output. Through proper data base design *you can eliminate the need for a sequential pass*. The parts store system's mail-order catalog program listed a subset of parts through a select set, neatly avoiding the processing of all part records.

The hard disk time for the data base batch load was three hours, but this could have been improved by optimum positioning of the data base file on disk. Because of long load times, it is important to do research and development with small prototype data bases. The three-hour load time translates to two seconds per part. If parts were being added interactively at a terminal, MDBS III would certainly have kept up with the fastest operator.

As for memory usage, a typical MDBS III memory map looks something like the following:

Run-time routines:	16K
MDBS III routines:	20K
Page buffer:	12K
Application program:	8K
CP/M operating sys:	8K
	64K

It may seem that 8K isn't a lot of program space, but TLB, Inc. puts a surprising amount of Solomon code in there, including the screen handler. The use of many overlays helps, and the overlays load quickly because only a short segment of code is involved.

Restrictions

MDBS III doesn't restrict what you do, but it imposes a certain discipline. You can make a system do anything you need, but plan to do the following:

- Buy and learn a programming language with which MDBS III interfaces.
- Buy or write your own screen handler. A screen handler called SCREEN is forthcoming from Micro Data Base Systems.
- Plan your data base structure well before starting to program. Advance planning and project management are necessary with any DBMS or without one, but RDBMS and FMS are more tolerant of frequent design changes.
- Deal with tight memory space by frequent chaining or overlay swapping, or use 16 bits.
- Endure the lack of a restructure utility. DRS, a data restructure utility, is forthcoming.

Security

MDBS III has excellent security capability. The only problem is that user names, passwords, and access codes are modifiable only with the MDBS-DMU utility. This precludes access from a main menu, an important requirement for turnkey systems operated by non-technical staff. The authors of the Solomon software solved this problem by shortcutting the internal MDBS security and programming their own system, storing the passwords in a special set in the data base. The password library can be updated by anyone who possesses the master password.

DATA MANIPULATION COMMANDS

Assignment Commands

SCM
  Set current of run unit based on member

SCN
  Set current of run unit to null

SCO
  Set current of run unit based on owner

SCU
  Set current of run unit based on user indicator

SMC
  Set member based on current of run unit

SME
  Set member to current of run unit (exception)

SMM
  Set member based on member

SMN
  Set member to null

SMO
  Set member based on owner

SMU
  Set member based on user indicator

SOC
  Set owner based on current of run unit

SOE
  Set owner to current of run unit (exception)

SOM
  Set owner based on member

SON
  Set owner to null

SOO
  Set owner based on owner

SOU
  Set owner based on user indicator

SUC
  Set user indicator to current of run unit

SUM
  Set user indicator to member

SUN
  Set user indicator to null

SUO
  Set user indicator to owner

SUU
  Set user indicator to user indicator

Boolean Commands

AMM
  And of members with members

AMO
  And of members with owners

AOM
  And of owners with members

AOO
  And of owners with owners

XMM
  Exclude members from members

XMO
  Exclude members from owners

XOM
  Exclude owners from members

DATA MANIPULATION
COMMANDS (Continued)

XOO
Exclude owners from owners

Connect Commands

IMS
Insert member into set

IOS
Insert owner into set

Creation Commands

CRA
Create record in area

CRS
Create record and store

Deletion Commands

DRC
Delete record that is current

DRM
Delete record that is member

DRO
Delete record that is owner

Disconnect Commands

RMS
Remove member from set

ROS
Remove owner from set

RSM
Remove all set members

RSO
Remove all set owners

Find Commands

FDRK
Find duplicate record based on calc key

FFM
Find first member

FFO
Find first owner

FFS
Find first sequential record

FLM
Find last member

FLO
Find last owner

FMI
Find member based on data item

FMSK
Find member based on sort key

FNM
Find next member

FNMI
Find next member based on data item

FNMSK
Find next member based on sort key

FNO
Find next owner

FNOI
Find next owner based on data item

FNOSK
Find next owner based on sort key

FNS
Find next sequential record

FOI
Find owner based on data item

FOSK
Find owner based on sort key

FPM
Find prior member

FPO
Find prior owner

FRK
Find record based on calc key

Modify Commands

PFC
Put data into field of current of run unit

DATA MANIPULATION COMMANDS (Continued)

PFM
  Put data into field of member

PFO
  Put data into field of owner

PUTC
  Put data into current of run unit

PUTM
  Put data into member

PUTO
  Put data into owner

Multiuser Locking Commands

The following locking commands are for multiuser operating systems only.

MAU
  Multiuser active user indicators

MCC
  Multiuser current contention count

MCF
  Multiuser current of run unit free

MCP
  Multiuser current of run unit protect

MRTF
  Multiuser record type free

MRTP
  Multiuser record type protect

MSF
  Multiuser set free

MSP
  Multiuser set protect

Recovery Commands

The following recovery commands are for use with the RTL option only.

LGCPLX
  Log start of complex transactions

LGENDX
  Log END complex transactions

LGFILE
  Log FILE specification

LGFLSH
  Log file buffer flush

LGMSG
  Log file message

PIFD
  Page-image file declaration

TRABT
  Transaction abort

TRBGN
  Transaction begin

TRCOM
  Transaction commit

Retrieval Commands

GETC
  Get data from current of run unit

GETM
  Get data from member

GETO
  Get data from owner

GFC
  Get field from current on run unit

GFM
  Get field from member

GFO
  Get field from owner

Special Commands

ALTEOS
  Alter end of set

DEFINE
  Define data block

EXTEND
  Extend data block

SETPBF
  Set page buffer region

DATA MANIPULATION
COMMANDS (Continued)

UNDEF
  Undefine data blocks

VARCS
  Variable for command status

Utility Commands

AUI
  Allocate user indicators

CCU
  Check current of run unit against user indicator

DBCLS
  Data base close

DBCLSA
  Data base close for area

DBENV
  Data base environment

DBOPN
  Data base open

DBOPNA
  Data base open area

DBSAVE
  Data base save

DBSTAT
  Data base statistics

GMC
  Get member count

GOC
  Get owner count

GTC
  Get type of member

GTO
  Get type of owner

NCI
  Null all currency indicators

TCT
  Test current of run unit type

TMT
  Test member type

TOT
  Test owner type

8

More Data Base Management Software

ondor, dBASE II, FMS-80, and MDBS III are not the only data base management system packages for CP/M microcomputers. There are at least a dozen other products on the market, and new products are announced every month. This chapter summarizes those other packages that are already popular in the software marketplace. A product is described here instead of in its own chapter because it doesn't meet enough of the DBMS objectives established in Chapter 2 to warrant a full chapter, or because it is similar to one or more of the thoroughly described products.

If one package has two pages of description and another has only a paragraph, don't conclude that the first is better than the second. The "big four" DBMS packages serve as a *frame of reference* for this chapter. Unless you've bypassed Chapters 4 through 7, phrases such as "similar to Condor" will have meaning.

Again, don't make value judgements; Condor, dBASE II, FMS-80, and MDBS III were thoroughly documented because they were immediately available for extensive research, not because they are better or worse than the packages described in this chapter.

MACHINE SPECIFIC PACKAGES

Apple and Commodore Computers

You've probably noticed there are no references to software for Apple or Commodore computers. CP/M-compatible software, including the DBMS packages, will run on those machines with add-on microprocessor hardware such as the Microsoft Softcard. In addition, there are more than a few other data base management programs available for unmodified Apple and Commodore systems. Some of these programs fall into the DBMS category, and nearly all are less expensive than their CP/M counterparts. You'll have to do your own research, but Chapters 1 through 3 provide the theory and standards you need.

TRS-80 Computers

The ubiquitous Radio Shack systems are a special case. Model II and Model 16 run CP/M-compatible software with no modification, and Models I and III run it with some hardware changes. If you use the TRSDOS operating system or its variants, you enter another software world with its own set of data base management software. One TRS-80 package, Profile, is discussed here because its ease of use and low price deserve some recognition.

The IBM Personal Computer

This microcomputer is too big to ignore. Software firms have been working overtime adapting their programs to run on this machine and its Japanese and American "clones." As a result, most of the CP/M data base management packages are available or will be available soon for the personal computer. And all CP/M-80 DBMS packages will run on the IBM PC with the "Baby Blue" CP/M-80 emulator card.

DATASTAR

Price (6/82)

$350

Source

MicroPro International
1299 4th St.
San Rafael, CA 94901
(415) 457-8990

System Requirements

56K CP/M

DataStar was designed as a *data entry* system to be used as a "front end" for programs written in BASIC, COBOL, and other languages. When you use DataStar with a report generator program, such as ACCESS/80 by Friends Software, or MicroPro's own new InfoStar, you have the equivalent of a complete MDBS. DataStar helps you enter the data dictionary,

guides you through data entry, and permits sequential searching and instant keyed access. Limited multifile capability pushes DataStar into the data base world. Because DataStar's files are directly readable by BASIC programs, you don't need a built-in or a host language.

The Data Dictionary

DataStar's FORMGEN module lets you design your data entry *form* (serving as a data dictionary) directly on the CRT. You enter field descriptions such as CUSTOMER or PRODUCT CODE, then indicate fields with underscores. A six-digit product code field is represented by six underscores. This works like Condor's form definition shown in Figures 4-1 and 4-2. Data-Star doesn't name the fields as Condor does, but tracks them by relative number in the record as does FMS-80. Your DataStar field descriptions don't have to correspond to any internal field names.

Once you have laid out a screen, you move the cursor to each field and type ^R. DataStar then prompts you for all field characteristics which include

- Field derivation
  - a. Direct operator input
  - b. From external list or file
  - c. Calculated from other fields
  - d. Operator override of external data
  - e. Required entry
- Justification
  - a. Right or left
- Pad character
  - a. For incompletely entered fields
- Floating character
- Verification
  - a. Sight
  - b. Retype
  - c. Using external list or file

- Check digits
- Range check
  - *a.* Lower and upper limits
- Edit mask
  - *a.* Entry control mask
  - *b.* Content control mask

As you can see, there is more to DataStar's data dictionary than the ordinary DBMS data dictionary. This is because DataStar began as an inexpensive substitute for dedicated data entry machines. You can enter and modify your forms with surprising ease because of Data-Star's clever use of control keys; if you have used WordStar, you will feel right at home. A status line at the top of the screen shows cursor line and column number plus field lengths and the cursor's relative position in the field. There are plenty of instructional HELP screens available, so DataStar can be classified as *menu-driven.*

Key Fields

DataStar requires you to select one or more fields as a record *key*. While working in FORMGEN, you position the cursor over the target field, type ^K, then specify whether duplicate keys are allowed. The key field will later allow you to access data sequentially in key order, and it will permit quick direct access by key. If duplicate keys are forbidden, you won't be able to enter the same key twice.

Data Entry

DataStar makes optimum use of full-screen editing for data entry. You may move freely among fields and within fields, and you can insert and delete characters. This is handy if you left out a character at the beginning of a long description and you don't want to retype

it. This is similar to the dBASE II data entry method. DataStar also lets you pick up a field value from the corresponding field in the previous record.

Query Facility

Scanning lets you sequentially step through a file, one record at a time. You may scan in data file order (the order in which data was first entered) or in index order (according to the key field). In both cases you can select all records or a subset defined by a scan mask. The scan mask is an image of a form with all the fields initially set to asterisks. The asterisks are wild card characters matching anything. As an example, consider a two-field record consisting of a six-digit product code and a 20-character description. The scan mask starts out as follows:

```
PRODUCT: ******DESCRIPTION: ************
```

If you didn't touch the mask, you would be sequencing through all the records, but if you changed it to

```
PRODUCT: 6*****DESCRIPTION: WINTER*******
```

you would see only those products with first digit 6 *and* with description starting with WINTER.

You can *select* a particular record directly by entering its key, then you can switch to scan mode and sequence backward or forward from that point.

Multifile Lookup

DataStar will reference data from other files *during data entry.* If you are entering sales data, for instance, you can pick up a product description and unit price from a master file, keyed on product code. If the master file is large, the lookup can take a second or two, but if the file is small enough to fit in memory (a list of states' codes, for instance) lookup is instantaneous. You can use DataStar's calculate option to multiply unit price (from the product master) by units sold (operator entered) to get sales amount. FMS-80 and dBASE II can do this via their built-in languages, but Condor requires separate JOIN and COMPUTE passes as described in Chapter 4.

Technical Information

DataStar uses an *index* to permit indexed-sequential scanning and direct selection. This index is a separate disk file with a function somewhere in between a pointer file and B-tree index (see Chapter 3). An FMS-80 pointer file won't let you add new entries in the middle, but DataStar's index lets you add *some* new entries. Soon performance is degraded and the file and index must be *reorganized*. DataStar's index method adds new entries onto the end of the index file with *chain pointers* from the points where the entries "should have been."

Interface to Other Programs

Part of DataStar's attraction is its file compatibility. DataStar's files can be read directly by programs written in most programming languages, including report generator packages such as ACCESS/80. Since the index file can't be used, you must *sort* any DataStar file prior to outside use. DataStar's own reorganization function will do the trick, but MicroPro recommends that you use their SuperSort program for faster processing. A report generator will probably have its own high-speed sort.

Restrictions

DataStar restricts you to one form per file. Each field in the file must appear on the screen;

there are no undisplayed fields. You can't have a sales order header followed by a series of product details; you must enter all the headers in one file, then all the details in another. A BASIC or COBOL program merges them together after data entry is complete.

There is no possibility for program interaction during data entry, but the sophisticated file lookup and computation facilities may make programming unnecessary. All operations with complete files must be done with stand-alone programs. There is no equivalent to the relational JOIN and PROJECT commands, for instance.

Because the index method isn't based on B-tree methods, you must endure frequent file reorganizations if the volume of added records is high.

PROFILE II

Price
$179

Source
Radio Shack Division of the Tandy Corporation
One Tandy Center
Fort Worth, Texas 76102

System Requirements
A Radio Shack TRS-80 Model II
    microcomputer

This is *not* a CP/M-compatible program. It runs on the Radio Shack TRS-80 Model II microcomputer under the TRSDOS operating system. (The Model II can also run CP/M.) CP/M software authors should look closely at Profile because it has some features missing that are available in many CP/M data base management packages—notably low price and ease of use.

Just for the record, there is a new Profile update for the Model II called *Profile Plus* with added indexing, arithmetic, and menu functions, which sells for $299. There are also less expensive Profile versions available for the Models I and III.

Profile calls itself an "electronic filing system," not a data base. The absence of a multifile capability firmly excludes it from the DBMS class as defined by this book.

The Menu

Perhaps the best way to understand Profile is to look at its main menu. (This is a menu-driven system.)

```
PROFILE II

MENU SELECTION


0 - Profile Directory
1 - Define Data Formats
2 - Define Screen Formats
3 - Define Report Formats
4 - Define Label Formats
5 - Define Selection Formats
6 - Expand Existing File
7 - Inquire, Update, Add
8 - Print Reports
9 - Print Labels
A - Select Records
X - Exit
```

Profile is structured like FMS-80, allowing smooth screen and report definition, but providing no indexed lookup or built-in language. Profile's files may be extracted for use by BASIC programs and by Radio Shack's SCRIPSIT word processor program.

Data Dictionary
(Define Data Formats)

In keeping with Profile's simplified way of doing business, name and length are the only field attributes. Records are limited to 853

characters, the first 85 (or fewer) of which act as a combination index and data file. Those 85 characters can be split into as many as 36 fields for query and report selection. The other 768 characters may be used for non-select fields with a maximum field size of 256 bytes.

The fields are entered sequentially, one at a time, with a number assigned to each one. You must print out the field list because you reference the field numbers later in screen and report definition. Changing an already entered data dictionary is very difficult.

Screen Design
(Define Screen Formats)

Screen formats are entered in full-screen mode with the cursor. Operator prompts are typed directly on the screen, and fields are identified by number and data type, which includes numeric, alphanumeric, and two-place decimal. There can be as many as five *password-protected* screen formats per data file, allowing sensitive data to be separated from ordinary data. When data is entered into the screen format, full movement within and among fields is permitted.

Query Facility
(Inquire, Update, Add)

Profile stores records in data entry order. Queries are *sequential*, displaying data one screen at a time, in the *original* order. You are prompted to *select* on any combination of fields in the first 85 characters, with simple "and-or" connectives. There are wild card and range options, plus the standard "greater than," "less than," and so on. Once you define the selection criteria, you can step through the selected records and update them. You must enter the selection criteria each time you use them;

there's no way to store the criteria except in conjunction with a SCRIPSIT extract.

There is always *direct* access to records by record number, made easy by Profile's optional printing of record number on reports. The inquire, update, and add screens always show you the current number at the bottom.

Reporting (Define Report Formats, Print Report)

The report generator on Profile works like that on Condor, permitting you to lay out the report directly on the screen. *Horizontal scrolling* lets you use 132 columns. There is one sub-total level allowed with mandatory page breaks. There is no provision for subheadings and sub-total captions. Fields are identified by number, just as they are in screen definition.

Report printing is preceded first by a select, then by an optional sort on one field or a portion of a field. This permits reports to appear in sorted order, even though the data file is not sorted. Profile sorts are limited by memory, so you're not allowed to print a report over 1272 records if your sort key size is 20 characters. Careful use of selection criteria and control of sort key length will get you out of most binds.

Other Features

Profile lets you define and print *mailing labels* with as many as six across the page. The process is similar to that for report definition and printing, with the same effective use of the screen.

You can create a *limited menu* with access allowed only to the Inquire, Update, Add, and various print functions of the program. With proper use of *passwords* and *protected fields*, you can limit unauthorized persons' access to your data.

Technical Information

What looks at first like one Profile data file is really as many as four subfiles, or *segments*, split vertically down field boundaries. The first segment contains the select fields up to the maximum of 85 characters and serves as a pointer file as well as part of the data file. The other three optional segments contain up to 256 characters per subrecord and can be located on different disk drives, allowing maximum data storage on a diskette-based system.

The first segment is processed during queries and report printing. If a record is selected, its corresponding subrecords in the other segments can be brought in. Each segment has its own data dictionary; thus, a new segment with extra fields can be added onto an already existing data file. A given screen can access fields from any of the segments.

The number of records, as well as the number of segments, is defined when setting up the file. If your initial guess isn't large enough, you can always *expand* the file later. It's best to keep the total number of records as small as possible because sequential queries search through *all* the allocated records.

Restrictions

Profile does a lot for being so simple a system. If you keep its electronic filing in mind you should be happy, but if you step outside this framework you could be frustrated. There's no multifile capability, no way to post transactions, and no way to print complicated reports. All file access is either sequential or direct, and a size restricted sort is required each time a report is printed.

PEARL LEVEL 3

Price

$495

Source

Relational Systems International Corp.
  (formerly Computer Pathways Unlimited)
5002 Commercial S.E.
Salem, OR 97306
(503) 363-8929

System Requirements

A 56K CP/M system with the CBASIC2 language

Pearl Level 3 is a *program generator* and not technically a DBMS. You specify a data dictionary and report formats just as you would with an FMS; then you enter data and print reports.

How does a program generator differ from a DBMS? In the DBMS, all the programs that handle data are general-purpose, extracting data dictionary and report layout information from disk files, considered part of the data base. Normally there is system unique code only if you write programs in a built-in or host language. Pearl, on the other hand, produces a series of CBASIC2 programs customized specifically to your application.

If you have specified a five-field name and address file, for instance, Pearl makes a program which prompts for FIRST NAME, accepts ten alphabetic characters into a variable called FIRST.NAME$, prompts for LAST NAME, and so forth—just like a program you would write from scratch.

Pearl doesn't stop at data entry; it makes report programs, posting programs, and reorganization programs, all tied together with menu programs. The data dictionary and report layout information are not stored in the data base but *coded into the programs*.

The end results of Pearl and an FMS are the same, but each approach has its advantages and disadvantages. Pearl takes time to generate the code, and the CBASIC2 compiler takes time to compile it. This is 40 minutes over what an FMS requires, but you get well-structured, *easily modified* programs. Imagine that you have just finished a complex report using the Report Generator of FMS-80. Your client now wants one small addition which is just outside FMS-80's scope, forcing you to start from scratch with an EFM program. If you had been using Pearl instead, you could have modified the Pearl-generated CBASIC2 report program, solving the problem in minutes rather than hours.

Suppose you want to sell a vertical market package to manufacturers of tomato sauce. If you use a DBMS, you would have to sell a copy of the DBMS package to every purchaser, adding many dollars to the total price. With Pearl, the purchaser needs only CBASIC2 which he or she probably already owns. Relational Systems demands *no royalties* on sales of Pearl-generated systems.

Pearl Level 3, together with its predecessors Level 2 and Level 1, were among the first applications development packages. They're not so common now because CBASIC2, a semi-compiled language, is being replaced with faster fully compiled languages. Fortunately, Digital Research has developed CB-80, a compatible high-speed upgrade of CBASIC2, and Relational Systems plans to upgrade Pearl accordingly, giving it a new lease on life.

Relational Systems has just introduced a new package, *Personal Pearl,* which is not a program generator at all, but something close to a DBMS. It only costs $295 and is worth looking into; however, don't confuse it with Pearl Level 3.

Data Dictionary

Pearl's menu-driven data dictionary defines the following:

- Sequence number
- Variable description (heading)
- Variable code name (for CBASIC2)
- Number of occurrences (short arrays)
- Storage format
  - *a.* Floating point
  - *b.* Integer
  - *c.* String
  - *d.* Date
  - *e.* Money
  - *f.* Computational (dummy element, derived from others)
- Length of field (max 60)
- Low range
- High range
- Edit mask
- Edit control option
  - *a.* No restrictions
  - *b.* Edit during add only
  - *c.* Display only
  - *d.* Suppress display/edit
- Validation control option
  - *a.* No selection
  - *b.* Yes/no selection
  - *c.* Alpha single character
  - *d.* Phrase selection
  - *e.* Cross file key validation
- Key option
  - *a.* Not applicable
  - *b.* Primary key
  - *c.* Secondary key

Nowhere does Pearl use cursor addressing. Data dictionary entry and subsequent data entry is all scroll mode with frequent screen clearing. At least there's no need for screen formatting. Each field is given a sequence number, usually in increments of ten, enabling insertion of new fields.

Report Generator

Pearl's report definition procedure is almost identical to that of FMS-80. You get all the usual subtotal and grand total features plus computation in the detail lines. In addition, you can insert lines of CBASIC2 code, including IF statements. This is necessary because Pearl doesn't have the *select* features found in true DBMS packages. All select instructions must be directly coded into the report programs.

The report generator accommodates a *primary* file and an optional *secondary* file. A report could list sales transactions along with product descriptions taken from a master file. The FMS-80 Report Generator won't do this.

Query Facility

Query processing limits you to viewing one record at a time through the "change" mode in data entry. You can modify a generated report program to print to the screen, and you can "hard code" that report to select only certain records. Pearl is not as flexible as a DBMS, but it gets the job done.

File Access

Pearl is geared for business applications and supports the following file types:

- Indexed Master File
- Transaction File
- Historical Transaction File
- Random (direct access) File
- Sequential Sort File

The indexed master file is used most often. As in dBASE II, there is a data file plus one or more B$^+$-tree index files. Pearl provides all the CBASIC2 code to manipulate the indexes, so you really don't know they're there. If you were using Pearl to build a general ledger system, the master file would be your account file, with account number as the key. The sequential transaction file would contain journal vouchers, and the historical transaction file would contain those vouchers after they were posted to the accounts. After receiving your detailed instructions, Pearl generates the code to maintain the account file, enter and modify the transactions, post the transactions to the accounts, and close out the accounts at month's end.

Random files may be used when it's convenient to use the record number as the key.

Pearl works in conjunction with an assembly language sort program to produce reports sorted in any order. If you wanted an alphabetical list of customers from a master file of customer numbers, Pearl would call the sort program and pass the sorted result to a report program.

Technical Information

How does Pearl work? When you first run Pearl to define the system, a series of programs, written in CBASIC2, takes control and asks you questions through menus. The result of the definition phase is a set of disk files defining your particular system. The next step, generation, uses another series of programs to convert those control files into CBASIC2 source code. Some of this code is generated from scratch while the rest, such as index manipulation routines, is brought in from a "library" and merged into the custom code.

Pearl produces a SUBMIT file which controls compilation of all the generated source modules. The end result is a menu-driven system consisting of more than a dozen programs all chained together.

If your generated system isn't exactly the way you want it, you can change the CBASIC2 source code and recompile, or you can regenerate all or part of the system. The control files are still there and can be modified through the Pearl definition module. If you need to add a new field to a file you have no choice but to regenerate.

Once you have started to customize the CBASIC2 source code, you can't regenerate the system unless you are prepared to reinsert all your customizations into the new code.

Restrictions

Fundamental restrictions are Pearl's record size limit of 249 characters and field quantity limit of 22. Make sure your application fits before using Pearl. The lack of cursor addressing is also a hindrance.

In theory, all Pearl restrictions may be overcome by modifying the generated programs. This isn't practical, however, because of the work involved.

QUICKCODE

Price

$295

Source

Fox & Geller
P.O. Box 1053
Teaneck, NJ 07666
(201) 837-0142

System Requirements

The dBASE II program and a
  CP/M system

Quickcode is a program generator for dBASE II which lets you crank out free-standing applications similar to those of FMS-80, using on-screen format generation similar to that of Condor.

Quickcode evolved from an earlier product, Quickscreen, which produced chunks of dBASE II code (in the built-in language) for full-screen editing. Remember that the dBASE EDIT command allows only one field per line (Figure 5-1) and that programming a screen with SAY-GET instructions is a lot of work. With Quick-screen you still had to build a program around the generated screen code. Quickcode automates construction of a working system of programs, a menu-driven update/inquiry/report system with mailing labels, and a word processor connection. You can take the system as it comes, customize it, or use pieces of the generated dBASE code in your own programs.

Data Dictionary

Quickcode begins with a blank screen; a detailed HELP screen appears when you press the "?" key. This is the blank sheet on which you sketch your data entry form. You have full cursor control; you can insert and delete characters and lines, display a grid, and even take text from word processor files. You type descriptive information on the screen just as it must appear later, and you specify dBASE II field names by preceding them with a semi-colon. If your four-field customer database has fields called NAME, ADDRESS, ZIP:CODE, and PHONE, then your Quickcode screen might look like the following:

```
**** CUSTOMER FILE ****

Customer Name     ;NAME
Address           ;ADDRESS
Zip Code          ;ZIP:CODE Phone Number ;PHONE
```

This is *Quickscreen* mode which specifies where fields start on the screen. *Fields* mode, switched on and off by typing ^B, lets you finish the data dictionary definition by specifying field length, type, and so on. Fields mode displays a list of all fields. An example of this is shown in Figure 8-1.

#	FIELD NAME	T	LEN	F DEFAULT	MINIMUM	MAXIMUM	ERROR MESSAGE	VAL	ER/
1	NAME	C	24	*NONE*	*NONE*	*NONE*	*NONE*	*	0
2	ADDRESS	C	24	*NONE*	*NONE*	*NONE*	*NONE*	*	0
3	ZIP:CODE	I	5	98105	00000	99999	ILLEGAL ZIP	*	0
4	PHONE	T	13	*NONE*	*NONE*	*NONE*	*NONE*	*	0

FIGURE 8-1.
Fields mode

The layout of Figure 8-1 resembles a data dictionary. The data types in the "T" column are

N—Numeric (1 decimal place)

I—Integer

C—Character (alphanumeric)

$—Money (2 places)

D—Date (mm/dd/yy)

T—Telephone (aaa)bbb-cccc

S—Social Security (aaa-bb-cccc)

L—Logical (1 character)

The "F" column specifies the field as a database *key* and the "VAL" column permits *validating* a field against a short list or against another database.

The data dictionary is stored on disk forever, allowing you to rearrange screens and change field characteristics. You can switch back and forth between Fields mode, Quickscreen mode, and Help mode.

The Basic Generated System

When you're through with the screen and data dictionary, Quickcode generates your dBASE code in about one minute. Upon entering dBASE II, you see the following menu:

```
          SYSTEM: CUSTOMERS
            FILE: CUSTOMERS
          PLEASE CHOOSE ONE:

  A to ADD data
  G to GET/EDIT data
  R to RUN report
  W to make WordStar Connection
  L to print mailing LABELS/forms
  Q to QUIT (exit to CP/M)
```

This gives a good picture of a Quickcode system. The ADD and GET/EDIT screens look like the ones you entered along with the data dictionary. The GET/EDIT is the query processor, letting you move forward and backward in the file and allowing you to *search* for records sequentially or by key using the dBASE II index method.

Quickcode doesn't do reports, but rather defers to the dBASE II Report Generator. You specify the name of the previously set up report form file, or you define a new one on the spot.

The WordStar Connection creates a .DOC and .DAT file for MailMerge with no option for selecting records. The mailing labels are slightly doctored data entry screen images printed on paper.

Quickcode as a Programmer's Tool

Quickcode's basic system isn't overwhelming. If you buy Quickcode and dBASE only to do simple mailing lists, you've wasted your money. dBASE is good for more complex systems, but those systems invariably have simple parts which can benefit from Quickcode's automatic code generation. Using as an example the dBASE sales order system outlined in Chapter 5, Quickcode could produce all the code for customer and product file maintenance, and it could generate the screens for sales order headers and details. The programmer merges the generated code with custom code, saving time over programming everything from scratch.

Quickcode optionally allows generation of disjoint program modules, those not tied together from a menu. It also has a *menu generator* for custom menus.

Technical Information

Quickcode first generates an empty database file (.DBF) with all fields defined. Since dBASE doesn't know about Social Security numbers, telephone numbers, and dates, these are set up as ordinary character fields. The generated programs perform the required translation.

The programs Quickcode produces are as follows:

CMD	Display main menu and call appropriate module
IO	Display and enter data for one record
OUT	Display one database record
ADD	Control the adding of records to the database
RPT	Control printing of reports
WS	Create the WordStar data file
LBL	Print mailing labels or forms
GET	Find a particular record
ED	Edit an existing record
FAU	Set the defaults
VAL	Validate each input field
GO	Set up the index for a keyed database

Restrictions

All dBASE II's restrictions apply to Quickcode-generated systems. Any Quickcode restrictions can be overcome by modifying the generated dBASE II code. If you use multiple indexes, you must alter the code so that dBASE updates them all.

ACCESS/80

Price

$295, $495, or $995,
    depending on options

Source

Friends Software
P.O. Box 527
Berkeley, CA 94701
(415) 540-7282

System Requirements

48K CP/M system, CP/M-86
    version available

ACCESS/80, begun as a *report generator*, has since become an Information Management System. The report generator is the core and is worth examining. It's driven by *commands*, making it entirely different from on-screen and table-driven report generators. Most formatting is automatic, and files may be treated as arrays which may be searched, sorted, and tabulated. An IF-THEN-ELSE construct provides flexibility, and multiple reports may be printed from one pass of the data file.

The commands, forming a structured high-level language, can be stored for repetitive execution, classifying ACCESS/80 as a program-driven and command-driven system. ACCESS/80 can produce reports from fixed-length or variable-length record files produced by BASIC or COBOL.

The data base portion of ACCESS/80 uses full-screen data entry and updating along with multiple-key B-tree indexing; it can extend files over multiple disk drives, diskettes, or both. Record length is limited only by memory size. The ability to load an entire file into a table for searching counts as ACCESS/80's multifile capability.

SELECTOR V

Price

$495

Source

Micro-Ap, Inc.
7033 Village Parkway, Suite 206
Dublin, CA 94566
(415) 828-6697

System Requirements

A 48K CP/M system

Like Louis XIV, Selector V descended from a long line of Roman numerals. Selector I, II, III, and IV were systems based on CBASIC2. They received high marks from users but were awfully slow. CB-80, the native code CBASIC2 equivalent, made Selector V possible, eliminating the speed problem of earlier versions.

Selector V is a menu-driven system in two parts, Definition and Execution, and requires no built-in or host language. It works well with multifile access, processing up to six files at once. A unique feature is the simultaneous processing of a group of records having a non-unique key. This means you could ask for all names beginning with the letter "K," for example, and Selector V would get them all without a sequential pass of the whole file. Data files are standard ASCII, readable by other programs.

There are two *report generators*, one for row and column work with subtotals and computations, and the other for page work, suitable for invoices, checks, and other forms. Selector V is definitely a DBMS, but it has features from RDBMS, FMS, and NDBMS, making it difficult to classify.

There is one application package, a general ledger system called GLector V, based on Selector V and available from MicroAp.

THE QUAD

Price

$495

Source

QuanTeckna Research Corporation
6902 220th St. S.W.
Mountlake Terrace, WA 98043

System Requirements

A CP/M system

This FMS-type data base management system uses the features of your word processor to add fancy printing to your reports and to produce customized form letters. It comes complete with an accounts receivable application.

MICRO B$^+$

Price

$260

Source

FairCom
2606 Johnson Drive
Colombia, MO 65201
(314) 445-3304

System Requirements

A CP/M system

This is only one component of a DBMS, but it's an important one. If you are using an established language like BASIC, FORTRAN, PL/I-80, or Pascal and you don't need the power and expense of MDBS III, Micro B$^+$ might help with data handling. With this system, you can efficiently maintain B$^+$-tree indexes (see Chapter 3) to data files. Your programs communicate with the FairCom assembly language routines by means of CALL statements, allowing you to find, add, and delete specific keys. The key *delete* operation is fully supported, a feature often left out of DBMS packages.

SEQUITUR

Price

$3495

Source

Pacific Software Manufacturing Company
2608 Eighth Street
Berkeley, CA 94710
(415) 540-5000

System Requirements

An Onyx, Plexus, PDP 11, or VAX 11 computer with the UNIX operating system

Here's a *non-CP/M* relational data base management system which harnesses the power of 16- and 32-bit computers. Because you'll soon have your own 16-bit machine, this is the sort of software you'll be using. Hopefully the price will come down as the 16-bit computer population grows.

Sequitur is a command-driven program with the flavor of Condor, but it has more power, incorporating many of the features of a large RDBMS. To begin with, record and field size limits disappear, and the number of fields per record (columns) increases to 1024.

A Sequitur feature not yet seen in CP/M RDBMS is *query by example* (QBE). This feature allows you to fill in a skeleton of a table on the screen. In Condor you select all books from publisher BYT with inventory quantity 50 or less by typing the command

```
SELECT BOOKS ST PUBLISHER =
   'BYT' AND QUANTITY.ON.HAND <= 50
```

In a QBE system, you see a blank table like the following:

Publisher	Catalog No.	Title	Qty. on Hand

Next you fill in the blanks

Publisher	Catalog No.	Title	Qty. on Hand
BYT			<= 50

and the computer returns

Publisher	Catalog No.	Title	Qty. on Hand
BYT	0960	Ciarcia's Circuit Cellar	40
BYT	1040	Layman's Guide to SBC's	46
BYT	4925	You Just Bought a Personl	42

Sequitur can perform *virtual operations* as mentioned in Chapter 2. When you JOIN two databases, there is no duplicate table created. This conserves disk space and insures that any update goes to the correct database because there is *only* one database.

There's an integrated word processor program, and that's important because Sequitur can handle whole pages of text, not just 255-byte chunks. You can produce form letters, storing the body of the letter in the data base as well as the names and addresses.

9

Future Trends

If you're browsing through this book in a computer junk shop circa 2020, please don't laugh at the predictions made in this chapter. Previous generations have made their predictions for the future as well. Perhaps you've seen a 1940 drawing of cities full of 200-story neoclassical skyscrapers, complete with terra-cotta gargoyles. Well, this chapter is far more conservative; it covers only the next ten years; after 1992 all bets are off.

Microcomputers Versus Large Systems

If you buy a Cray 1, a popular supercomputer selling for several million dollars, you can program only in FORTRAN or assembler, and you can't run a DBMS. With a $3000 microcomputer, you can choose from a dozen languages, all the DBMS systems in this book, plus several others. While the Cray runs faster, speed may be incidental to your application. In any case, the Motorola 68000 16-bit microprocessor has been tested at 25Mhz (three times normal), and a software-compatible 32-bit version has been announced. You can soon own a personal computer more powerful than today's large systems.

Recall the first Altair computer. At the time of its introduction, 4K (4096 bytes) of RAM (random access memory) were considered a big deal, and only cassettes and paper tape were available as mass storage devices. Today, the latest semiconductor technology offers inexpensive one-megabyte microcomputer memories, and disks are increasing in capacity and decreasing in cost. Hard disks of 100 or more megabytes are appearing, and these could cost less than $1000 by the end of the decade.

Where does this leave the manufacturers of minicomputers and large systems? It may become pointless for them to develop an expensive CPU (central processing unit) when a nearby semiconductor plant is turning out millions of $10 chips with more power than their in-house product. Microprocessors and high-density memories are available at the same price to manufacturers of both microsystems and mainframes. Only a few companies will continue to make state-of-the-art supercomputers. Most computers will be built from a very few microprocessor families. Just think, your home computer may be software compatible with the computer that prints your bank statement.

Look at the pages of any recent computer magazine. You'll see advertisements for hundreds of programs you can buy for CP/M-based machines as well as for Apple, PET, TRS-80, and other systems. Next visualize the January, 1992, edition of *BYTE* magazine. Eight-bit machines have become relics, and all software will run on the latest multi-megabyte 16- or 32-bit personal computer, one that will be compatible with almost all business computers, large and small. In the year 1992, advertisements will illustrate that the "software gap" between micros and large systems has vanished; microcomputer software, including the DBMS, will have become state-of-the-art.

The Short Term

In the next few years 8-bit DBMS systems will continue to improve, with new features and corrected bugs. Several new low-priced packages may appear, and the prices of existing programs will drop. The push, however, will be to publish DBMS for the 16-bit machines, like the IBM Personal Computer and its imitators. The PC, whose 8088 chip is not much faster than a Z-80, can conveniently address large amounts of memory—several megabytes instead of the standard 64K of the Z-80. This removes the DBMS author's restraints, permitting him or her to write a powerful, fast, and "user-friendly" package.

These second generation DBMS will include all the existing 8-bit features, borrow some extras from the large-system packages, and then break new ground in ease of use.

Microcomputer systems based on the 68000, Z8000, and 8086 chips are natural for multiuser operations. Many DBMS authors are now converting their programs for this environment. DBMS are appearing on multiprocessor 8-bit systems, but eventually the 16-bit explosion should overshadow this effort.

Associative Memories

A normal computer memory permits data retrieval by *address*. If you have 1000 names in memory, you can get any one of them by specifying a number from 000 through 999, or you can sequentially process them 000, 001, 002, 003, and so on. An associative memory works the opposite way. You specify "Marco Polo" and the memory returns the address 532. "Smith" electronically produces 683, 684, 685, and 686, the addresses of all the cells containing that name. If your whole database were in an associative memory, think how quick a "sequential pass" would be. The "crossword puzzle" system of Chapter 4 would give results instantly, eliminating the one minute wait for each selection of words.

Associative memories are still a curiosity, even though at least one has appeared in microcomputer-compatible S-100 form. To be useful, these memories must be large—several megabytes—and this requires the undivided attention of the semiconductor houses that are otherwise occupied with more popular devices. A computer company would do well to produce an associative-memory machine along with the RDBMS software to run it.

Distributed Data Base

A week doesn't go by without the announcement of a new "executive work station" aimed at the management of wealthy corporations. Just what will executives do with their new toys? They can stay out of trouble running spread sheets and preparing PERT schedules, or they can use their systems as $700 "dumb" terminals, attached to the behemoth (that's the computer, not the data entry supervisor) in the basement. The machines can be hooked together for electronic mail, but this involves the secretary rather than the executive. But this "electronic office" turns out to be little more than a multiterminal word processor.

Many of the "work stations" (the new name for personal computers) contain 16-bit microprocessors, permitting them to run sophisticated DBMS software. How could this relate to the data base already sitting in the company's central computer? *Distributed processing* is the answer, best understood by studying an example. A seafood company processed and distributed canned salmon through a nationwide chain of warehouses. The salmon was stored in numbered lots (batches) within each warehouse, facilitating quick FDA recall. A ten-year-old set of computer programs at the company's main office traced which cases were in each bay (area) of each warehouse. As the company grew, the inventory files got larger until daily processing took 25 hours of computer time. A crew of salespeople tried to convince the president to buy a larger and very expensive new computer, but a bright young consultant prevailed with a new idea.

Why not have a two-tiered computer system? A remote computer at each warehouse would store detailed information such as which lots are in which bays, and the central computer would store summary information such as which lots are in which warehouses. The central computer would interrogate the warehouse computers for specific details. The remote computers would do order entry and invoicing, further reducing the head office's computer load. This plan was adopted, a half-dozen minicomputers were ordered, and a programming team was hired.

The design team had selected some database minicomputer inventory software for the warehouses and had specified a data base for the home office computer. Had the plan begun they would have been faced with the awesome task

of tying the two software components together, a process requiring a year's work by several people. The future design team will use 16- or 32-bit microcomputers at the warehouses, and each will support several terminals. The antique office mainframe computer will be replaced by a new desk-top, microprocessor-based machine, that is fully software-compatible with the remote systems. The software will be distributed data base, one integrated system in all the company's offices and warehouses across the country.

Just what does a distributed data base look like? Choose any network DBMS schema from Chapter 7, then split the nodes among different computers. If a program or person needs information from a different location, the DBMS automatically goes and gets it. If telephone bills are a problem, the system can be configured to automatically update the central summary data base once each night. As far as the programmer is concerned, there is just one big computer with one big data base.

Distributed relational data bases are possible too; a given data base could have records in different places. Users would know that queries for remote data would be more "expensive" because of the communication costs.

How does the executive work station fit in? Computer-literate sales managers could query the company distributed data base, down loading selected information into their own desktop units. They could then use the data in a spread sheet program to make sales projections or budgets and then transfer these figures to a word processor file to publish a report.

You're probably wondering why distributed processing hasn't taken hold already. Some manufacturers of large systems sell integrated· hardware and software for distributed processing, but these systems are expensive and not always compatible with the systems companies already own. There is at present no preeminent distributed data base management system (DDBMS), although some of the major manufacturers are addressing the problem. The steady influx of microcomputers into large corporations should insure a market for a good DDBMS, but such systems won't be written in someone's garage. Only a serious, concentrated effort by a major software firm may produce a package by the end of the 1980s.

A

dBASE II from Ashton-Tate—Programs

The figures in this appendix pertain to Chapter 5 programs.

```
* BOOKS.CMD - mainline command module for retrieval system
SET TALK OFF                            * no troubleshooting data
USE BOOKS                               * open the primary database
SELECT SECONDARY
USE KEYWORDS INDEX KW-KEY               * open the secondary database
STORE ´ ´ TO code
DO WHILE code <> ´X´                    * define main program loop
    ERASE                               * clear the screen
    @ 0,20 SAY ´LIBRARY RETRIEVAL SYSTEM´
    @ 4,20 SAY ´<I> INQUIRE´           * display the menu
    @ 5,20 SAY ´<A> ADD    ´
    @ 6,20 SAY ´<X> EXIT   ´
    @ 0,0
    WAIT TO code                        * accept operator´s choice
    STORE !(code) TO code               * force it to upper case
    DO CASE
        CASE code = ´I´
            DO INQUIRE                  * select ´INQUIRE´ or ´ADD´
        CASE code = ´A´
            DO ADD
    ENDCASE
ENDDO
RETURN                                  * back to dBASE on ´X´

* INQUIRE.CMD - for book retrieval system - called from BOOKS
STORE ´ ´ TO icode
```
(continued)

FIGURE A-1.
A data retrieval example

241

```
DO WHILE icode <> 'X'                           * main loop
    ERASE                                       * clear screen
    @ 0,20 SAY 'INQUIRE'
    DO GETKEYS                                  * get the keys to var 'search'
    DO DISPBOOKS                                * display matching records
    @ 1,0 SAY 'TYPE "X" TO EXIT, OTHER KEY TO CONTINUE'
    WAIT TO icode
    STORE !(icode) TO icode                     * allow an exit to BOOKS
ENDDO
RETURN


* ADD.CMD - add records to book database - called from BOOKS
STORE ' ' TO acode
DO WHILE acode <> 'X'
    ERASE                                       * clear screen
    @ 0,20 SAY 'ADD'
    DO GETKEYS                                  * get the keys to var SEARCH
    SELECT PRIMARY
    APPEND BLANK                                * define a new record
    REPLACE bk:keys WITH search                 * use 'search' as the key
    @ 12,0 SAY 'SOURCE' GET bk:source
    @ 13,0 SAY 'DATE' GET bk:date               * allow full-screen data entry
    @ 14,0 SAY 'ABSTRACT' GET bk:abstrac
    @ 15,0 SAY 'TITLE' GET bk:title
    @ 16,0 SAY 'AUTHOR' GET bk:author
    READ
    @ 1,0 SAY 'ENTER "X" TO EXIT, OTHER KEY TO CONTINUE'
    WAIT TO acode                               * allow an exit to BOOKS
    STORE !(acode) TO acode
ENDDO
RETURN


* GETKEYS.CMD   gets 8 keys into 'search' - called from INQUIRE and ADD
    STORE ' ' TO k1,k2,k3,k4,k5,k6,k7,k8        * initialize 8 subkey variables
    SELECT SECONDARY                            *    to blanks
    STORE F TO ctl
    DO WHILE .NOT. ctl                          * main loop for entering all 8 subkeys
        STORE 1 TO i
        @ 5,20 SAY 'Enter up to 8 keys'
        @ 6,20 SAY 'USE CARRIAGE RET TO PLACE CURSOR'
        @ 7,20 SAY 'BELOW LAST BLANK LINE AFTER DATA IS ENTERED.'
        DO WHILE i <= 8                         * loop for entering each of 8 subkeys
            STORE STR(I,1) TO isub              * manufacture a variable name and
            STORE STR(I+2,2) TO irow            *  row number from counter 'i'
            STORE i+1 TO i                      * (k1,k2,k3, etc.)
            @ &irow,0 GET K&isub                * get the subkey
        ENDDO
        READ
*
        STORE 1 TO i
```

(continued)

FIGURE A-1.
A data retrieval example
(continued)

```
          DO WHILE i <= 8                      * main loop for displaying all
              STORE STR(I,1) TO isub           *   8 words corresponding to subkeys
              STORE STR(I+2,2) TO irow
              STORE i+1 TO i
              STORE !(k&isub) TO k&isub        * upper case
              STORE k&isub TO key
              IF key <> ' '
                  FIND &key                    * lookup keyword
                  iF #=0                        * # is not 0 if found
                      @ &irow,8
                      ?? 'NOT FOUND '
                      STORE ' ' TO k&isub
                  ELSE
                      @ &irow,8 SAY kw:word     * display word
                  ENDIF
              ELSE
                  @ &irow,8
                  ?? '              '           * display a blank if no subkey
              ENDIF
          ENDDO
          @ 9,20 SAY 'ALL OK?' GET ctl
          READ
          @ 11,0          _                     * position for display
      ENDDO
      RETURN
*
      STORE 1 TO i                              * combine the 8 subkeys to form
      STORE ' ' TO search                       *   a string called 'search' with
      DO WHILE i <= 8                           *   dots between subkeys
          STORE STR(I,1) TO isub
          STORE i+1 TO i
          iF K&isub <> ' '                      * use only non-blank subkeys
              STORE search - K&isub - '.' TO search
          ENDIF
      ENDDO
      RETURN

* DISPBOOKS.CMD - display all books with matching keys 'search'
SELECT PRIMARY                                  * called from INQUIRE
GO TOP                                          * top of the book database
STORE LEN(search) TO length                     * length of the search key
DO WHILE .NOT. EOF                              * check @all@ the records
    STORE 1 TO pos                              *   in the BOOK database
    DO WHILE pos < length                       * '$' is the substring operator
        IF .NOT. $(search,pos,2) $ bk:keys
            STORE 99 TO pos                      * see if @each@ subkey in 'search'
        ELSE                                     *   is included in the key from
            STORE pos+3 TO pos                    *   the database record
        ENDIF
    ENDDO
    IF pos <> 99                                * display the selected book's
```

(continued)

FIGURE A-1.

A data retrieval example
(continued)

```
        DISPLAY bk:keys bk:source bk:date
        DISPLAY bk:abstrac OFF              *      data on three lines
        DISPLAY bk:title bk:author OFF
    ENDIF
    SKIP                                    * get the next record
ENDDO
RETURN
\NP
    --------------------------------------------------------------------
```

FIGURE A-1.
A data retrieval example
(continued)

```
* REPORT.CMD - demonstration on-order report
FRASE
SET TALK OFF
SELECT PRIMARY
USE RD-FILE INDEX RD-INDX2              * sales order detail file
SELECT SECONDARY
USE RH-FILE INDEX RH-INDEX             * sales order header file
SELECT PRIMARY
SET FORMAT TO print                    * turn printer on, screen off
STORE 0 TO line                        * initialize all variables
STORE '@ '+STR(line,2)+',' TO print
STORE T TO first
STORE 0 TO page
STORE 0 TO oldproduct
STORE 0 TO ptotal
STORE 0 TO gtotal
GOTO TOP                               * first record in index
DO WHILE .NOT. EOF                     * main loop for all records
    IF line > 55 .OR. first
        DO NEWPAGE                     * page headings
    ENDIF
    IF rd:product <> oldproduct
        IF oldproduct <> 0
            &print 10 SAY 'PRODUCT TOTAL'      * product totals
            &print 36 SAY ptotal USING '999,999'
            STORE gtotal+ptotal TO gtotal
            STORE 0 TO ptotal
            STORE line+2 TO line
            STORE '@ '+STR(line,2)+',' TO print
        ENDIF
        &print 0 SAY 'PRODUCT'                 * new product header
```

(continued)

FIGURE A-2.
Demonstration report program

```
            &print 8 SAY rd:product
            &print 18 SAY rd:desc
            STORE line+2 TO line
            STORE '@ '+STR(line,2)+',' TO print
            STORE rd:product TO oldproduct
        ENDIF
        SELECT SECONDARY
        STORE STR(rd:order,6) TO ORDER
        FIND &ORDER                          * find header corresponding to
        SELECT PRIMARY                       *   this detail
        &print 00 SAY rh:name                * customer name from header
        &print 27 SAY rd:order
        &print 35 SAY rd:sequnce             * order detail information
        &print 39 SAY rd:qordrd
        &print 47 SAY rd:uprice
        &print 55 SAY rd:amount
        STORE STR(rh:dtord,6) TO date        * convert yymmdd to mm/dd/yy
        STORE $(date,3,2)+'/'+$(date,5,2)+'/'+$(date,1,2) TO date
        &print 65 SAY date
        STORE STR(rh:dtdelv,6) TO date
        STORE $(date,3,2)+'/'+$(date,5,2)+'/'+$(date,1,2) TO date
        &print 75 SAY date
        STORE line+1 TO line                 * new line
        STORE '@ '+STR(line,2)+',' TO print
        STORE ptotal+rd:qordrd TO ptotal
        SKIP
    ENDDO
    &print 10 SAY 'PRODUCT TOTAL'            * total for last product
    &print 36 SAY ptotal USING '999,999'
    STORE gtotal+ptotal TO gtotal
    STORE line+2 TO line
    STORE '@ '+STR(line,2)+',' TO print
    &print 10 SAY 'GRAND TOTAL'              * grand total for report
    &print 36 SAY gtotal USING '999,999'
    STORE line+1 TO line
    STORE '@ '+STR(line,2)+',' TO print
    SET FORMAT TO SCREEN                     * turn printer off, screen on
    RETURN

    * NEWPAGE.CMD - eject and print page headings - called from REPORT
        STORE F TO first
        &print 0
        EJECT
        STORE 0 TO line
        STORE '@ '+STR(line,2)+',' TO print
        STORE page + 1 TO page
        &print 20 SAY 'On-order Detail Report'
        &print 63 SAY 'Page'
        &print 69 SAY page USING '##'
        STORE line+2 TO line
```

(continued)

FIGURE A-2.

Demonstration report program
(continued)

```
          STORE '@ '+STR(line,2)+',' TO print
          &print 5 SAY 'CUSTOMER'
          &print 27 SAY 'ORDER #'
          &print 35 SAY 'SEQ'
          &print 39 SAY 'Q ORDRD'
          &print 47 SAY 'U PRICE'
          &print 55 SAY 'AMOUNT'
          &print 65 SAY 'DT ORDRD'
          &print 75 SAY 'DELVY DT'
          STORE line+2 TO line
          STORE '@ '+STR(line,2)+',' TO print
          RETURN

      \NP
      ---------------------------------------------------------------------
```

FIGURE A-2.
Demonstration report program
(continued)

```
* DISPDETS.CMD - display all details for an order
@ 09,00 SAY 'SEQ ORDRD  SHPD     PROD'   * heading for detail display
@ 09,26 SAY 'DESCRIPTION'
@ 09,53 SAY 'DISC   PRICE      AMT'
@ 09,0
STORE T TO true                          * initialize variables
STORE 0 TO totamt
STORE 0 TO oldrec
FIND &order                              * find first detail for this order
IF # = 0                                 * "#" is the current record number
    STORE F TO true                      * no details for this order
ENDIF
STORE # TO oldrec
DO WHILE true
    STORE rd:amount+totamt TO totamt     * keep running total for order
    DISPLAY rd:sequnce, rd:qordrd, rd:qshipd, rd:product, $(rd:desc,1,28),;
            rd:disc, rd:uprice, rd:amount OFF
    SKIP                                  * display 1 line for the detail
    IF STR(rd:order,6) <> order .OR. # = oldrec
        STORE F TO true                  * all finished if the next order
        LOOP                             *   comes up or if there are
    ENDIF                                *   no more details in the file
    STORE # TO oldrec
ENDDO
DISPLAY '                                        ORDER TOTAL      ',;
        '  ', STR(totamt,9,2) OFF        * display the order total
RETURN
```

FIGURE A-3.
Sample program from
order processing system

B

FMS-80 from
DJR Associates—Programs

The figures in this appendix pertain to Chapter 6 programs.

```
/* RIDERZER.EFM zeros out all everything after the season
 */
"",a,1                        /* the place for the 'Y/N' to go */
input (riders.idx)
output ()

    noauto;                   /* inhibit automatic file reading
                                 we'll do it ourselves, thank you */
    clear;
    display 'This step clears all riders, both season and evening totals!';
ask:
    curse 3,1; clearln;
    display 'Do you really want to do it? (Y/N) ';
    enteru 0,1;               /* accept Y or N in upper case */
    if 0,1 = 'N'
        goto exit;
    endif
    if 0,1 != 'Y'             /* loop until 'Y' or 'N' */
        goto ask;
    endif
    curse 5,1;
    display 'Clearing rider ......';
    nread 1 1;                /* read the first rider record */
fileloop:
    curse 5,22; display 1,1;
    1,(7-40) = 0;             /* notice how easy it is to zero everything? */
    rewrite 1;                /* save rider record back on disk */
    nread next 1;             /* get the next record */
    if error 1
        goto exit;            /* test for end of file */
    endif
    goto fileloop;
exit:
    stop;
    end;
```

FIGURE B-1.
End-of-season total zero program

```
/* RIDERCMP.EFM adds season totals by rider
               adds evening totals by rider
     necessary only if totals are changed by 'modify'
 */
input (riders.idx)
output ()

    noauto;                    /* inhibit automatic file reading
                                  we'll do it ourselves, thank you */
    clear;                     /* the screen */
    curse 3,1; display 'Totalling rider ........';
    nread 1 1;                 /* read the first rider record */
fileloop:
    V=11; W=12;                /* index for first event */
    curse 3,22; display 1,1; /* display rider number on screen */
    1,7 = 0;                   /* zero evening total */
    1,8 = 0;                   /* zero season total */
eventloop:
    1,7 = 1,7 + 1,V;           /* total evening points */
    1,8 = 1,8 + 1,W;           /* total season points */
    V=V+2; W=W+2;
    if V < 40
        goto eventloop;
    endif
    rewrite 1;                 /* save rider record back on disk */
    nread next 1;              /* get the next record */
    if error 1
        goto exit;             /* test for end of file */
    endif
    goto fileloop;
exit:
    stop;
    end;
```

FIGURE B-2.
Rider total recompute program

```
/* RIDERUPD.EFM updates RIDERS.TRX to RIDERS.DAT
                adds evening points to season points
                adds season totals by rider
                adds evening totals by rider
        automatic processing of transaction records
 */
input (riders.trx,riders.fd; riders.idx)
/* first file is transactions, second is data file */
output ()

    clear; curse 3,1;
    display 'Updating rider .....' 1,1;
    2,1 = 1,1;              /* set up the key for rider retrieval */
    kread 2;                /* find the rider record */
    if error 2
        goto exit;          /* can't find it!  */
    endif
    V=11;                   /* index for first event */
    W=12;
    display 1,1 1,2 1,3;    /* put something on the screen */
    2,7 = 0;                /* zero evening total */
    2,8 = 0;                /* zero season total */
    2,6 = date;             /* set date last race = today */
eventloop:
    2,W = 2,W + 1,V;        /* add evening points to season (master)*/
    2,V = 1,V;              /* move evening points to master */
    2,7 = 2,7 + 2,V;        /* total evening points */
    2,8 = 2,8 + 2,W;        /* total season points */
    V=V+2;
    W=W+2;
    if V < 40               /* loop through all events */
        goto eventloop;
    endif
    rewrite 2;              /* save rider record back on disk */
exit:
    end;                    /* get the next transaction automatically */
```

FIGURE B-3.
Race total update program

```
/* RIDERSUM.EFM print the rider summary report
        main module
    C = previous class
    N = top ten counter
    P = page counter
    R,D,F = rider pointer
    S,E,G = season total pointer
    W = event pointer in file - starts at 12
 */
"",d,3,'XXX^'
        ...
   (there are actually 90 of these!)
        ...
"",d,3,'XXX^'
"",d,3,'XXX^'

input (riderclr.idx; riders.idx)
/* file 1 is riders indexed by class ranked season total (descending)
 * file 2 is riders indexed by rider number */
output ()
    noauto;
    nread 1 1;    /* first record from file */
    C=999;        /* previous class */
    P=1;          /* page count */
fileloop:
    if 1,2 != C   /* test for class break */
        call heading;
        C = 1,2;
    endif
    if N < 11
        call printline;          /* line of 'top ten' */
    endif
    call tablestore;        /* data into the table */
    nread next 1;      /* read next rider record */
    if error 1
        goto exit;      /* test for end of file */
    endif
    goto fileloop;
exit:
    call tableprint;       /* last table */
    eject;
    stop;

/*************************************************************
 * module to print the page heading for a new class
 */
heading:
    if C != 999
        call tableprint;    /* not first time thru */
    endif
    eject;
```

(continued)

FIGURE B-4.
Rider summary report program

```
    print at(50) 'R+E CYCLE TRACK STATISTICS';
    print at(118) 'DATE ' date;
    print;
    print at(52) '5627 UNIVERSITY WAY NE';
    print at(125) 'PAGE ' P;
    print; print;
    print at(1) 'TOP TEN IN THE ';
    switch 1,2
        case 2:
            print at(16) 'II';
            break;
        case 3:
            print at(16) 'III';
            break;
        case 4:
            print at(16) 'IV';
            break;
        case 5:
            print at(16) 'Women & Junior';
            break;
        default:
            print at(16) 'unknown';
            break;
    endswitch
    print ' CLASS'; print;
    print 'rider number     name              season points';
    print;
    P=P+1;          /* page count */
    N=1;            /* top ten counter */
    0,(1-90)=0;     /* zero out the table */
    return;

/*********************************************************
 * module to print one line of the top ten
 */
printline:
    print at(1) 'NO. ' N;
    print at(3) 1,1 '    ' 1,4;
    print at(23) 1,3 1,8;
    print;
    N=N+1;
    return;

/*********************************************************
 * module to store one rider's information in the table
 *    rider number and season event totals are stored in the table
 */
tablestore:
    W=12;
    R=1; S=46;              /* initialize pointers in the table */
```

(continued)

FIGURE B-4.
Rider summary report program
(continued)

```
    D=2;  E=47;
    F=3;  G=48;
eventloop:
    if 1,W > 0,S          /* rider better than first */
        0,F = 0,D; 0,G = 0,E;
        0,D = 0,R; 0,E = 0,S;    /* 2 to 3, 1 to 2, new to 1 */
        0,R = 1,1; 0,S = 1,W;
        goto nextevent;
    endif
    if 1,W > 0,E          /* rider better than second */
        0,F = 0,D; 0,G = 0,E;
        0,D = 1,1; 0,E = 1,W;    /* 2 to 3, new to 2 */
        goto nextevent;
    endif
    if 1,W > 0,G          /* rider better than third */
        0,F = 1,1; 0,G = 1,W;    /* new to 3 */
        goto nextevent;
    endif
nextevent:
    D=D+3; E=E+3;          /* index to next event */
    F=F+3; G=G+3;
    R=R+3; S=S+3;
    W=W+2;
    if W < 41
        goto eventloop;
    endif
    return;


/*******************************************************
 * module to print the 1,2,3 place table
 *  rider nbrs and season event totals are stored in the table
 *  first and last names are looked up from file 2 when printed
 */
tableprint:
    print;                     /* table headings */
    print at(1) 'EVENT';
    print at(30) 'FIRST';
    print at(65) 'SECOND';
    print at(100) 'THIRD';
    print; print;
    W=12;
    R=1; S=46;
    D=2; E=47;
    F=3; G=48;
    flush 1;                   /* this seems essential */
tableloop:
    print at(1) h(1,W);
    if 0,R = 0                 /* skip rider print if no rider */
        goto tskip1;
```

(continued)

FIGURE B-4.
Rider summary report program
(continued)

```
       endif
       2,1 = 0,R;                   /* rider # is the key for name lookup */
       kread 2;                     /* first place */
       print at(20) 2,4 2,3 0,S;    /* first, last name, season total */
tskip1:
       if 0,D = 0
           goto tskip2;
       endif
       2,1 = 0,D;
       kread 2;                     /* second place */
       print at(55) 2,4 2,3 0,E;
tskip2:
       if 0,F = 0
           goto tskip3;
       endif
       2,1 = 0,F;
       kread 2;                     /* third place */
       print at(90) 2,4 2,3 0,G;
tskip3:
       print; print;
       D=D+3; E=E+3;                /* index to next event */
       F=F+3; G=G+3;
       R=R+3; S=S+3;
       W=W+2;
       if W < 41
           goto tableloop;          /* loop for all 15 events */
       endif
       return;
       end;
```

FIGURE B-4.
Rider summary report program
(continued)

C

Annotated Bibliography

If you are looking for books specifically on data bases for microcomputers you won't find them listed here; this is one of the first. If you would like to know more about data base theory and mainframe implementations, there are a few good books to consider.

The first is by James Martin, *Computer Data-Base Organization*, 2nd ed. (Englewood Cliffs, N.J.: Prentice-Hall, 1977). The first half of this two-part book describes the logical organization of the data base including the theory behind hierarchical, network, and relational data models. It also describes the CODASYL data description language and IBM's Data Language/I for the IMS data base. The second half of the book extensively details the physical data structures—useful information if you are actually writing a DBMS. Hundreds of tables and diagrams in two colors help convey the material.

Another good book is *An Introduction to Data Base Systems*, 3rd ed. by C.J. Date of IBM (Reading, Mass.: Addison-Wesley, 1981). Date emphasizes the logical aspect of data base and, after some preliminaries, describes in detail the three principal approaches. Unlike other authors, he describes the rela-tional model before the hierarchical and net-work models, giving that approach more credi-bility than it has received in the past. Indeed, the author theorizes that relational data bases are superior to network/hierarchical data bases and that the latter became entrenched because of the high cost and slow access of early disk drives. The main value of the book is the description of two "commercial" relational DBMS systems that gives a glimpse into the future of microcomputer data base.

Written on a slightly lower technical level are two books by David Kroenke, *Database Processing* (Chicago: SRA, 1977) and *Database: A Professional's Primer* (1978). These books are oriented toward specific commercial Data Base Management Systems and case studies.

There have been a number of magazine arti-cles about microcomputer data bases, and a good one concerning Network/Hierarchical Data Base Management Systems is "Data-Base Management Systems: Powerful Newcomers to MicroComputers" from *BYTE* magazine, November, 1981. A reprint of this article is available from ISE, publishers of MDBS III.

Faircom, publisher of the Micro B$^+$ file access package, distributes a reprint from the

Association for Computing Machinery journal with lots of useful B-tree information ("The Ubiquitous B-Tree," *ACM Computing Surveys*, Vol. 11, No. 2, June 1979). There are 38 references included in case you want to get scholarly.

Index

Other Osborne/McGraw-Hill Publications

An Introduction to Microcomputers: Volume 0—The Beginner's Book, 3rd Edition
An Introduction to Microcomputers: Volume 1—Basic Concepts, 2nd Edition
Osborne 4 & 8-Bit Microprocessor Handbook
Osborne 16-Bit Microprocessor Handbook
8089 I/O Processor Handbook
CRT Controller Handbook
68000 Microprocessor Handbook
8080A/8085 Assembly Language Programming
6800 Assembly Language Programming
Z80 ® Assembly Language Programming
6502 Assembly Language Programming
Z8000 ® Assembly Language Programming
6809 Assembly Language Programming
Running Wild—The Next Industrial Revolution
The 8086 Book
PET ®/CBM™ and the IEEE 488 Bus (GPIB)
PET ® Personal Computer Guide
CBM™ Professional Computer Guide
Business System Buyer's Guide
Osborne CP/M ® User Guide, 2nd Edition
Apple II ® User's Guide
Microprocessors for Measurement and Control
Some Common BASIC Programs
Some Common BASIC Programs—PET™/CBM™ Edition
Some Common BASIC Programs—Atari ® Edition
Some Common BASIC Programs—TRS-80™ Level II Edition
Some Common BASIC Programs—Apple II ® Edition
Some Common BASIC Programs—IBM ® Personal Computer Edition
Some Common Pascal Programs
Practical BASIC Programs
Practical BASIC Programs—TRS-80™ Level Edition
Practical BASIC Programs—Apple II ® Edition
Practical BASIC Programs—IBM ® Personal Computer Edition
Practical Pascal Programs
Payroll with Cost Accounting
Accounts Payable and Accounts Receivable
Accounts Payable and Accounts Receivable CBASIC
General Ledger
CBASIC™ User Guide
Science and Engineering Programs—Apple II ® Edition
Interfacing to S-100/IEEE 696 Microcomputers
A User Guide to the UNIX™ System
PET ® Fun and Games
Trade Secrets: How to Protect Your Ideas and Assets
Assembly Language Programming for the Apple II ®
VisiCalc ®: Home and Office Companion
Discover FORTH
6502 Assembly Language Subroutines
Your ATARI ® Computer
The HP-IL System
WordStar ® Made Easy, 2nd Edition
Armchair BASIC